"Kimber's courageous memoir fills a gap in the literature, exposing both the preoccupied suffering of an eating disorder and the healing that occurs when she satiates her spiritual hunger with the practice of yoga. As a therapist who works extensively with these issues, I highly recommend *Full* to anyone struggling with an eating disorder or who desires to strengthen their relationship to food, body, and self."

—**Signe Darpinian,** author of *Knock Out Dieting*

"If you can read only one memoir about eating disorder recovery, read *Full.* Kimber's writing is generously dosed with humor and wisdom, filled with marvelous insight, and never shies away from the difficulty of the undertaking. She brings the struggle and recovery alive on the page and makes it feel possible for all of us."

—**Tamara Gerlach,** author of *Cultivating Radiance*

"Step away from the scale, ditch the measuring tape, and chuck the BMI chart. Then settle in with a cup of tea and let Kimber guide you on her humorous and touching journey to leave diet talk behind and learn to listen to—and love—her body. *Full* is a nourishing feast for the soul."

—**Linda Bacon, PhD,** coauthor of *Body Respect*

"*Full* is an exceptionally raw and honest sharing of Kimber Simpkins's struggle with anorexia, body image, and relationship with food, and how she overcame her negative thinking and found freedom and happiness within her body. I could relate to so much of what she wrote. If you have ever struggled with food or body image issues, I recommend Kimber's book as an insightful, inspiring resource for you!"

—**Dina Proctor,** author of *Madly Chasing Peace*

"Kimber Simpkins is an authentic force for change on this planet, and this book is her torch. She leads the way in a new generation of women committed to removing the veil of shame and secrecy around our relationship to our body, food, and feelings. This book resonated with me on a deep level as a woman and a spiritual practitioner. I *highly* recommend Kimber's book for any woman who is ready to let down the burden of food and self-esteem issues. It has the potential to act as a catalytic force toward healing, and ultimately to living a more authentic life."

—**Katie Silcox,** author of *Healthy, Happy, Sexy*

"There is a hunger in all of us for satisfaction, and in this beautiful book we follow Kimber on her Odyssey through the actual hunger of the body, only to discover that it lives in the mind as well. This is a very moving, and often funny, story about Kimber's struggles with her 'inner anorexic'; a story which points all of us toward healing. *Full* is stuffed with wit and wisdom."

—**Wes "Scoop" Nisker**

"As insightful for the person with an eating disorder or the clinician, *Full* gets you inside the underpinnings of the illness and its challenging recovery. Ms. Simpkins astutely walks you through her successful integration of opposite parts of her Self with passion and humor. A testimony to the power of imagination and a must-read for everyone who desires to love his or her body for what it is."

—**Eric Bottino,** clinician at the Young Adult and Family Center's eating disorder program at the University of California, San Francisco

"In *Full*, Kimber Simpkins opens her heart and offers her experience in an honest and heartfelt memoir. It will serve as a support and guide for all those who feel less than good enough. Anytime you pick up Full, you will be reminded that you are in good company on the path."

—**Sharon Salzberg,** cofounder of the Insight Meditation Society in Barre, MA, and author of *Real Happiness* and *Real Happiness at Work*

"*Full* beautifully illustrates that anorexia is starvation of the soul as well as the body. The author portrays with hope and humor the labyrinthine path of recovery from an eating disorder, one that ultimately must include a loving partnership with one's own body."

—**Tamara Traeder, LMFT, LPCC**

"I fell in love with *Full*'s honesty and its humor. Kimber writes with a passion conveying her experiences intimately. I felt her presence, her struggles, and her success as if she were sitting next to me whispering into my ear! This book is certain to be a refuge and bible for all women struggling with body image."

—**Angela Farmer,** world-renowned yoga teacher

"*Full* should be savored like a long hike with a cherished friend. Kimber invites readers into her inner world, sharing her journey from secret body hating to public body loving, finally converting us into allies for self-acceptance and bodily celebration. This transformative book shows, and tells, readers how to cultivate a loving relationship with our bodies. A must-read for anyone who has struggled with body image."

—**Nishanga Bliss, DSc, LAc,** author of *Real Food All Year*

full

HOW I LEARNED *to* SATISFY
MY INSATIABLE HUNGER
and FEED MY SOUL

KIMBER SIMPKINS

New Harbinger Publications, Inc.

Publisher's Note

This publication is designed to provide accurate and authoritative information in regard to the subject matter covered. It is sold with the understanding that the publisher is not engaged in rendering psychological, financial, legal, or other professional services. If expert assistance or counseling is needed, the services of a competent professional should be sought.

Distributed in Canada by Raincoast Books

Cover design by Amy Shoup; Text design by Michele Waters-Kermes; Acquired by Catharine Meyers; Edited by Ken Knabb

Library of Congress Cataloging-in-Publication Data

Simpkins, Kimber.
  Full : how I learned to satisfy my insatiable hunger and feed my soul / Kimber Simpkins.
    pages cm
  ISBN 978-1-62625-227-1 (hardback) -- ISBN 978-1-62625-228-8 (pdf e-book) -- ISBN 978-1-62625-229-5 (epub) 1. Simpkins, Kimber--Mental health. 2. Anorexia--Patients--Biography. 3. Anorexia--Patients--Religious life. 4. Yoga--Therapeutic use. 5. Buddhism. I. Title.
  RC552.A5S57 2015
  616.85'2620092--dc23
  [B]
                       2014042454

Printed in the United States of America

17   16   15

10 9 8 7 6 5 4 3 2 1   First printing

The danger is not that the soul should doubt whether there is any bread, but that, by a lie, it should persuade itself that it is not hungry.

—Simone Weil

Contents

Acknowledgments

Thank you to Peter Blanchard, the teacher who told me he couldn't wait to read my first book. Thank you to Liz Thurber, Miryam Sas, and Kenyatta Monroe-Sinkler, my writers group, who kept the dream of this book alive through the lean times. Without them, I couldn't have found my wings. To Lisa Tener, who helped me remember where I'd left my wings and showed me they were good and flight-worthy. To Chris Simpkins, the branch I return to when the miles have run out, supporting me in my wildest dreams. Thank you, love.

I couldn't have written this book without the professional, personal, and spiritual support of so many, and yet I know I will inevitably forget a few here and there. I am sorry for the oversight; please forgive me and know you are loved and appreciated even without mention. I am deeply grateful to Katchie Ananda, my beloved teacher, for these years of crazy wisdom, patience, and friendship; to John Friend, Noah Maze, Sianna Sherman, and Jim and Ruthie Bernaert for their *asana* and inspiration; to Carlos Pomeda, Pema Chödrön, Douglas Brooks, Sally Kempton, Jack Kornfield, Wes Nisker, Kevin Griffin for their wise words that spark my heart; and to Scott Blossom, Kimberly Leo, Mae Boscana, Saraswati Clere, and Kim Adams for all the yoga love and support. Profound gratitude also to Stephanie Zone, Andrew Rivin, Anna Brait, Dru Rivers, Judith Redmond, Paul Muller, Andrew Brait, Thomas Nelson, Kim Steinmann, Celine Lazaro and the Garcia and Lazaro families, Kat Kozik, Allison Hardy, Bente Petersen, Eric Anthony, Bert Herrlinger, Karen Schulman-Bear, Gina Matero, June Jordan, Sal Risinger, Jodi Hirata, Melanie Cogburn, Shoshanna Marks, Darshana Weill, Rosie Love, Amber Charne, Cecily Greenfield, Christina Sell, Katie Hern, Teri Mae Rutledge, Abby Tucker, Simmin Joy Holland, Rajen Thapa and the staff of Taste of the Himalayas, the whole staff, crew, and family at Full Belly Farm, and all my long-lost friends in Poland.

For their inspiration and insight, deep thanks to Eve Ensler, Anne Lamott, Elizabeth Gilbert, John Gottman, and Katie and her dad. Thank you to all those who have encouraged, supported, and made this work possible: Lora Mills, Suesi Pomeda, Richard Berger, Ginger Moran, Martha Murphy, Teresa Burns Gunther, Luiza Silva, Lindsey Cohn, Linda Bacon, Marilyn Wann, Ragen Chastain, Signe Darpinian, Tamara Gerlach, Kathleen Antonia, Sarah Kurhajetz, Teja Watson, Peter Engel, Ellen Lafferty, Linda Eifer, Maud Nadler, Meredith Rom, Deborah Volkots, Jen McDonald-Peltier, Irene Sazar, Heather and Benji Wertheimer of Shantala, Cyndy McClay, Marissa Baumann, Valerie Tookes, Dylan Hawhee, Jonna Hensley, Julia Feldman, Laura Brunsvold, Sarah Hinds, Dee Dee Tanner, Hayley Ebersole, all our friends at Camp It Up!, all the Love Your Body workshop participants, and all my students, near and far.

Much gratitude to Catharine Meyers, Jess Beebe, Vicraj Gill, Adia Colar, Karen Hathaway, Jessica Dore, Bevin Donahue, Amy Shoup, and the whole team at New Harbinger Publications for embracing *Full* and its message so—well—"fully." And to Stephanie Haffner, Cooper Simpkins, Carolyn Brown, Jennifer Simpson-Manske, and my beloved parents: thank you so much for your guidance, patience, and forgiveness. Each one of you has played an important role in the unfolding of this journey. Any wisdom in this book can be wholly attributed to you. Any mistakes or silliness are entirely my own.

In the interest of inclusion, the they-singular pronoun has been used on occasion.

Many names used in the book have been changed.

May this book be of benefit to all beings everywhere.

Introduction

What you hold in your hands is the result of more than three years of revision, seven years of writing, and thirty-odd years of angst about my body. It's not been so much a roller-coaster ride as a million-hour day at the anti-amusement park, endlessly riding the whiplash bumper cars and spinning forever in tea cups. I thought my struggle with the remnants of anorexia would never end, that my whole life would continue its eternal ups and downs of joy over being temporarily thinner and self-loathing for not being thin enough.

This book is the saga of how I escaped. It wasn't a short path and it was most definitely not straight. In these pages, there are no tidy ten steps to leaving an eating disorder behind, each epiphany neatly fitting over the last and all tied up with a pretty bow. My recovery, like that of many others, was messy, awkward, and fabulous. And it's still going on.

Every gentle movement forward was accompanied by a gut-wrenching setback. Every brilliant insight resigned itself to the heart-breaking resistance to act on it. If what you want is a real life story about how difficult it is to undo years of hating oneself and how frustrating it is to unravel the habits that make it hard to do anything but fall back into the same old ruts, you're in the right place. There is a happy ending, though. A genuine one that every step backward has made even sweeter.

What I hope you receive from the book is this: the inspiration to find your own way through life's distorted funhouse mirrors and scary clowns, to emerge from the other side knowing yourself a little better than before, and to make up your own ending, happy or otherwise.

The story unfolds over a long period of time, so don't worry too much about how all the different pieces fit together chronologically. There's no quiz at the end. In yoga class, I often tell my students, "Soften toward yourself. Enjoy your breath." Softening your expectations increases your enjoyment of almost everything, including this book. It all mostly happened just this way, pretty much in this order, except where otherwise specified.

Take a deep breath. And come along for the ride.

chapter one

Hungry All the Time

My mother hates it when I say I was anorexic. I try to reassure her that my reasonably well adjusted, happy childhood was the only thing that allowed me to emerge from that period of my life relatively unscathed. Still, she worries that someone will blame and judge her for my attempt to starve myself as a teenager. Will someone blame and judge her because I gave up law to become a yoga teacher? I did that too, but no one's likely to cross her name off their holiday card list as a result.

Part of me rationalizes that I only half-starved myself. I had a well-planned, if not downright neurotic, ritual of eating. One green apple for breakfast, salad—lettuce only, no dressing—for lunch. For dinner a "normal" meal for my parents' benefit, a few vegetables, some rice. Mostly I remember being hungry all the time and totally obsessed with whatever I planned to eat next, or more specifically, what I planned not to eat. After a year or so of dedicated noneating, I mysteriously returned to seminormal mealtime habits when I turned sixteen. But that feeling of being endlessly hungry at the all-you-can-eat buffet table of life never went away.

I believed being hungry was just what my life was. In fact, I assumed this was what everybody's life was: everyone went around being hungry all the time, doing the best they could not to eat everything in sight. Chips—no, salads—yes, fill up on those greens, say no to the bread, and God forbid! the butter. Then why are there thin people, fat people, and all kinds in between, you might ask? I decided some of us must just be better at this eating thing than others, some with willpower and some not, some with metabolisms that could keep up with their lack of willpower and some, unfortunately, without. I placed myself somewhere between Homer Simpson and Princess the Elephant: willpower deficient, low metabolism, big bones, and a tendency to eat whatever was thrown at me. To look like those happy, pizza-deprived models on the cover of *Seventeen* magazine, I decided my only choice was to simply stop eating. From scouring diet books and exercise routines, I figured everyone faced the same dilemma. Either eat and be "fat" or starve and be "normal." Endless hunger as the human condition, like a page out of Dante or Sartre. Hell is other people, hell is ourselves, hell is cycling through concentric circles of deprivation and bingeing. Life is hell, and hell is being hungry.

Then one evening several years ago after eating dinner with friends, we stood outside the restaurant on the sidewalk in the cool evening, chatting and saying our good-byes. I launched into an enthusiastic description of the next restaurant where we should eat, how fantastic their desserts were, what tasty appetizers they served on those little plates.

"How can you talk about food right now?" my friend Pete laughed, his eyes a mixture of amazement and teasing. "I'm stuffed full!"

He held onto his stomach like it might burst open. I stopped and looked away, embarrassed.

"I don't know," I stammered. "I'm still kinda hungry, I guess."

Avoiding his glance, I stared down at the cracks in the sidewalk. In that moment I realized that even with all the yummy Ethiopian food we'd consumed over the last hour or so, some corner of my belly still wanted more. Mortifyingly, I realized I could sit right down and eat the entire meal over again, from start to finish.

Later at home, when the initial feeling of shame passed, a sense of amazement crept over me. Pete was genuinely full—in fact he was surprised I wasn't! He didn't feel hungry all the time, especially not right after a meal. Did this mean that eternal hunger isn't the human condition after all? Could I figure out how to not be hungry all the time? No way. But if some people could do it, why not me? Could I sit down at a meal and push away my plate, full and satisfied, without the wish that I could just repeat the whole experience of eating over again, right then?

I started taking an informal poll of my friends. At dinner, as we dipped our spoons into bowls of steaming polenta and marinara sauce sprinkled with creamy goat cheese, I'd casually ask, "So, do you feel hungry all the time, or just sometimes? Do you ever feel full or do you mostly feel unsatisfied?"

Some friends were just as surprised as I. "You mean, some people only get hungry every once in a while?" my friend Patricia mused. "I wonder what that's like."

"Yeah, it's true," I assured her, nodding emphatically before her doubtful expression, as if I'd shared with her my visit to a Seussian foreign country where the people I'd met really did wear shoes on their heads.

Other friends looked at me with the same amazement that Pete evinced that night under the streetlights. "You're hungry all the time? Even after you've just eaten? All day long?" Then I'd know I was talking to one of those visitors from that far away land called Fullness, an exotic place I'd never visited, but longed to learn everything about. The times I felt closest to full were not at the dinner table but on my yoga mat. The sense of wholeness that crept up and settled briefly into my heart while lying on my back at the end of class led me to conclude that yoga might be the ship on which I could stow away to search for the lost island where "full" wasn't just a mark on the fuel gauge.

After many years of practicing yoga and meditation, I learned that noticing matters—observing what you do, how you do it, what triggers you, what comforts you. Notice if you check out when your legs feel tired in triangle pose. Notice if you compete with your neighbor to see whose head gets closer to their knees. Notice if your mind starts to spin off about how heavily your fellow meditator is breathing: *What's wrong with him, does he have a cold, or is he making an obscene phone call? Oh my God, is he snoring? Should I open one eye and make sure he's even awake? Maybe I should jostle him or better yet, move somewhere else. My foot hurts anyway. Wait a second, it's been like ten minutes since I even noticed my own breath. Ugh, I'll never get the hang of this! Wait, I'm not supposed to be criticizing myself, either. Sigh. Just breathe. In, out, in...out...*

"Be mindful of your thoughts on the mat and your actions off the mat." I heard these words over and over from the mouths of my yoga teachers—and meditation teachers, too, substituting "cushion" for "mat." What I found in my head were the same thoughts, again and again, a broken record skipping back to the awkward refrain, *Am I doing it right? Are people looking at me? Do they think I'm fat?*

They say some 90% of our thoughts are the same every single day. *Some new thoughts would be welcome over here! Preferably less self-obsessed. Kinder would be nice, too.* Mindfulness was painful, but illuminating.

During my yoga practice, I noticed for the first time my own idiosyncrasies. Usually I competed with everyone around me, but if no one was nearby to egg me on, I competed with myself. *Come on, Kimber. You got your leg straighter yesterday...last week...last month... when you were ten!* The pain finally got my attention, forcing me to recognize how hard I pushed myself, even to the point of injury. I would heal my lower back and then boom! injure my shoulder yet again trying to get myself into some fancy arm balance. And for what, the yoga Olympic trials? Finally, after years of gentle attention, I started to undo the pushy habit, and found myself able to practice without hurting myself again and again. If my mind-body habit of self-injury could slowly unravel itself under yoga's persistent gaze, perhaps I could apply the same technique of attentiveness to my eating habits as well and discover a forgotten map, a secret route to the hidden island of Fullness.

When I say, "I want to be full," what do I mean exactly? The desire to fill myself up with food has less to do with what I've eaten during the day and more to do with filling some emotional or spiritual hole that's never satisfied. My emptiness feels like the pothole down the street from my house. Every once in a while a city road crew comes by and fills it with asphalt, smoothing out the edges. Within days, the hole, having digested its tarry meal, reopens, the edges parting their raw black teeth as if to say, "I'm back! Feed me more!" I imagine that pothole leads directly to the molten core of the earth, like my belly, the gateway to my unquenchable digestive fires.

What I want is this: I want to feel full all the time. Never too full, never too empty. To know exactly how much food my body needs. To not have to think about food that much. To be able to enjoy a barbecue picnic, a catered wedding, or a friend's first baking experiment. I want my body to be a highly tuned machine, taking in exactly what it needs, no more and no less. I want to go out with my friends to the new Moroccan or Korean restaurant and eat exactly what my body wants, be it chocolate cream puffs or steamed bamboo shoots. And I don't want to obsess about food all the time, or restrict myself endlessly. Who wants to be the party pooper who announces, "I can't eat your homemade sweet potato fries and aioli blended with herbs from your garden, they're not on my diet"? Not me.

Also, it's time to renounce my enrollment in the Secret Body-Haters Club. I've been a devoted card-carrying member for decades. One April morning, not long after my conversation with Pete on the sidewalk, as a new, nervous teacher, I taught a yoga class to a group of wonderful students of all ages, telling them, "You should love your body. Look at how much it does for you. It's amazing and beautiful. It deserves your kindness." And I meant every syllable.

And here's the crazy thing: as I exited the studio and walked down the stairs to my car, I caught a glimpse of myself in the mirror. *You need to go on a diet. Maybe you should try that clay, charcoal, and salt water cleanse that yoga teacher told you about yesterday.* Sticking my key in the car door I looked down at my pillowy thighs. *God! You're so fat! How can any student take you seriously as a yoga teacher?*

Seeing my reflection in the car window, the horror of what I was doing finally dawned on me. *I'm doing exactly what I told my students not to do. I'm a total freaking hypocrite.*

What do they call that? Cognitive dissonance. I know I shouldn't hate myself. But I can't seem to put a cork in it. Maybe when I arrive on the island of Full, they'll make me relinquish my card for good, and magictastically I'll embody the kindness toward myself I tell everyone else to apply to themselves.

I want to feel good, healthy, and strong. To enjoy life. And no more diets! There's some kindness in that, right? How about a long-term approach that can adjust to different times of my life and varying circumstances? To feel full enough to match and overwhelm the emptiness of my hunger. Sure it's a big dream, contradictory and wild. But is it really too much to ask?

To begin with, I wanted to notice what was going in my mouth, and when and how and why. Unfortunately, right away this effort pulled me back to my days of teenage dieting and calorie counting. Butter has too many fat calories! *Mmm, that'll be dry toast for me. Crunch, crunch.* But this time it wasn't about counting calories, tallying things up. To truly come to understand my underlying eating habits, I needed to loosen the hold of my judgmental mind and notice my patterns around food in a very open way. Frank questions would have to be asked about why I ate this and not that, with honest and direct responses even if the answers embarrassed me.

What is "full" exactly, what does it feel like? In those elusive moments when a brief feeling of fullness might settle into my body like a butterfly on the back of a gardener's gloved hand, I wanted to figure out how to hold very still and let the butterfly linger a bit longer, opening and closing its wings.

So far I'd noticed a wide array of factors that led me to a lack of feeling full:

1. Seeing new bags, wrinkles, and spots under my eyes while brushing my teeth.

2. Someone giving me the finger after I've made some unforgivable driving mistake, like pulling into the intersection for a left turn too slowly for their taste.

3. Waking up bleary-eyed at 3:00 a.m. and worrying about whether our naughty wandering cat had gotten into another nasty and expensive fight with a raccoon.

4. Skipping my yoga practice because I woke up too late after having chewed on my pillow for four hours after I woke up at 3:00 a.m. worrying about the cat.

5. Hurrying through meals, through the day, through my life.

Only one of these things related to food! Surely everything in my life didn't have to go perfectly in order for my stomach to feel full. What could I do to help fullness feel more like a welcome guest and less like an elusive ghost?

No one knew the answers but me. I sensed the answers were tied up in an elaborate knot, twisted and stretched like the loops that encompass a rubber band ball. Instead of letting the ball bounce through the house, knocking over plants and breaking vases, I wanted to take it into my hands and pull off one band at a time. What would I find at the center? When you take a rubber band ball apart, you end up with a pile of twisted, stringy rubber. The center—gone. Once all my questions had been loosened, pulled back, and left lying on the floor, I hoped my hunger would vanish just as mysteriously.

Years ago, I vacationed in Hawaii with my partner and my parents. For many people, this might seem like a terrible idea: they go off on vacation to get away from their parents, not to shack up with them. Fortunately, my parents are pretty fun, and we all mostly enjoyed it, despite the following interaction with my mom.

In our lovely rented beachside condo, we were all putting on shorts, sundresses, sandals, on our way out to dinner, when I wandered into my parents' room to borrow my mother's hair dryer.

My mother, brushing her hair, said to me, "I can't believe you tell people you're anorexic. You're not anorexic."

Whoa! My stomach recoiled as if I'd been punched. I had offhandedly mentioned something at dinner the previous night about how dipping bread into olive oil would have seemed gross when I was anorexic, but now I loved it.

"Not now, Mom. *As a teenager.*"

"You were *not*," she replied, steadying her gaze on her own tanned face in the mirror as she roughly pulled the sharp bristles through blond-gray hair.

Stunned into silence, I found myself caught between (1) defending myself with eloquent arguments and journal entries, (2) restraining my desire to alternately throw something at her or laugh at her, (3) realizing how ridiculous it was to try to convince her of something she had no intention of believing, and (4) hauling myself off to some tiled corner of the apartment to sob for the remainder of the humid afternoon with the inviting beach lying just a few steps away.

Fortunately, my partner overheard our exchange and a quick commiserating roll of the eyes was enough for me to let it go, at least until some point in the future when I could pin Mom down in a location more ideal for forcing her to admit I had a teenage eating disorder. Like maybe buckled into a long trans-Pacific flight while the captain has illuminated the overhead "Fasten Seatbelt" sign.

I hadn't always been hungry. Once upon a time I was a big, happy newborn. Nine and a half pounds of sleepy, smiley baby goodness. Born big enough to be self-feeding, Mom says, like the newly hatched chicks with their yolk sacs who can be packed into boxes like golf balls and shipped across the country, needing no food or water along the way. After two years of dealing with my colicky sister (amazing they even thought about having a second kid—Hey, this one screams and cries all the time, let's make another one!), they were shocked when I came out all contented and peaceful. At the hospital, when

Mom woke up after my delivery, she asked if I needed her and the nurse assured her, "No, she's fine, sleeping."

"Are you sure she's okay?" Mom asked again.

At my mother's disbelieving insistence, the nurse brought me in to see if I would breastfeed. I opened my eyes a moment, nuzzled her swollen nipple, and quietly fell back to sleep.

A couple of months later, the story goes, Mom brought me in for a checkup.

"Tell me what's wrong with her," she begged the pediatrician. "She never cries, she hardly eats, she sleeps all the time, is she…?"

I'm pretty sure the old-school word that she might have mouthed across the examination room in 1970 was "retarded." Mom wanted to know if I was *slow*, you know, mentally challenged, as we might say in our more sensitive age. Jenny, their oldest, cranky daughter had shown signs of brilliance already, therefore high-maintenance meant high-functioning. Low-maintenance meant…well, you get the idea.

The pediatrician assured her I was just peachy. Not a thing wrong with me. My parents could hardly believe their luck. Even beyond the age when most people grow sick of hearing their parents tell their baby stories, I never grow tired of hearing about being born a fat little Buddha, contented, full, and easy.

My parents loved me. They moved away from what they considered the fast-hippy-divorce-and-drug culture of southern California and back to the small conservative steel town in Ohio where they had both grown up. Since they'd done well by growing up in the country air and winding roads, they figured Jenny and I would do the same. Mom and Dad told me I could become anything I wanted. They both worked, running their own businesses: Dad seeing patients as an ear, nose, and throat doctor, Mom fitting hearing aids as an audiologist. We ate dinner together every night.

I loved my parents right back. They attended every play I was in, every softball game. As health professionals, they encouraged us to eat lots of fruits and vegetables. Salad, made with bowling ball–sized heads of iceberg lettuce and pink hothouse tomatoes, was an everyday occurrence. I never thought much about food, or my body, or my weight, or my attractiveness. Jenny and I leapt around the house singing at the top of our lungs the soundtracks from *The Sound of Music* and *Fiddler on the Roof*. We begged Mom and Dad to make popcorn and let us stay up to watch evening movies. Our little gang of skinny kids roamed the manicured lawns of the neighborhood, riding our bikes around the cul-de-sacs, hiding out under trees, making a fort out of discarded plywood in someone's backyard.

On snow days during our Midwestern winters, Jenny and I got a big metal mixing bowl out from the bottom kitchen cabinet and waded out to the center of the yard in our boots and coats to scoop up wads of freshly fallen snow. We hurried it back into the house and with our cold hands mixed sugar and dark vanilla into the flaky crystals. Huddled under blankets on the floor next to the couch, we ate, shivering, spooning our homemade treat from bowls cradled in our laps.

The first moment I discovered I didn't like my body was a shock, like getting my finger stuck in the funny bone opening of our Operation game. (I always hated that game; I couldn't figure out why it was fun to risk electrocution—however mild—for the thrill of using tweezers to extricate tiny plastic bones out of a hairy flat guy.) At our kitchen table one fall afternoon in sixth grade, Mom excitedly showed me a stack of photos from our August trip to Sanibel Island in Florida. I loved Sanibel, with its warm waves and pelicans, but most of all I relished the freedom to ride my bike out to the lighthouse, from one sandy end of the lush tropical island to the other.

Mom pointed out our new friends in the pictures, shots of pelicans napping on the piers, a bank of storm clouds threatening overhead, and then she left me at the kitchen table to put away the groceries while I idly fingered my way to the bottom of the pile.

I stopped at a photo that showed me standing among several people—it was the photo that changed me forever. As if looking through a microscope, I only saw myself, my companions disappearing into blurry shadows. Long, straggly hair listlessly hung over my shoulders. A wide, goofy smile spread across my face, eyes squinting. I stood wide-legged in the thick Bermuda grass behind the condo we rented. My entire posture was childish; the girl—me—utterly unaware of anything but the sun in her eyes and the grass tickling the sides of her feet.

But here's the part that really rammed my finger into the wall socket of mortifying self-consciousness: my full belly filled my T-shirt, sticking out over the top of my skirt like the Pillsbury Dough Boy, for everyone to see. I looked fat. I stared at the picture in disbelief. *Is that me?* I held my breath. And refused to exhale. I held my belly close, tucking it back against its organs, with a warning that I'd be keeping an eye on it and it better behave. Or else. My belly never hung out again.

One night not long after, we ate out at a 1920s-themed fast food restaurant, one of our family's favorite spots. I loved their PB&J: thick slices of real strawberries atop crunchy peanut butter and soft, heavy white bread. Enjoying my sandwich, talking at the table with my parents and sister, I watched as a woman came into the restaurant with her husband and two kids. They looked just like an average family, except the woman was very fat and had an exceptionally pretty face: blonde hair, huge blue eyes, and a gorgeous smile. Except for her weight, her face might have smiled from the cover of any of the fashion magazines I'd begun to gaze at enviously.

The first thought that emerged from my adolescent mind was, *Whoa, doesn't that woman know how beautiful she'd be if she were skinnier?*

I watched her, fascinated, as I considered ordering a second PB&J. (I'd inhaled the first.) I was appalled by the apparent tragic loss of opportunity her size presented, but then I noticed that she didn't seem self-conscious at all. She moved with ease in her body, content with the attentions of her husband, unconcerned about the snotty judgments of pubescent strangers. Even while my eyes took in what was clearly a happy and beautiful fat woman, my mind fired relentless barbs: *How awful, to be so lovely and trapped in a huge body,* or, *If I looked like that, I'd throw myself under a train.*

Here was a clear sign in front of me that you didn't have to be skinny to be happy and loved, and I couldn't see it, beyond the veil of my own prejudice and nascent self-hatred. Still, the memory was preserved, maybe as a life raft to hold on to when I needed it most.

Not long after that, I had my first binge. I was fourteen, home from school on a weekday, some random holiday like Columbus Day or Teachers' Enrichment Day. Up in my attic room, lying on the lime-green carpet in front of the television, I shoveled mint chocolate chip ice cream into my mouth straight out of the half-gallon box. I ate half of it and swore to myself that I would stop, that I would walk down the stairs and put the rest back in the freezer. I walked all the way down two flights of stairs to the kitchen and put it back on its shelf. Minutes later, like an ice cream–fueled zombie, I found myself standing in front of the freezer, pulling the container out, and running back upstairs with it cradled under my arm. Just one more bite. Maybe two.

Part of me felt disgusted and another part had given up, saying, *You've eaten so much already, what's a little more?* Long before any further thoughts of *Stop, look what you're doing!* could arise, my spoon

15

scraped the bottom of the container. *Oh well, just a couple more bites left. Might as well finish it.*

Later, I lay on the floor with my aching belly, a bloated blob of self-loathing. Once the creeping horror of what I'd just done sunk in, I dragged my body over to stand on the mini trampoline in front of the mirror. Time to burn off all those evil fat calories. Three bounces later, I flopped back on the floor. No use. Too nauseated and too full to bounce. Bleah.

While bingeing, my mind was empty, not thinking about anything, not even the ice cream itself, just enjoying the rhythm of scooping the ice cream out, icy creamy coolness in my mouth, sweet and mine, all mine. Scoop, in, swallow, scoop, in, swallow, barely tasting anymore, certainly no awareness of how bloated my stomach was growing, not thinking for a moment about whether I felt hungry or already totally beyond full.

I resented having to think about whether I was hungry. Of course I wasn't hungry. I just wanted to eat. *I want, I want, I want.* Any wee flutter of self-control deserted me. My mind and my body were operating on their own strange agenda. Later I used the tactile memory of green nausea from green ice cream over green carpet to persuade myself not to eat. *This is who you are, out of control.* The only way to control that intense longing for *more*, I decided, was to shut it down. *Remember what a big fat pig you are/were/can be. You don't want to feel that way again, do you?* I traded loss of control for total domination, chaos for totalitarianism.

chapter two

The Year of Eating Dangerously

One Monday morning after everyone has folded their hands to join me in a final "Om" to close our yoga class, my yoga friend Adrienne invites me to lunch to talk about food. A "yoga friend" is someone you notice rolling their mat out on the other side of the room, attending the same teachers' classes, trying to maneuver their leg behind their head nearby, and sighing in *savasana*, the nap pose at the end of class. You start to notice when they're not there, and you greet them joyfully when they return. Finally, after months of seeing each other, you exchange names and, some time after that, you might even get to see them without their yoga clothes on. Not naked. Just with normal clothes: jeans and sweaters and shoes. Sometimes you can hardly recognize a fellow classmate unless they're sweaty, upside-down, and wearing stretch pants. You meet for tea and learn more about them than whether or not they like standing on their head.

Adrienne and I met while putting on our shoes after our favorite teacher Katchie's class. When I started to teach, Adrienne showed up at my classes, too. Her presence in my classes was flattering—*She has good taste in teachers. Why is she here? Oh.*—and provided much-needed encouragement for my growing teaching skills.

"I liked your article," she says as we stand in the tea-scented lobby after yoga.

"Thanks." My face flushes. She's read it? Embarrassment steals my breath. Months before, I had written an article for *Yogi Times* called "Sit, Eat, and Be Full," about eating mindfully. As open as I am with my students about my personal life, my writing feels like standing naked in front of a crowd. So I hadn't told anyone about the article, though why I should be surprised to find that a *yoga* friend has read a *yoga* magazine, I have no idea. What did I imagine, that they would publish only one copy of the magazine and hand it over, gift-wrapped, to me?

"I'm a psychologist and eating disorders specialist," she says, beaming at me. "I'd love to talk to you more about food and yoga." I'm more delighted than if she'd told me she was an incarnation of the goddess Athena, arrived to share her wisdom and weaving tips with me.

We walk to a café across the street from the yoga studio, and eat our salads to the rhythmic roar of the coffee roasters in the back. I ask Adrienne how she diagnoses anorexia. Can she retroactively diagnose my eating disorder from twenty years ago? She mentions that the folks who are in charge of these things are planning to change the definition of anorexia to include more patients, and then lists for me the four main criteria for a current diagnosis of anorexia nervosa:

1. Intense fear of gaining weight

2. Body image distortion

3. Amenorrhea (no monthly period) or hormonal irregularity

4. Refusal to maintain a "normal" weight, instead staying about 15% below a healthy weight

Scribbling in my notebook, I pause to consider the list. I imagine myself back in the narrow hollow that was my fifteen-year-old body. It doesn't take me long to figure it out:

1. The idea of gaining weight caused the floor to melt under me and brought the sensation of sliding into a Hieronymus Bosch black void filled with shiny, beetle-shaped demons and beaked minions with sticks.

2. My body looked huge and ugly to me, no matter how much weight I lost.

3. I didn't even notice that my period had stopped. But it had, a mere three years after it started. Which was quite convenient for someone exerting ruthless control over her body.

4. I stopped weighing myself and was never diagnosed. I refused for a time to maintain a normal body weight, but no one even noticed. Then I stopped refusing.

"Just so you know," Adrienne says, "lots of eating disorders don't even have a label. There are binge-exercisers, people who eat only at night, people who can't eat in front of other people, or people who simply don't meet the exact criteria for anorexia or bulimia, but who have an eating disorder nonetheless. They're all placed in a big amorphous category called Eating Disorder, NOS: Not Otherwise Specified."

Adrienne's words offered me the relief of the label "anorexic" but took away the need for a label at all. It's as if, after having tried to stuff my square peg self into a round hole all my life, someone comes up behind me and whispers, "Hey Kimber, you're *square*, honey, not round. And stop bothering with the holes." I had lived through an eating disorder, period. An eating disorder as individual as I am.

In tenth grade as a sulky fifteen-year-old, I began to deliberately conceal from my parents what I was and wasn't eating. Every night I ate a "normal" meal without complaint to avoid questions, using the time-tested method of mushing the food around into compact piles, choreographing well-timed bites when I had someone's attention. "So, Mom, how were things at the office today?" Smile, bite. "Dad, did you remember to make me a dentist's appointment?" Pause. He looks up, okay, now lift, open mouth, bite, chew, swallow.

Except for the occasional apple and bit of lettuce, I fasted when no one was watching. Sometimes I "lost" my inner battle to the hungry demons and ate a bowl of popcorn or a bag of chips. Once the cheating started by swallowing one mouthful, I'd eat the whole container. I was committed until the bottom emerged into the light. Meat and fat reminded me of the very substances I most wanted to excise from my body. I became a vegetarian. At night, I exercised as if all the world's inner and outer demons could be chased away in the few minutes allotted before bed. My routine of 100 crunches, several hundred leg lifts in different formations, and military push-ups took about 25 minutes. Taking a page from the playbook of my militaristic former softball coach, I forced myself to do them even when sick or exhausted.

That winter, my tonsils swelled up into goopy red hacky sacks in the back of my throat, and my dad scheduled surgery during the winter break so I wouldn't miss school. Lying in the hospital bed in my backless gown, I was delighted by both the constant chatter of the nurses bringing me ice water and how nicely the surgery and recovery fit into my routine: no solid food for one week. Only soft foods for two to three weeks after that. Perfect! When the nurses moved on to other patients, I edged my feet down onto the cold floor and crept over to swing the door shut, then scampered back over to the bed to perform my centuplicate sit-ups and leg lifts in the hospital bed. I didn't care that the movement's stress caused a blood vessel to swell up in the back of my newly raw throat. They had to wheel me back into surgery for an extra procedure to relieve the pressure.

Visiting with armfuls of balloons and flowers, my parents offered me ice cream and popsicles. The nurses produced wads of green Jell-O and pints of whole milk. I waved it all away and instead sucked on ice and diet apple soda. At some point my dad must have noticed that I wasn't eating much, and I caught him sneaking regular soda into my cup. Without complaining, I always poured my own after that. *He has no idea how little I'm eating.*

Committed to starving myself, the sensation of "full" and my stomach were separated by about 250,000 miles—the distance to the moon's bright surface from earth's night shadow. Savory mushrooms over creamy pasta? No thank you. More watery tasteless gruel for me, please. My embrace of emptiness, the vaguely demanding hollowness in my belly, was a desperate effort to squelch the desire for fullness altogether. My hunger cheered me—a sign that my efforts at starvation were working. *Good, you're hungry*, I thought to myself. *You deserve it.*

In reality, the anorexia probably drove my desire to feel full to a deeper level, even a cellular level, creating in my body the fear of starvation, to which it responded by later increasing my fat stores. According to Linda Bacon, PhD, in her book *Health at Every Size: The Surprising Truth About Your Weight*, the body typically responds to starvation, whether inflicted intentionally or otherwise, by setting its weight set point higher, as in heavier: the body's way of hoarding for the next famine. Unbeknownst to me, all my fat cells sat grumbling to themselves, waiting for the next feast, their chance to jump on the tables, kick up their heels, and belt out a rousing, drunken rendition of "I Will Survive."

Even as my body howled at me for sustenance, I closed my ears and turned away from its pleas. Anorexia is the ultimate insensitivity. By consciously denying my needs, desires, and feelings, I systematically dulled my mind's sensitivity to my body. My only focus was a mental picture of what I wanted my body to look like: as skinny as possible, skinnier than anyone else was or could ever safely be. Skin and bones, bones and skin. I wouldn't be satisfied until that was all that was left.

I can still remember the pressure of a young child's belt that I wore underneath my clothes. A friend had given it to me as we stood in her closet finding clothes to wear to the middle school dance. I was holding the skinny white belt with the tiny gold buckle and she looked over and said, "That's too small for me. You can have it if you want."

It was too small for me, too. But I took it home anyway and a few years later found that I could cinch it high around my waist to its tightest point as an early warning system for my anorexic defense. Every moment of the day, I knew whether my stomach remained flat and hollow, or curved outward, pressing uncomfortably against the leather, indicating I'd eaten too much, or anything at all. My baggy shirts and sweaters hid it from my parents, my sister, my classmates, everyone. Later, in college, I learned about hair shirts, the rough, uncomfortable underclothes that monks and zealots would wear to remind them of their devotion to God. I understood immediately, intuitively, the motivation behind wearing a hair shirt. That belt was my hair shirt, reminding me in each moment of my commitment to not eat, to let nothing between my lips that would give me pleasure or offer comfort.

Like a novice nun, I was mortifyingly modest. No one would ever have glimpsed my belt-cum-hair shirt. After school, when my class-mates changed out of their school uniforms in the bathroom, I wouldn't let anyone see a single naked square inch. I hid in a tiny bathroom stall, legs balanced over the toilet, acrobatically trying to keep my limbs and clothes out of the lidless bowl and out of view as I changed. The other girls would gather in the area between the sinks and stalls while they slipped into street clothes and gossiped— *Did you hear that Robert's brother totaled his mom's car on Saturday by driving it through the garage door?*—but I couldn't join them. I cringed at the thought that someone might glance my way and glimpse my too-fat but secretly dwindling flesh.

No effort was too extreme when it came to avoiding food, espe-cially my favorites: chocolate frosted brownies, iced cookies, and cake of any shape, size, or flavor. When a friend brought a box of cupcakes to class for her birthday, I excused myself to the bathroom the minute my eye caught sight of the pink cardboard box. On bake sale days, the senior girls manned the table in the hallway right in front of the entrance; I would sneak out a back door and walk all the way around three wings of the school to wait for my ride on the curb. My distance from food distanced me from my friends as well. *No, I don't want any pizza. No, I don't want to split a Coke. No, I can't come to your birthday party...not if there's cake involved.*

Once during a trip to the bathroom during English class, I real-ized that my underwear didn't fit anymore. It was sliding off my hips under my pants—the elastic simply had nothing to hold on to. Words can't describe the weirdness of trying to hitch up my panties through my slacks to keep them from creeping down my legs. Couldn't everyone see the sides of my undies trying to escape down my legs? But no, they somehow managed to stay tethered between my legs, helplessly garroted by the crotch of my pants.

In a moment of forgetful pride, I told one person about how much, well, how *little* I was eating—Mr. Warney, one of the French teachers. He wasn't one of my teachers, but he always praised my performances in our school plays. One day as I strode out of the lunchroom, while everyone else lingered, eating and conversing, Mr. Warney leaned against the doorway, raised an implausibly furry eyebrow at me, and asked what I'd had for lunch. Rarely did anyone ask what I ate, and I was delighted to brag about my self-control.

"Plain salad, no dressing. And an apple for breakfast."

He looked at me funny; a shadow of disbelief crossed his eyes and then he tilted his head in surprise. Something in my expression told him I was serious, and did I detect a hint of admiration in his smile?

"That's enough for you, huh?" he asked. I suddenly felt naked, worried that I'd revealed too much. What if he told someone? My gaze dropped to the floor and I scooted off to my library hideout for the rest of lunch period.

Settling into the nook under the library stairs, I scoured magazines until the bell rang. The pages of *Newsweek*, *Life*, and *National Geographic* provided various tidbits of information to help me in my quest to grow ever thinner. *What's your weight's set point? Eating an apple every day can lower your appetite! Tribal adults in Africa survive on less than a cup of grain per day.* Immersed in my plans for self-annihilation, a small part of me wished Mr. Warney *would* tell someone—the school nurse, my parents, anyone. Another part of me knew that as I and my classmates memorized calorie charts and evinced disdain for blue cheese dressing and whipped cream, all to look like the ideal of thin adolescent beauty on magazine covers and big screens, many of the adults in nearby universes expected no less of us. Mr. Warney never told.

One magazine in my library stash explained that nervous fidgeting burned a significant number of calories per day. I set out to become a champion fidgeter. Whenever my legs were crossed, under a desk or table, my top shin bounced. When reading, I tapped my foot or wiggled my ankles or toes. Leaning on a table or counter, I drummed my fingers, or flipped my pencil. Anything to burn a few extra calories here or there. I guess that's where the *nervosa* part of anorexia comes in.

My day was filled with hundreds of bizarre little rituals. I became oddly superstitious, believing that whenever I saw the clock read the same number all the way across, 4:44 or 11:11, I had to make a wish. I always wished for the same thing: to be thin. To die thin. To be so thin that even if the world couldn't agree on nuclear weapons or whether God exists, they could all agree on one thing: Kimber is not fat. Same thing when a shooting star streaked across the sky. All my wishes came down to one thing. Nothing else was important. Wishing myself thin became so reflexive that even now, years later, when I look at a digital clock and see the numbers repeated across the display, I still remember the girl who made the wish, over and over, to die thin.

For every reflective surface I passed, I made a sport of flinging insults at my body. *You big, fat pig* was a classic favorite. Though I gave myself points for creativity: *You're a giant walking sausage in princess flats. Next week they're having tryouts for a Roman play. You're a shoe-in for Mount Olympus.*

I felt sorry for all the people who had to look at my ugly body. How could they stand it, when I couldn't? My worst nightmare was to end up in an accident where the paramedics would cut the clothes off my dying body and, seeing my huge balloon thighs, say to each other, "Such a shame, look at how fat she is!" Being judged fat, to my empathy-shriveled mind, was much worse than being judged dead. Of course at some point being thin and being dead would inevitably be the same thing, but that didn't faze me. *Better dead and thin than fat and alive.*

The only way to guarantee that food didn't linger on my legs and hips was to eat way less than my body needed. Tucked away under the library stairs, reading an article about World War II concentration camps, I learned that prisoners were fed less than 1000 calories a day, barely enough to survive. Interesting. Those folks were pretty skinny. The gears in my head made a diabolical clicking sound. *I'll eat like I'm in a concentration camp.*

Taking into account the ethics of this approach didn't occur to me. New strategy in hand, I counted out my calories grudgingly, like a prison guard measuring out the smallest number of calories needed to keep his prisoner alive. If I didn't know how many calories something had, I couldn't eat it. If I did know, I probably wouldn't eat it. Given how fuzzy the whole calorie thing was anyway—*Uh-oh, today's green apple is bigger than yesterday's, I'll have to do another round of sit-ups*—I tried to eat way fewer than 1000 calories a day, often less than 900 if I could manage it.

While actively anorexic, I actually asked for help: "HELLO! I'm trying to kill myself here!" No, the request wasn't quite that explicit, but my secret was starting to scare me. Damp, squashed tissues filled my backpack and multiplied under the bed. I denied the tears, hiding them from everyone but my pillow. Waking up in the morning, all I wanted to do was crawl back under the covers and play dead. In my dreams I neither ate nor starved myself. In my dreams I was not at war with my body.

"Can I see a psychiatrist?" I asked my parents one night as we cleared the table after a dinner of marinated chicken breasts and reheated frozen broccoli. They stopped, bemused for a moment, and looked at each other before turning their gazes back to me.

"What for?" Dad asked, wiping his forehead with the back of his hand. Mom developed a sudden interest in scrubbing an invisible spot on the kitchen table.

"I just need someone to talk to. About stuff."

"Paul, I told you she wasn't acting right..." Mom said.

"Mona." He gently waved her quiet. "Is everything okay?" His voice deepened.

"Yeah. I just need someone to talk to. About stuff. Please."

Dad looked at Mom again with a shrug, and said, "We'll ask Dr. Miles for a recommendation and get you in to see someone right away."

Dr. Miles had been my parents' marriage counselor for years. After many weekend afternoons spent paging through mind-numbing magazines in his waiting room while my parents hashed out whatever was driving them crazy about each other, I figured Mom and Dad wouldn't hassle me about asking for an appointment for myself. I didn't ask them about why they needed a marriage counselor or what happened behind their closed door. I hoped they wouldn't ask me about mine.

The woman Dr. Miles found was supposedly an expert in adolescent medicine. She was nice enough. But deeply oblivious. She was shorter than me, with frizzy dark hair, very fat, middle-aged, and friendly, but not warm. I had done the work of getting myself to her, so I waited for her to do her part.....*Ask me what I eat, how much I weigh, ask me to tell you why I'm so sad all the time. Ask me why I'm trying to kill myself, slowly, quietly, tidily.* Why the waves of desperation flowing off me didn't knock her to the floor, I'll never know.

Imagine—a sterile examination room, an obese female psychiatrist in one chair, across the room a skinny fifteen-year-old girl, crossing her legs and sucking them up into her body away from the icy tile floor. The psychiatrist pulls a pen from the surprisingly diverse selection that gaps from the pocket of her lab coat and starts writing into her chart. They talk, awkwardly. The doctor barely looks up from her scribbling. The girl tries to hide her gaze under the exam table, the door, the shadow of the doctor's shoe on the floor. They never make eye contact.

"How's your school work going?"

"Fine."

"How's your family?"

"Fine."

"How are your plans for college?"

"Fine."

"Studying for the SATs?"

"Yeah."

Does the psychiatrist ask what the girl had for breakfast? Does she weigh the girl? Does she ask her a single question about her self-image? No. Three sessions of stiff, chilly conversation later, the psychiatrist informs the girl her problem is she's afraid to go to college: "You should tell your parents you don't want to go."

Hold on. WHAT? I was devastated. I had the guts and the self-awareness to tell someone I was depressed, and this is what I get? Someone to kick my only life preserver away and leave me to drown? My sister would soon graduate high school and leave for college—without me, of course. Who wants to take their little sister to college? Since birth, I'd followed my big sister everywhere, to the bathroom, to kindergarten, to the prom in her corsage and tulle. She hated it for years, but then slowly grew to tolerate her adoring fan. But now she was going someplace I couldn't follow.

Not only was I wrecked by the reality of Jen moving away, but college was important to me for the very reason I'd asked to see the psychiatrist in the first place. From the distance I stood, I thought maybe, if my eyes squinted just right, I could see a green-lit sign hanging over the doorway to college marked "EXIT MISERY." College, I imagined, would loosen me from my straitjacket of perfection, or would at least provide some new scenery out of the tiny, barred windows I'd built for myself.

I had barely been exposed to Sartre, but I feared that if my parents heard the psychiatrist's bizarre theory that the idea of college was stressing me out, that sign would blink red and inexplicably change to "*HUIS CLOS*—NO EXIT, SUCKER!" I ran away from that woman as fast as I could. No way was someone going to block off my emergency exit. I didn't tell my parents why I refused to see her again: "I'm fine now. All better."

I didn't want them to entertain even the remotest possibility that my path might not follow my sister's through that brightly lit doorway. Two and a half more years to go.

So. Asking for help didn't work out that well. What next?

Mornings were an exhausting hell. The first thought as my eyes opened was: *Only sixteen more hours and then I can go back to sleep.* Every day I robotically performed elaborate rituals. Pee, scale, shower, shave, dress, pack for school, grab apple, leave, get to school, locker, class, lettuce lunch, head to library, read, class, chorus, softball practice, go home, pretend to eat dinner, homework, exercise, bed. Ad nauseam. I was doing my best to fit into the coffin of expectations I had built for myself. It was a tight fit, but I was taking care of that problem by making myself smaller.

At softball practice, we ran endless sprints, with military-like taunts from the coaches and vicious teasing from the older girls if your shorts rode up into your butt crease or if you hadn't shaved your legs that morning. I hated softball. The best part was standing in the outfield, watching the bees try to extract pollen from the tightly furled clover, waiting for the fly ball that never came. I was always yelled at for running too slowly when we were called up to bat.

Tests of deprivation stretched into weeks and months. I ate no sugar of any kind, but occasionally would let myself binge on potato chips or Doritos after not having eaten anything else all day. And then I used a sharpened, pitiless stick of self-loathing to prod myself into eating only my prisoner's fare the next day.

I worry whether someone reading this book might borrow the horrifying tricks I played on myself to develop or reinforce their own process of becoming anorexic. Because that's what I did—my anorexic bible was a cheap teen novel called *Polly's Secret*. Picking it up, I imagined Polly's secret would turn out to be a passageway to a magical world, or a fantastic wish-fulfilling tree, or maybe her crush on some geeky guy. But it led me to a different world altogether. Though the paperback was intended as a morality tale warning young girls against the dangers of anorexia, I treated it as a how-to book, imitating Polly's quirks, compulsions, and mindset. To this day, I don't know how much of my weird starvation routine came from Polly or emerged out of my own twisted imagination.

Teen magazines were another great source of tidbits for a budding (withering?) anorexic. I remember reading about a teenage model who said she hadn't eaten pizza in over a year…so I put that on my list of no-nos. No pizza. I gave up lots of things, even raisins. Raisins are high in zinc, and zinc enhances appetite. No raisins for me.

My body was a lab animal, my diet an experiment. My research focused not on how to take care of my body, nurture it, and help it thrive, but how to best bend it to my will and make it look like a size zero air-brushed model at whatever cost to my health and well-being.

Okay, not whatever cost. Perfection was the goal and that entailed having bowel function and enamel on my teeth. Laxatives and vomiting were out. It had to be perfectly secret, accomplished without drawing anyone's attention to the deadly experiment. Without letting it get too far out of control. It was all about control.

So if you're reading this and catch yourself thinking, "I could use some of these tricks as diet tips," drop this book and go find an eating disorders support group. Now. Seriously. Yeah, you're thinking, "I don't have an eating disorder, I just want to lose a few pounds, blah, blah, blah." It's freaky, isn't it, how seductive it is? "If I could just lose ten pounds, then I'd be happier, then people will like me, then I can really start living."

Or, you could forget about the diet and start living right now. You could sit back, laugh at how ridiculously easy it is to get caught up in wishing our bodies away, and enjoy the rest of the book. Just an idea.

At fifteen years and hungry, the scale was the hourglass of my life, telling me how close or far away I remained from my goal weight. Every morning I weighed myself first thing—well, after peeing usually, only before peeing if I felt especially sadistic that day. Barefoot, naked, I woke up to the first judgment of the day, and its verdict was never good. *You're one pound heavier than yesterday, you ugly, stupid thing.* Or, *You're two pounds lighter, let's see if you can keep it off, no treat of diet hot chocolate for you today.*

The morning the scale finally showed the numbers of my "ideal" weight, instead of celebrating, I despaired. My chilled feet stood shivering on the white plastic slab that determined my fate, my mood, my day. Looking down at those accusing numbers, I realized my body still had muscle covering its bones. "Too fat" was the verdict. I kept going.

It seems morbid, but to be honest, my target weight was zero. No weight was skinny enough for me. I wasn't grossed out by pictures of people whose bones jutted out against taut skin. I envied them. Zero was my goal, and no one could stop me.

As an adult, I was not surprised to find out that anorexia is one of the deadliest illnesses for young women between 15 and 24. Many don't escape it alive. Only about a third of anorexics ever fully leave their flirtation with death behind. And even that number is debatable. Zero is not a life-sustaining weight.

The scale taunted me. Zero seemed impossibly far away. But I knew my efforts were working. I would eat only *half* an apple, do *200* sit ups, never *ever* binge, exert exacting control over myself at *every* level, until I was an unstoppable calorie-burning machine. At that moment I realized I didn't need a scale anymore. It only reminded me of how far away my end point was.

Indeed, if the scale gave me an opportunity to rejoice about my progress, it might undercut my ability to lose even more weight. I had already honed the blade of my mental self-insult machine. The scale became redundant, unnecessary, even perhaps a liability. I never stepped on a scale voluntarily again.

More than twenty years later, a thorough search of my house will not unearth a scale, not even in the dustiest recesses of the basement. Perhaps I don't trust myself not to become obsessed by it, like a recovering alcoholic not keeping booze around. Perfectly sensible, really. For years, if I saw a scale peeking out from under the sink in someone's bathroom, a creepy feeling came over me, as if it were whispering, *Kimber, look at me, I'm right here under the sink. You could pull me out and step on me for just a second. It won't hurt a bit. Come on, just one little step? You know you want to.*

Yeah, nice try, I'd think, deliberately pulling my gaze away. Tucking my hair behind my ear in the mirror, I'd wonder momentarily if other people imagined themselves being solicited by a bathroom scale. Do other people have *normal* interactions with the bathroom scale? *Hey, how's it going, nice to see you, thanks for the info, see ya later?* Instead of a sinister menace crouching in the shadows, ready to take them down in a blaze of claws and fury, they just see an inert hunk of plastic and metal, useful for its convenience and function? Must be nice.

Aside from my tendency to assign the bathroom scale a malevolent personality, what it really represented was an all-too-convenient putdown. *Feeling pretty good? Step on the scale, that'll cure any delusions of happiness. Feeling bad already? Only a footstep away from feeling a helluva lot worse.*

After renouncing the scale, security grew even tighter around what was eaten and not eaten, and I protected my naked body from view as if it had vital state secrets tattooed all over it. Was it extreme modesty, or just hiding out? Very few photos of me exist from that time. No pictures, no evidence, no before and after shots. No one could compare me to myself or anyone else. Photos tended to unleash in me a torrent of self-recriminations for my apparent failure to resemble magazine models. It didn't matter, because soon I would vanish anyway.

One picture from that time still haunts me—a prom photo, taken in the hotel room my parents had rented so we wouldn't have to drive home from the party late at night. At my small high school, all the students were invited to the prom, and most showed up as part of an awkward, overdressed couple who deserted each other later for the company of their same-sex friends. I went with Brian, my perfect platonic boyfriend, the handsome blond male version of me. Model skinny. Quiet, with a good sense of humor. Intensely private. Nonthreatening. I had planned the whole thing months in advance. In the fall, I had decided we would make a cute couple and had pursued him, to the end of achieving the gold star standard of perfection I had set for myself. Perfect grades, perfect body, perfect smile, perfect boyfriend. Perfect date for the prom.

My practiced smile shines out of that photo, but the rest is oddly gloomy. I sit stiffly, alone, made up, leaning away from the camera slightly. The hotel chair is dark, with shadows looming in the corner, and the tall window to the right glows with an unearthly pale light. The low-cut neck of my satiny white dress, bought and taken in only a month before, gapes open at the chest, barely held up by my narrowing shoulders, as if the dress would issue not the tiniest whisper of a complaint were its occupant to float quietly up out of its folds and be sucked out the window on a draft.

As May turned to June, I was about to leave on a school trip to France, about to turn sixteen, about to lose the iron-clad grip over myself I had cultivated so viciously for a year. I had no sense of my actual weight, but my favorite jeans kept getting baggier, and I found myself spending longer and longer stretches away from food and out of touch with my body. Perhaps I sensed that my finely tuned control would soon slip silently through my fingers, because the day before we left for France, no nourishment passed through my lips at all.

I wanted to see if I could do it.

Skipping breakfast, my dogged companion hunger and I walked to the drugstore down the street and bought a box of fiber pills to bring along on the trip. *Today I will eat nothing but fiber pills. Maybe I can feel full while eating nothing at all.* Opening the bottle on the way back up the street, I sniffed the contents; their rich, scratchy, concentrated aroma nearly made me gag on the sidewalk. They looked like hamster pellets. Smelled like hamster pellets. Tasted like them too. *Someone is making a ton of money repackaging this crap.* I forced a couple down anyway. My feet felt airy; the soles of my Keds barely touched the ground. Like I might launch at any moment. I concealed my latest vanishing strategy in my bulky shirt and, at home, arranged the bottle inside a pair of socks at the bottom of my suitcase. Some other teenager might be excited about seeing the Eiffel Tower for the first time. My only thoughts were for whether I could maintain my weird diet on the other side of the Atlantic.

Anorexia was a war I waged on myself; by force of will I tore myself apart from the inside, bit by bit. Even years later, part of me longed for that war—the war against my own body. Though I could no longer muster up the razor-edged self-hatred required to voluntarily starve myself, I missed the twisted delight of self-imposed deprivation. Like a hostage with Stockholm syndrome, I defended the brutal tactics of my inner anorexic with apologetic fervor. *Sure, she tied me to a chair, taunted me mercilessly, and starved me senseless, but it's not her fault. I wanted her to do it. She did it for my own good.*

Fortunately, before my inner abductor and her collaborator could carry their plan to its inevitable conclusion, some reservoir of self-preservation must have kicked in: the desire to live, even "fat." I held my parents responsible for feeding that reservoir with the steady, constant assurance that I was a worthy, well-loved, wholesome person. So I backed away from the edge of that slow suicide, however unwillingly.

Several years into my journey to find fullness, I finally told my dad on the phone one afternoon that I'd been anorexic as a teenager.

"We didn't know," he said. "We would have tried to help."

"You did try to help. I asked you to let me see a shrink and you did. But she was terrible. She never asked me about what I was eating or how I felt about my body."

35

"You should have told us. We would have sent you to someone else. Someone better."

"I know. But I couldn't. I was afraid to tell you why I needed someone different. She told me I was depressed because I didn't want to go to college and I was terrified you guys wouldn't let me go if you knew. So I told you everything was fine."

"We never...we wouldn't ever have kept you from leaving for college."

"I know. I'm sorry. I should have told you."

"No." My dad's voice cracked. "I'm sorry. I'm sorry this happened to you. I'm sorry we couldn't help you more."

We were both silent for a moment, trying not to cry into the receiver.

"Dad? I'm afraid to tell Mom."

"She won't like it."

"I'm writing a book about it, she's going to find out sooner or later."

"Just don't rub her nose in it."

The message sunk in. He felt badly about what happened and he didn't want Mom to feel bad, too. Telling her *is* rubbing her nose in it. I sighed. My impulse to protect Mom from anything bad, anything upsetting, came directly from Dad's contributing X chromosome. Why was it *my* job to protect *her*?

chapter three

Lost: Willpower

During another one of our post-yoga lunches, Adrie nne tells me
that when she meets someone who has recovered from an eating
disorder, she always wants to know how they got out of it. I wish I
could give her some pithy answer like, "What worked for me was
sauna sweats. Ginger chews. Whale blubber treatments. And I read
this great book called *How I Went to France, Got a Life, and Lost My
Eating Disorder.*"

If such a book existed, it would have oddly presaged the outcome
of that summer. I'm not entirely sure how my eating disorder got lost,
only that it disappeared suddenly in the humid breeze, just as the
gray dirt of winter gives way to spring's wide swaths of pungent grass
all over Midwestern suburbia.

Luckily for me, our trip to southern France would later land us in
Paris in time to celebrate my sweet sixteenth in late June. A couple
of years before, we had hosted a French girl, Danielle, at our house
for a month, and her family had invited me to stay at her home in
the town of Oloron later that summer. My second visit a year later
would be as the only girl on the annual tenth grade school-organized

exchange trip (all our other classmates had been scared off by the recent hijacking of a French airliner): just me and three boys (including Brian, my sweet, still-platonic boyfriend, David, a nice geeky kid in my grade, and Ethan, our de facto leader, a tall handsome boy a year older) chaperoned by a gray-bearded teacher, Mr. Wheaten. Fortunately Mr. Wheaten was so involved in catching up with his own *amis* and imbibing his annual ration of French vintages that we were left unsupervised and free to explore the joys and dangers of Paris according to the whims of our teenage hearts.

Not having laid eyes on me since the previous summer when I had first met Danielle's family, my French parents greeted me at the baggage claim of the tiny regional airport with choruses of "*Trop maigre!* Too thin! *Tu ne manges rien. Mange, mange-toi!* Eat, eat!" Hélène and Henri, Danielle's parents, and Mouchette, her grandmother, were shocked to see my skinny self. Their high-pitched chatter of outrage mystified me; my friends and family back home had barely noted the gradual change from month to month. Danielle's family vowed to fatten me up "like a *foie gras.*" If I'd known at the time how foie gras is made—by force-feeding geese enormous quantities of mashed corn—I might have turned around and come home.

Their attentions were received with a mixture of pleasure and horror. No two words had ever sounded so beautiful in French than *trop maigre*, too thin. *Say it again.*

But horror overcame delight when I realized how seriously they were taking their duty to put meat back on my bones. And with the twin pressures of novelty and politeness, I found it hard to resist the temptations around me. Much harder than I'd imagined. Nutella on bread. Café au lait. Sheep cheese made only in the local mountains. Chocolates so delicate they could be crafted only in wintertime. A rich, flaky dessert mysteriously called La Russe: paper-thin layers of sugar-dusted pastry with creamy chocolate and, yes, hazelnut filling.

Perhaps my inner prison guard didn't speak enough French to understand what exactly was happening. But part of my mind remained with the fiber pills, in their cushioned hiding place inside my suitcase. Tomorrow I'll eat nothing, I told myself. *Demain.*

Danielle had a scale in her spacious attic bathroom, but it was in indecipherable kilograms, and I didn't trouble myself to make the conversion. I'd stopped counting calories and no one else counted either. Life in France was such a departure from everyday reality, I could start over again from scratch. We ate lunch and dinner outside on the Garcias' porch, the neighbor's cow hanging its head over the hedge to watch. They held two pre-birthday parties in my honor, complete with champagne (in the middle of the day, no less)—one for just the family, one for our whole group of students and friends. Even my inner anorexic couldn't say no to a cake frosted and lit in my honor, and hell, it was French, and hell, it tasted good. I feasted.

One night I filled my plate with salad, but tiny Hélène looked at me with big brown eyes that said in a language that required no translation: *My sweet American guest, I made this tender delicacy especially for you and if you don't eat it I might cry right here.* With a sigh and an inner promise, I let her serve me scallops baked in sweet tomato sauce from the table platter. I loved my French family for how much they loved me, and given my limited skills in *la langue française*, I could only show my full appreciation by oohing and ahhing over the amazing meal, a universal language of the tongue's delight.

At night they refilled my wineglass until I slurred my words, and Danielle and our group's other student hosts taught us drinking songs until the wee hours. *When I die, may I be buried / In a cellar where they keep good wine / Both feet up against the wall / And my head under the tap.* It sounds quite poetic in French. The families we stayed with conspired to keep our little group on a busy schedule of outings and meals, and, without the possibility of setting up a routine I could control or manipulate, I was forced to eat like a normal person. And shockingly enough, I liked it. *Hmm. Hamster pellets? Or another serving of anchovy-stuffed olives?* My mind reassured, *You can revert back to your personal famine when you get home.* Compared to the daily home-cooked fare from Hélène's kitchen, the rodent-grass-flavored fiber pills seemed absurd.

A week or so into our trip, I sat beside Danielle in the back seat of the family car, gazing out the window at the strange but soothingly familiar landscape. The road looped and turned away from the lush emerald gorges we had just visited, when suddenly a black Citroën sped around the corner at us. Swerving, we hit the gravel on the tiny shoulder and skidded sharply. A loud shriek cut across my ears as the far back wheel nearly dipped beyond the point of no return, taking the rest of the car with it off the edge of the steep, golden hillside; but the other three wheels clung valiantly to the tiny shoulder. Leaning toward the road, Henri, Danielle's father, gripped the wheel and swerved away from the ravine. We all held our breath for a moment, and the black sedan jerked back onto the road. Curses I couldn't translate with my high school French spewed from the driver's seat as we sped away.

At that moment of near-disaster it occurred to me for the first time that you never know what might happen in the next instant. One minute you're thrilled, looking up into thick green blankets of vegetation draped over steep ravines, the next you're trapped under a twisted pile of metal, looking at sky where the ground is supposed to be, gasping your last breath.

Steadying my breath, I decided then and there that I could never commit suicide—having found my own personal answer to the only truly serious philosophical problem, according to Camus. Why not commit suicide? Because each moment offers the opportunity to embrace the unexpected. I had been slowly, stealthily cutting away at myself with an invisible knife whose blade I knew would eventually reach bone. Perhaps this marked the point at which I gave up starving myself.

Having said moist-eyed good-byes to our host families in the south, my suitcase full of jars of homemade *foie gras* that Mouchette insisted my parents needed, we bundled ourselves onto a plane to Orly airport. Only hours later I settled into my Parisian hotel room, with its luxuriously large bed, tall, lace-curtained window, and my own bathroom: the perk of being the only girl. Sprawled across the matelassé coverlet, I reveled in my adultlike privacy, feeling only a tiny bit sorry for the three boys who had to share a much smaller room across the hall, with two twin beds and a dusty cot.

Our trip was almost over, and I stayed behind one afternoon to pack while the boys went exploring. I intended to carefully iron the beautiful pale yellow skirt and jacket that my French family had given me, so that I could sit in it for hours on the airplane and get it all wrinkled. In the foyer I asked the friendly concierge for an iron, and he promised to bring one up right away. Up in my room, after wrestling the ironing board's legs out and setting it shakily beside the wall outlet, I heard a knock. I opened the door and reached for the iron the concierge held against his chest, saying, "Merci…"

But the concierge brushed past me and dropped the iron on the bed. I followed him into the room, confused for a moment. He turned toward me, grasped my arms by my sides, pressed his lips onto mine, and tried to stick his tongue down my throat. With eyes open, startled to the bone, I saw my reflection in the closet mirror as I tried to free myself from his crushing embrace, and wondered, *What I have I done to deserve this?* I felt his hips and torso force me toward the bed as my arms pushed him away. Compared to him, my body felt small and fragile, though the adrenaline leaping through my veins like a thousand electric eels gave me the energy to fight back.

God only knows which words of my fragile French persuaded him to leave, which of my frantic actions convinced him that my objection to his advances was not modesty, but a profound lack of interest bordering on disgust. As the door shut behind him, the sticky smell of his cologne clung to my face and neck and hair, but my clothes remained on and my virginity intact. Relieved by his departure, sitting on the floor with my head in my trembling hands, I was shaken out of my shock when I realized: *He has the key to my room.*

I grabbed my backpack, fumbled with my now-pointless key, and hurried off to find my male companions. Wandering down the winding cobblestone streets, ignoring the taxis, oblivious to the street cafés and market stalls, my thoughts sped ahead of my feet. *What would I tell the boys? Would they even believe me?*

To my relief, I caught sight of Brian and Ethan loitering on the stairs in front of the museum I had declined to visit. David stood only a few feet away, wiping the summer sweat from his forehead with his sleeve. I hurried up the steps to meet them. They seemed unsurprised to see me, and falling into step behind them, I kept my eyes down, trying to distract myself by counting cigarette butts flattened into the cobblestones as we walked. Ethan eyed the half-eaten baguette David had carried around in his backpack all day and decided we should eat. We wandered down alleyways, coming out onto a side street near the Champs-Élysées, and headed toward a cheap café serving sandwiches for an early dinner. I placed one foot in front of the other, each step a numb attempt to put more distance between me and the concierge's probing hands. I resolved to say nothing about what had happened in my room. I would suck it up, like my belly. Brian slowed down a bit to walk next to me, telling me about the museum and the funny guide who had assisted them in Russian-accented French.

My resolve didn't last. "Brian? If I called out in the middle of the night, would you come help me?"

"It depends." He lightly punched me in the arm.

My lower lip quivered. "No, I'm serious, if I screamed from my room in the middle of the night, would you come help me?" I imagined the three of them breaking the door down and leaping in, swords drawn like the teenage musketeers.

"What are you talking about?"

Brian tried to capture my gaze, but I knew if I looked him in the eye, the flood of tears would be unstoppable. The fear in my voice must have transmitted what words could not. He put his arm around me and I turned to him, and wept into his shoulder. Ethan and David surrounded us, awkwardly comforting, and sat down with me on a carved stone bench. The story, along with my tears, spilled out on the sidewalk overlooking the Seine.

To the boys' credit, I remember being sufficiently reassured to return with them to the hotel later that evening. We stayed up all night long, singing every French drinking song we could remember, our bodies draped across the generous bed in my room, sipping dirt-cheap wine we'd picked up for a buck fifty at the *épicerie*. The lecherous concierge failed to make an appearance. As the sun rose we ventured out to find the first street vendor selling hot *pommes frites*, packed our bags, and took our hangovers to the airport and back to our parents' blissful ignorance.

In the broiling July weeks following my return to suburbia, I discovered that along with my sense of physical safety, I had lost my willpower not to eat. Something intangible had shifted; the inner force that held sweets at a distance and compelled me to exercise as if pursued by demons had vanished. Maybe some survival-based corner of my brain blamed my thin, carefully tended body for inviting the concierge's attention and comforted me with the conclusion that by layering on fat and pounds I could shield and defend myself again. Or perhaps my brain's love for life had simply seen its chance and permanently disarmed my attempt to starve myself to death.

My anorexic mindset remained undisturbed; self-loathing piled on with every bite that went into my mouth. My inner prison guard fumed over the turn of events, emasculated and railing with frustrated impotence. Even my inner prisoner seemed confused about what to do next. Accustomed to beatings and humiliation from her tormentor, she had no inner compass, no direction; abuse was the only relationship she knew.

Perversely, my inner prisoner seemed to miss the attention, and aggravated the guard every chance she got. Tied his shoelaces together, giggling. Painted his lips red while he slept, and filled his hands with shaving cream. She'd prod him awake with the same stick he'd thrashed her with. *Watch me eat this entire box of Thin Mints,* she'd laugh. *What's that you said? Stop? I'm sorry, you'll have to speak up, I can't hear you over the sound of tearing cardboard and crinkling plastic. They're thin. They're minty! Want one?* Her laughter reverberated across the bars of the empty cell. The smeared and hobbled guard lay immobilized, an absurd, venomous clown, staring at her.

One sultry July afternoon a few weeks before junior year was to begin, alone in the pink-carpeted TV room of our home, I consumed an entire bag of greasy potato chips. Crunchy, salty, oil-laden—they tasted divine on my fat-deprived tongue. At least the first twenty did. The next fifty or so, I didn't taste at all.

You are fat. Gross. Horrible.

The only suitable punishment was a self-flagellating jog. After hiding the crumpled bag in the bottom of the trash, I put on my gym shorts to go for a run in the humid Midwestern afternoon. The heavy

44

maple branches dripped with moist, felted leaves, and as I pounded the sidewalk with my body's enormous mass, I imagined their looming trunks were passersby smug with the knowledge of my failure, sniggering at my loss of self-control, and grimly satisfied by my defeat. With them as my witnesses, I would run until my legs gave out, and only then would I drag myself home on my elbows, clean myself up, and not eat anything else for the rest of the week.

Just one block into my forced march, my anger and quadriceps faltered, leaving only disgust and an icky taste in my mouth. I trudged home in humiliation, my failure completed by the inability to carry out a just punishment. Three weeks of French food, being fattened up as promised, had caught up with me. But only temporarily, I hoped. Alas, by the time school began in mid-August, I had not yet relocated my lost willpower. If someone picked my willpower up out of the subway grate in Paris, dusted it off and took it home, I hope they used it for good, and not for ill.

If I had felt numb while starving myself, I felt doubly numb now. With Jen gone to college, the school carpool responsibilities fell on my shoulders, and my schedule filled with memorizing lines for the school play, student government meetings, college visits, and endless sleepless nights in front of the computer pounding out yet another paper I'd left until the last minute. My body gained weight, but I wouldn't let myself see it or feel it, except as an overall self-disgust dulled only by my relentless schedule. When I happened to glimpse my swelling form in the mirror, my mind spat, *You big, fat pig*, shrinking with the inward knowledge that this was no longer merely a motivating insult; it was true. Afraid to taste, afraid to feel, I tried to distance myself from what I ate or looked like. Inwardly I identified with the prison guard, furious that the rigors of hardship and thinness had come to an end. Slowly, my inner prisoner wandered away

from the prison grounds and explored the world, forgetting sometimes about the guard still searching for her, and the empty cell
awaiting her return.

After the tenth grade Hunger Year of not eating anything sweet,
during junior year my body began to freak out. One Saturday
morning in mid-January I found myself on the floor of the upstairs
bathroom, wet and naked, with a throbbing lump on the back of my
head. My mouth tasted like burlap, and my head lolled heavy with
blood and a black emptiness I found hard to shake off. I had fainted
as I stepped out of the hot water into the chilled air.

The following week while driving home from school alone one
evening, I tried to focus on the contrast between the glaring white
snow bank and the dark tarmac. The world slowly tilted, went black,
then righted itself again. With the road spinning around me, I pulled
into a nearby parking lot, shut off the engine, closed my eyes, and
holding onto the steering wheel as if my life depended on it, leaned
my head back against the blue velour seat. I waited for my control to
reappear from whatever void it had dropped into. *Please let me get
home*, I prayed to the lights on the dashboard, the curve of the steering wheel, the pale yellow beads of my knuckles. *Please.*

Forty-five minutes later I pulled into our driveway, grateful no
more black voids had appeared to suck me in along I-75. That evening
I told my dad about my episodes. Still wearing his lab coat and suit,
he looked at me, perplexed by the changes in his second daughter,
nearly grown but not yet a woman.

"We'll see what we can do."

Reassured, I crushed myself to his lapel and stifled a sigh. For a
moment, I let myself take in all his comforting dad smells, cologne
and pipe smoke underlying the clean crunch of his coat. He held me
tight for a moment, his big arms wrapped around my back. There

was so much to tell him, but the words stuck in my throat like wads of cotton.

"I love you, hon."

"I love you too, Dad."

A few days later he took me to the hospital, right around the corner from our house, for a glucose tolerance test. A fasting test. No food for twelve hours beforehand. I arrived fuzzy-headed and irritable, and the nurse gave me a cup of orange-colored juice to drink, or what *looked* like juice. From the first tentative sip, my mouth told me this was *not* juice. A thick, gag-inducing sludge, like Tang mixed with Karo's corn syrup. Nothing for breakfast, and now this? I choked it down, wondering first how many calories the vile stuff might contain, and second, what possible diagnosis required this treatment? After an interminable wait spent struggling with nausea and dizziness, they brought me to a long, sterile recliner and took my blood. I was surprised it came out red and not goopy orange.

A week later Dad sat down across from me in our TV room. "So, the results came back. You're hypoglycemic. We're not sure why."

He leaned forward and explained that my body was producing too much insulin and not properly regulating the amount of sugar in my bloodstream. I nodded vaguely, not quite following his doctorly description of glucose intake and pancreatic function. The treatment recommendations were: No fasting, and keep a little food around all the time. I didn't understand. *Fasting had caused the blackouts? But I was fasting less now than the year before. He doesn't know I was starving myself.* I leaned against the back of the chair, sucking my lips between my teeth, keeping them shut and sealed. Part of me wanted to share everything. But a bigger part of me was too frightened to expose him to the carefully hidden monsters of my inner anorexic and her cohorts.

Juggling snacks and schoolwork, stashing a bag of pretzels in the car, a granola bar at the bottom of my backpack, I didn't consciously connect my reactions to sugar and fasting with my former deprivations. Now I wonder if my body didn't lose the ability to process sugar properly during its year off—maybe it forgot how to manage the Ho Hos and Snickers, and all the various combinations of sucrose, glucose, and fructose that the typical American diet entails.

My body held internal scars, perhaps, just as my mind did.

chapter four

The Anorexic in Me

If I had been completely composed that September day in Hawaii when my mom asserted, "You were not anorexic," instead of replying, "Not now, Mom. *As a teenager*," I would have dragged up from inside the complete, shocking truth: "Mom, I'm still anorexic."

At that time, I was a newly minted lawyer, and had lived for years just from the neck up. Body? What body? You don't need a *body* to be a *lawyer*, do you? As long as my body didn't get in the way of long hours bent over casebooks and the computer keyboard, I guess I wouldn't *mind* having it, but it damn well better not *need* anything.

Technically, I no longer starved myself. Regular meals, snacks, desserts, everything was once again on the menu. On the outside my body appeared healthy enough, though somewhat chubby (to my eyes, anyway). But some unspoken part of me longed to be anorexic again and waited in the dark for its opportunity to arise.

Secretly, I avoided mirrors, and if my body did get caught in one, I quickly glanced away to avoid seeing my thighs. I couldn't look at them without wincing at their too-muchness. Seeing my body in a mirror instantly brought up unconscious comparisons to the magazine images plastered onto the back of my skull. *My hips pooch out all over, my thighs rub together, my butt hangs too low.* In a bathing suit, my self-consciousness ballooned up like SpongeBob in the Macy's Thanksgiving Day parade, except I would have paid good money to have skinny, knobby legs like his. Who envies SpongeBob's legs? Me. Cartoon legs would be awesome, erasable and redrawn as needed.

My body didn't measure up to the "ideal," and I found it deeply shameful. Even in a tropical paradise with my family, enjoying ourselves by the pool or at the beach, I had to subtly psych myself up to head out into public view. A litany of faint reassurance and mild scolding usually did the trick. *Nobody is looking at you, nobody cares, forget what anyone else thinks about you. Don't be such a baby. If you look like you don't care, no one else will either.* And off to the pool with a towel wrapped tightly around my waist. *Suck that belly in, you'll be fine.*

I wouldn't admit to anyone how much my wide thighs grossed me out. No one could have convinced me they weren't disgusting. Anyone who would say my thighs weren't ugly was obviously blind. And I certainly didn't want to hear the opposite reaction— confirmation that my thighs were indeed huge. Nothing would be more likely to propel me into a spasm of self-disgust than being damned with faint praise: "Your thighs are...fine. Really. Not... too...fat."

Once in college, I watched out of the corner of my eye as a woman in the gym lovingly applied lotion to her entire body, in front of a room-length mirror, apparently oblivious to anyone (me) nearby. She touched every part of her body (even her thighs, horrors!) as if she cared about every inch of skin with equal affection. As I sat on a bench a few feet away, midway to pulling a large bottle of shampoo out of my locker, her pleased smile caused my preconceptions to swerve and brake. *She isn't Kate Moss; she doesn't have some model's body, just an average woman's body in ordinary shape.* But she clearly loved her body unashamedly. She was enjoying it. I watched her surreptitiously, fascinated. *How does she do it? Can I figure out how to love my body that way?*

I couldn't. Not yet. But one day I hoped I would.

The August after graduation from high school, I arrived at college in Los Angeles (child psychiatrist be damned), a fresh-faced Midwestern girl, with a white Laura Ashley comforter with tiny pink roses to conceal the musty twin bed I inherited from a long line of previous freshmen. USC hadn't been my first choice, but I resigned myself to a year of sunlight and beaches until I could transfer someplace more serious. Debbi, my Japanese-American roommate in the honors dorm, was from Hawaii, which we figured out on my globe was just slightly further away from L.A. than Ohio. She showed me how to make ramen noodles and eat them with chopsticks out of a cup. We commiserated, both of us new transplants dropped into a city where life was lived with the dials turned all the way up, taps on full blast, maximum warp speed, and hang on tight!

One night that brutally hot fall, we amused ourselves making balloon animals, cross-legged on our beds, and found that after making the legs and the body, we'd run out of room to make the ears and the head. "It looks like a four-legged..."

"...Penis!"

Debbi and I shrieked with laughter, rolling over on our sides, holding our bellies, trying to breathe. We ended up with a collection of colorful walking penis balloons, a long, side-splitting enactment of the conversations and activities walking penises might enjoy, and an array of giddy walking penis jokes. "What did one walking penis say to the other?—'Hey, got a rubber?'"

"Two walking penises go into a bar. The bartender says, 'Sorry, we don't serve dickheads.'"

We laughed until we cried. Our walking penises became quite popular with our dorm mates, who popped in to see what had sent us into near-hyperventilation.

My new friends along the hallway signed up for yoga that semester, and together we headed across campus in our sweatpants, giggling and gossiping in the dimming September light. Marla, the instructor, was all fluttery scarves and musky incense and chakras— whatever the heck those were—and she might as well have taught the class entirely in Sanskrit; she was as alien to me as if she hailed from the planet Nirvana.

One afternoon I glimpsed her near the checkout at the grocery store, her basket full of exotic, unfamiliar items. Holding my breath, I ducked behind the endcap display of tortillas and skittered down the aisle, blushing. Risking even eye contact with her felt excruciatingly embarrassing. I didn't know the first thing to say to her. I imagined waving my hand in front of her softly focused eyes, saying, "Hellooo? Do you speak English? Midwestern, perhaps? How do you do?" We had no common language. I was certain that no bridge of any size, or length, or metaphorical content could possibly connect her experience to mine.

Marla did speak English and was as American as someone who fluidly pronounced "*supta padangustasana*" could be. Yet in class, our shared mother tongue mattered little, which, as it turned out, was not her fault, but mine. I could barely hear a word she said over the uproar in my own head, the endless cacophony of negative comparisons to my friends' bodies. *Look at your sausage legs, no wonder no one likes you. Suanna's thighs are tiny little twigs next to your massive logs.*

How many hours would you have to spend at the gym to end up with what she has living on candy bars and regular Coke? Even Leila's hips are narrower than yours! Everybody's looking at you. They're all so relieved they're not as lumpy as you are. Oh, God, why did I come here? Marla led us through a slow series of stretches, mostly on the floor. "Let the purple energy settle…let the red energy rise," she chanted. My California-grown dorm mates nodded at her, breathing deeply, like they had a clue. Meanwhile, my mind continued its rant: *I could be on the Stairmaster now, actually doing something about these thighs instead of just breathing at them.*

The only moment my mind desisted from its ceaseless complaining came at the end of class, when we all lay down on our backs with our eyes closed in savasana, and Marla talked us onto a beautiful imaginary beach, with the sand warming our toes, the palms gracefully fanning our siesta. If I couldn't see my body, no one else could either. I gratefully rested, relieved to be free of my own criticism for a handful of breaths.

A semester's worth of stretching and breathing left me with the sense that yoga was something disconcertingly, unfathomably foreign, and not even "real" exercise. Or at least not an exercise that would help me rebuild the barbed-wire-crowned walls of thinness. But part of me held fast to those moments of peace, of stillness, of relief from the relentless demonic carousel of my mind.

During that year I gained the freshman five. Then the freshman ten. And the freshman fifteen weren't far behind. My mind and my body no longer collaborated. In the gym, my mind berated my shaky legs to go another mile, but later at the cafeteria, my hands piled the plate high with pasta and brownies. At night I would curl up under my bed's white comforter, eating endless honey sesame sticks in the dark, as if my body could conceal itself from my mind like a child hiding her legs from the monster under the bed. No matter how many Diet Cokes I stacked up alongside my computer to fuel my paper-writing marathons, no matter how many hours I spent climbing stairs that never led anywhere, my body and mind just wouldn't cooperate in once again peeling back the raw, hungry edge of my anorexia.

In Russian class, my study mate showed me a translucent blotch on her homework before we handed it forward from our desks. "I spent all weekend at the pool. Do you think she'll mind the suntan lotion?" Who knows if our Russian teacher minded—I was not impressed. No wonder the library had seemed so quiet. Were classes just what everyone did between sunbathing sessions? At a garden party a few weeks before, our Russian teacher had introduced me to a visiting scholar of Russian History who taught at Smith College. Her tough-as-nails demeanor told me she would make me work hard and learn more than I thought possible. I was ready to turn my attention to something other than my cellulite.

My friends along the hallway teased me when they found out I'd decided to go to Smith College, following in my sister's footsteps: "A girls' school? What, are you a lesbian?" Secretly horrified, I shrugged it off. At least they weren't mocking my thighs. From my own outlook on Mount Self-Hatred, I couldn't see why anyone would want to be my friend anyway. I'd miss Debbi, though. She'd lived with me all year. She knew I wasn't a lesbian. Didn't she? No matter. The following August, I traded movie stars and tanning creams for the crisp deciduous hills of western Massachusetts.

Behind the lush, beautiful campus of Smith College, beyond the wooded meadow and boggy mill stream, loomed an abandoned "insane asylum," as the students called the nearby falling-down mental hospital—just for the thrill of hearing those words uttered together. Nothing like taking a stroll by it to send a shiver up one's spine on a dark evening. As undergraduates, we wandered through the trees, gazing up at the tilting, deserted windows as the sun set, and wondered what souls had been lost there. I imagined my own inner prisoner frantically running downhill through the underbrush in bare feet, only to skid to a halt, gasp for breath, look up, and find herself on a manicured lawn with Smith's Paradise Pond shimmering in the distance. A narrow escape. Or so I felt when I transferred to Smith from USC. An escape from who I was to who I would be.

I ignored the scales in each bathroom by pretending they didn't exist and that I couldn't care less about my weight. I cut my long hair to a stylish bob and started wearing boyish, baggy clothes, more or less successfully hiding my accumulated sins under a cultivated indifference to my body and appearance.

Smith was a relief. There were women of all different shapes and sizes, even women who seemed genuinely unconcerned about what other people thought of their bodies. Every woman I met seemed talented, intelligent, and utterly different from me, each her own unique self.

At that time, every residential house at Smith had a dining room with its own kitchen staff and chef, who did their best to fatten us up. They were marvelous at it, serving delicious, comforting dishes, even vegetarian fare, and as much butter and bread and dessert as you wanted. No cafeteria trays, just a buffet table, all-you-can-eat, three meals a day. Without my inner prison guard to give me direction, the inner prisoner went wild, breezing past my admonitions to stop and eat sensibly, so I just ate whatever she wanted, despite being unhappy with the size 14 results. Nobody would tell me what I could and couldn't eat, not even myself.

Meals became an ongoing source of stress for me. Unconsciously I compared what was on my plate with what my friends put on theirs.

I compared my body to each of my housemates in turn as they weaved their way through the chairs and tables, across the planked floor, and through my line of vision, plates in hand. *Shelly's pants fit pretty tight, but my thighs are fatter. Laura's belly bulges out some, but look, her legs are so skinny. Ugh, I can't believe how much food Amy's piled onto her plate. I hate her. She could be a runway model and eats like a starving animal.* I turned back to my plate, frowning. *What's wrong with me? Why can't I look like that and eat whatever I want?* That question was more palatable when shoved down with another cookie.

Fortunately, I could still shop in the extra-large sizes of regular stores, even if I loathed my fattening body in private. I remained in the range of normal; in fact, downright average compared to American women as a whole. And still under the radar. *Yep, everyone thinks I'm just fine. Damn.*

I made deals with myself. *You can have dessert, but only on weekends. You can have seconds, but only of fruit and vegetables. You can eat a little candy, but only if someone offers it. You ate that whole bag of corn chips yesterday, so from now on, no more junk food, ever. No more ice cream, no more cake, no more MORE.*

Then one Wednesday evening I found myself in the dining hall, standing in front of the dessert table. Grapes and yogurt and brown sugar. Mmm. I rationalized, *It's not really dessert. Just fruit and dairy.* During my third trip to the giant bowl of blush-green grapes that never seemed to dwindle, I convinced myself, *Not really dessert.* My inner anorexic furiously pounded away at my ribs with her fists: *Don't! Stop, you fatso!* But she couldn't make a sound through the din of creamy sweetness chewed, swallowed, and repeated. No amount of scolding and cajoling could restrain my hunger once it had escaped.

Later, up in my room, lying on my bed, staring up at the cracks in the ceiling extending into the shadowed corners, I pressed a pillow into my bloated stomach and wept. I had become that most loathsome and feared of all creatures, what my inner anorexic had always warned me about: a food weakling, an uncontrolled addict, unable to say no to the weakest craving or most passing desire. Wrapped in my damp, flowery quilt, I binged on self-hatred.

It was the worst of both worlds: I couldn't stop myself from eating, and I continued to hold scathingly judgmental opinions of those who could not control themselves around food. Most specifically, me. At least while starving myself, I had the chilly, superior comfort of looking down on those poor souls who didn't know better than to indulge themselves with food. Now I had the horrible, disjointed sense of looking at myself from both directions, judging myself cruelly while simultaneously unable to resist the next bite. The prison guard and anorexic on one shoulder, constantly berating the gluttonous prisoner on the other. Like other people have angels and devils. Their constant bitter sniping led to an itchy, uncomfortable feeling that only a creamy piece of chocolate could temporarily dissolve.

The vow of silence I'd taken during my hungry year remained in full force. Not a word of my discomfort and confusion, of my constant guilt around food and exercise, escaped my lips. Not a single friend had ventured inside the mental prison, abandoned but haunted, of my failed attempt to emulate inmates dying of maltreatment. I happily discussed with my friends whether to dress up as a guitar or a Grecian goddess for Halloween (I went with the guitar) and shared stories about Nate, my older boyfriend who worked for Greenpeace. Two of my friends first met him while he dangled from a tree branch, taking photos of a protest we were marching in—Is that your *boyfriend?* Uh, dunno, it's hard to tell from here. Um... yup, that's him. Your boyfriend climbs trees? That's dreamy! But start talking about eating pizza or enjoying sundaes, and the conversation was over. *My eating is fine. I am fine. If you're sick and you never tell anyone and you're never diagnosed, it's like you were never sick, right? Right.*

As a junior I went in for a checkup at the health center, and when the nurse went to weigh me I told her not to show me my weight. "Don't tell me, either." I stepped on the scale, with my back turned to the numbers.

She looked at me penetratingly for a moment and then took me aside into an examination room. She said, "Usually when women don't want to know how much they weigh, we worry about eating disorders." *Ha*, I thought. *Five years too late…*

"I was anorexic as a teenager."

For a moment the air tensed around me as if I had admitted to some terrible crime. But after I'd spoken the taboo words, relief spread through my legs and I felt the sudden need to sit down. I had given voice to something forbidden, unutterable.

Tears burned at the corners of my eyes. "My eating is fine now, I haven't starved myself for years, don't worry." I stared at the floor, feeling her gaze on my face. Did she believe me?

She seemed reassured by my explanation as she jotted something down in my file. "Feel free to come back if you need to talk about it," she said as she left me sitting on the cold vinyl of the examination table. "The doctor will see you shortly."

When the door closed behind her, leaving me alone, staring at the fluorescent-lit floor, I felt fatigued, shaky, and, in some corner of my heart, weirdly pleased. The acknowledgment of her gaze, which recognized something in me that everyone else had glossed over and ignored, made me want to cry from relief. My experience was real, not all in my head. I wasn't alone. I had lived through it and could see myself standing on the other side.

With only this one piece of information, this nurse knew me, my history, my story; she understood something crucial about my day-to-day life. My teachers and my friends hadn't seen it. The child psychiatrist hadn't seen it—couldn't see it when it was practically sitting in her lap—but this woman, this person who laid eyes on me once, could see it, even years after my most obvious symptoms had disappeared. Even my parents, with all their love, even they couldn't see this part of me. Yet some insightful stranger saw it in a moment. Hallelujah. Maybe I wasn't so inscrutable after all. Maybe I could even start to understand myself.

Many of my Smith friends were not model-thin, but were beautiful and lovable, and had healthy, friendly attitudes toward themselves. Sheila, an upperclasswoman who lived down the hall, leaned into my doorway one evening as I was arranging my clothes in the mirror to hide my body's flaws, and said, "Oh, you look great. So strong, so fit."

I couldn't hide my surprise. My mouth hung open. She couldn't be serious. Why didn't she see me as fat and ugly, the way I saw myself?

I blushed. "No, my thighs are too fat. I wish they looked more like yours." She smiled, shrugged, and disappeared behind the door. Gazing at the mirror's reflection, I replayed her words. Was it possible that my self-perception was vastly different from the perception of those around me? *Could it be true that I don't look as fat as I feel? Is it possible that I could be fat and attractive?* My thick layer of self-disgust tried to resist the possibility, but it had already begun to sink in.

For a long time, I had thought of my body as something decorative, an *objet d'art* to please other people—my parents, men, women, whoever was looking—no matter the cost to myself. I thought my body should be a miniature show poodle: well-behaved, inoffensive, charmingly small, and pleasant to look at.

At Smith, it occurred to me for the first time that I was not a poodle. Not miniature. Not well-behaved. The stately brick buildings, the lush lawns, groomed paths, and breathtaking Paradise Pond were all maintained for the benefit and appreciation of the women who walked to and from class beneath the arms of wide maples and sycamores. Educated women. Powerful women. Me.

In an environment whose every rock and signpost were placed for my benefit, I could finally ask myself questions that I'd never allowed to surface. *Who says my body is for pleasing others? Why can't my body be for pleasing myself? Why does my body have to be my enemy?*

Weakening self-hatred and my nascent female-oriented outlook shined a new spotlight on how to relate my body. A Bette Midler–like voice appeared in that spotlight, speaking quietly at first, but with promise: *Hey, this is my body! Who made the rule that because it's large, it's ugly? Who made the rule that I can't love my body even if it doesn't belong on the cover of some magazine?* I didn't know who the culprit was, but I suspected "they" were the kind of asshole who would purposely spill their Bloody Mary on your white shirt at a cocktail party, make fun of you for the resulting stain, then announce loudly that your shirt had gotten in the way of enjoying their drink. Who cared what they thought anyway?

This line of thinking led me to my journal one Sunday night. At the tall desk overlooking a tree-lined path below, I chewed on the end of my pen, and wrote:

Time to make up my own rules.

- First rule: *My body is just fine the way it is.*

- Second rule: *I am allowed to love my body if I choose.*

- Third rule: *Stop listening to anyone who tells me otherwise. Even if the voice is in my own head.*

I knew these rules made sense. I resolved to stick to them. But when push came to shoving my thighs into my jeans, would I still remember them? Could I choose to love my body...was it that simple? I didn't know if it was possible after looking at my body with disgust for so long or avoiding it altogether.

Later that night, in the dim light of my dorm shower stall, I tried to apply lotion to my naked body the way the woman at the gym had done. Even with no mirror to look into, little waves of anxiety appeared on my internal horizon.

First, a deep breath. Next, lotion on my arms. That seemed fine, no problem. Heck, I could even muster up a little affection for my arms, they seemed pretty normal, good enough. Breasts, a little tentative, but alright. Belly's okay for me, now back, fine. Another deep breath. On to my butt...I tensed, my hands felt suddenly clammy... maybe my hips, how about my thighs...*ugh*. I froze. I couldn't touch anything down there without wanting to pull away. *Sigh*. I skipped lower for a moment. Feet, yup; ankles, calves, no problem. *What's left? Oh, yeah, I still have to do my thighs, butt, and hips. Okay, so don't look at them, look at something else, think of something else. If you can't think something nice, don't think anything at all.* The nicest thing I could think of was: *I hope someday I can enjoy touching every part of myself.*

My hips, butt, and thighs. I had disliked them for so long. I aspired to like them, maybe even love them, but it was incredibly difficult. What was wrong with them? In truth, they worked pretty well. They carried me everywhere, they were useful to sit on, to run with, to walk with, they gave me very few problems really, except that I hated the way they looked in pants or shorts or naked. As long as I didn't see them in the mirror or look at them hanging out there below my pelvis, my judgments floated in suspended animation, like fish trapped in a frozen lake. The minute their shape crossed my retina, the ice cracked open, comparisons and insults flapping every-where. At least I was starting to see their usefulness aside from their appearance, and understand that it was up to me to decide to love them. To love me.

Unless I believed I was lovable, it wouldn't make any difference how thin or how fat my body was—I would never feel loved no matter how much someone adored me. I would never be able to trust love or kindness or devotion in someone else, always thinking that they couldn't mean it, because who could love a fat blob like me anyway? And if someone truly loved me—what the hell was wrong with them? If I wanted to experience the love I craved, that I longed for, I would have to love myself, be kind to myself, and start to see my own beauty. The beautiful fat woman in the fast food restaurant... that was her secret, some part of me knew. Not only did she know her husband loved her, but *she loved herself.* Could I get there too? It would be a long road, a journey across miles and waters.

Caught up in a whirlwind of classes on history and genocide, meetings at the Haymarket underground anarchist café, and fund-raisers for political refugees, it occurred to me that obsessing about "who's the fairest one of all" sapped my energy for connecting with the women I lived and studied alongside. Instead of competing with other women—to look good for men, for popularity, for power, or for money—we should be joining together to protest unequal wages for women, to help women out of poverty, and to shed light on the ongoing international slave trade in "brides" and prostitutes. We should be supporting each other to realize our wildest dreams. When there was so much work to be done, how could I be worried about whether my jeans were too tight? Like an idle top whose young owner had wandered away, the tightly wound spool of my endless comparisons about physical appearance slowly started to loosen and unravel.

"Boyfriend in a Tree" didn't hurt either. Nate had followed me to the campus café one night after a political play in Smith's tiny theater. He didn't seem to notice my hips and thighs. Or rather, he *did* notice and had no objections. Flattered by the attention of an older, sophisticated activist, I was easily talked into a first date. We went to see *Henry and June*. On the list of terrible first-date movies, this one has got to be at the top, unless of course the point of your date is to be so overstimulated by elaborate sex scenes that you end up naked in your date's arms at the end of the night. Which is what happened. We embarked on a four-month fling during which he was sure I was in love with him, though *obsessed*, I think, is the better word.

For hours I laid on the rug in my dorm room desperately hoping he'd call. On the rare occasions he did, I tried to match his jaded indifference.

"Hey Kimber. What's up?"

Sitting bolt upright, nearly upsetting the floor lamp next to me, I tried to squeeze every bit of relief and hope out of my voice.

"Nothing. Working on a paper."

"I'm busy tonight, but maybe we could hang out later."

"Sure, later. Later's fine."

Gritting my teeth, I hung up, furious at myself for not pinning him down, for being such a wimp, for wanting him to validate me. *To love me.*

Lying in Nate's arms one night after having sex in my single bed in the dorm, I stroked his back with my hands, and he murmured into my ear, "Are you a lesbian?"

Imagine. You've just had intercourse with a man, and he asks if you're a lesbian. Very flattering. And weirdly, I got the impression that he was asking me not because I hadn't enjoyed it, *but because I'd enjoyed it too much*. I still wanted to touch and cuddle. Is that what lesbians did? How on earth would he know? Bemused and smiling into his shoulder, I answered, "I don't think so."

The women around me were beautiful, and righteous. New variations on what made a woman appealing sprang up, fully formed. Getting a whole group of people cheering for a cause? Awe-inspiring. Fat, short, old, skinny, awkward, strong, it didn't matter—if a woman could rev up a crowd, write a ferociously funny political diatribe, or belt out a parody of a recent pop song, she was downright gorgeous in my book. Instead of looking out at a group of women and categorizing each of them as fatter or thinner than me, prettier than me, or not, I could see that the one there in the corner with the nose ring looks tough and fun, she'd be a good friend to have at a rally; the one with the turtleneck and glasses looks serious, maybe she'd like to join our progressive magazine's editorial board; and the one with the guitar T-shirt and spiky hair...damn, she's sexy! No longer beauty contest competitors, women could be allies, friends...maybe more. It didn't occur to me I might *be* one of those sexy, beautiful women. It did occur to me that if I wanted to change the world, becoming a lawyer might be a good way to do it...I could be fierce, righteous, and effective, even if I couldn't be thin.

Still, the freed prisoner and resentful prison guard ran circles around each other in my subconscious; could I get them to call a truce after all these years? Maybe a Truth-and-Reconciliation kind of thing? After my disjointed experience with the child psychiatrist several years earlier, I was terrified another expert would try to tell me how I felt instead of listening. If my emotions were being dictated to me by someone else, I wouldn't get anywhere near the perilous gate of my innermost feelings. Part of me wanted the help of a professional, but fled in terror at the potential invasiveness of a stranger's queries in the midst of my raw unsteadiness. The opportunity for some shift in my inner landscape existed, and yet some well-intentioned interloper could all too easily grab on, jiggle the frame, and cause the whole thing to collapse.

I had a very clear picture of the ideal therapist: she'd be brilliant, self-effacing, a great listener, and able to put up with my postadolescent smugness. Also she'd have to be warm and loving, with excellent boundaries. She wouldn't assume anything about me, wouldn't know any of my friends, would be unassociated with the college, could meet with me whenever and wherever I wanted, and would, of course, be free of charge.

It became clear that the ideal therapist existed only in my mind. Which was fine. I could meet with her there, in the office between my two ears. Taking out the hardbound writing journal that had been a gift from my sister, I wrote a dialogue of what questions the ideal therapist would ask to elicit what was simmering beneath my uneasy awareness. I noted in my journal that this type of therapy had the benefit of being "cheaper, and more self-revealing."

(Note the absence of pleasantries, another benefit to having an inner therapist.)

Therapist: Why have you come here?

Me: I'm not really sure sometimes, and sometimes I know exactly why, but there's too much to start with. I don't know where to begin.

Therapist: Take your time.

Me: I'm afraid. I've been told I have a problem with eating, and I think maybe it's true.

At this point I tell my therapist the story of the concierge in Paris…
my near-rape experience.

Therapist: So this was a traumatic event for you?

Me: Yes, it was. It took me a long time to tell anyone other
than Brian and the boys about it, and I wondered if
it was my fault. Did I lead him on? I mean, I wasn't
raped or anything, it wasn't that serious—shouldn't I
just be flattered? No. I know I didn't lead him
on—and I didn't feel flattered, just disgusted and terrified. The real issue, anyway, was that the year
before this trip I had lost a lot of weight (I had always
considered myself fat), maybe for the wrong reasons,
and since then I've always thought I'd probably been
anorexic at the time. After that experience, I guess
you could say I started eating and I haven't stopped
since. I lost weight because I hated my body. My
reason for gaining weight again wasn't any better.

(Isn't it great how the inner therapist never interrupts you when you
drone on?)

Therapist: What reason was that?

Me: The same reason, really—my body was beautiful,
even though I couldn't see it, but I couldn't control it.
I couldn't control the way other people—men—felt
about it. It scared me—I needed to be able to control
people's reactions to me! What could I do? If I gained
weight, maybe I wouldn't have to worry about strangers being attracted to my body—but now I hate
myself for being so ugly and out of shape. My body

feels unhealthy, but it's even more unhealthy in my mind. No diet is going to work for me until I cure what's wrong with my mind! But I always wonder—is what's wrong in my mind, or in our culture? I felt so weak at that moment, in that hotel room. Defenseless. If he had wanted to, at that moment—he could have done whatever he wanted. And am I supposed to thank him because he didn't?

Therapist: Who should you thank?

Me: Myself. For the instinct of self-preservation, for knowing not to give in.

My inner therapist apparently didn't have anything useful to say after that, because the journal entry ends there.

The following week, the dialogue continued briefly, with the same sort of vague hostility I imagined I might have with a real therapist.

Therapist: Have you thought any more about what we talked about last week?

Me: I don't have to think about it. I live it. I was just thinking today that the fear of being fat and my overall obsession with my body seems to put a buffer between me and the intensity of my life experiences, my relationships, my enjoyments, and my disappointments. It's an excuse for everything—for my lack of self-esteem, my self-consciousness—and it probably keeps me from facing some truths about myself and from discovering my full potential.

Wow, I thought. *This session has certainly been productive.* I had no idea those thoughts were *in there.*

You might think that my life would have changed drastically in the wake of realizing how I'd been cheating myself. You would be sadly wrong. The excuse of using my body to not embrace life fully was a habit too ingrained, written too deeply into my character's lines and movements, to undo in a single moment of clarity.

But I had learned that shrinking my own head was a fantastic exercise: listening to myself, gleaning from my own memories what events were important to evaluate, recognize, and gradually alter my mindset. I'd found my inner therapist—someone for my inner prisoner's team. She'd been outnumbered for far too long by the guard and his anorexic friend. It was incredibly healing—at last all these things that had been bugging me could come pouring out into a safe space for my fragile opening. At some point an actual, embodied therapist would be needed, someone whose wisdom and experience I could draw on. But not yet.

My senior year at Smith, I lived in Tenney House, a vegetarian co-op. It magnetically drew the most radically thinking women—like a dark-haired beatnik at an underground café, beret askew and fondling his French cigarette, who spouts Rimbaud and Marx like his first and second languages. No one could be certain…is he gay, straight, or asexual? Or even…male? With its ambiguity and promises of long, smoky diatribes, Tenney pulled us into its circle, attracted by like-minded souls, no idea too extreme to voice.

Nate had taken his camera and tree-climbing abilities off to Eastern Europe, and though he wrote me, clearly expecting that I would follow him there, my obsession wore off quickly in his absence, like a badly-named cologne. Before he left, he asked me for a picture to add to his bulletin board, pinned with dozens of his conquests. No way. I asked him for the speckled scarf he always wore on photo shoots. He looked at me as if I'd asked for his first-born child. That we both refused the other's request seemed an appropriate epilogue.

I plastered my room with Klimt artwork and political posters, an Indian bedspread, and a piece of clean white poster board on the wall to inscribe inspiring quotes and my own musings. *Humankind cannot bear very much reality. T. S. Eliot.* My housemates and I shopped together, cooked together, ate together. We made huge pots of ramen with peanut sauce out of Molly Katzen cookbooks, tripling, quadrupling the recipes to serve fourteen of us around circular wooden tables that had stood witness to decades of revelatory rants about the epidemic of violence against women, and years of drama over whose turn it was to wash the dishes. We railed against the system, how powerless we felt as activists to change anything. I joined the LBC, the campus Lesbian Bisexual Caucus, and not a single eyebrow raised anywhere. *Whatever.*

One afternoon, my housemate Krista and her friend Elin had taped flyers for an eating disorder support group on the back door, and I briefly noted that the date and time worked for me. As I turned the corner to head up the stairs, I found the two of them in the sitting room, Elin in her Goth makeup, as skinny and wistful as a modern Twiggy, and Krista, looking wholesome and thoughtful, her shape, size, and weight perfectly "normal"—neither fat nor skinny, but, of course, thinner than me. *They have eating disorders?* I inwardly shrugged as I clomped my heavy black oxfords up the stairs.

The day of the meeting, the three of us walked over to the hall, Krista and Elin conspiratorially whispering to each other a few feet ahead of me. My rational mind knew they were planning the group's agenda, nervous about how it would go, but the more paranoid part of my brain was determined to torture me. *They're saying that they can't believe you're hijacking the meeting. They've seen you eat. They know you don't have an eating disorder. They don't believe you were anorexic. They're wondering what kind of weirdo goes around pretending to be a recovering anorexic.* I recognized that voice. It was my inner anorexic, smugly rolling her eyes, arms crossed in front of her sunken chest. *Told you this would happen,* she hissed.

By the time we arrived at the meeting, I couldn't speak. Me, the first one in kindergarten to raise her hand ("Kimi, let's let someone else answer this one"), who lived for the spotlight and applause, who loved to win over a crowd with a smile and a bit of self-deprecating humor. I had slid to the bottom of a dark hole and couldn't make even the tiniest sound to ask to be pulled out. They wouldn't believe me. If I were them, I wouldn't believe me either. They were all thinner than me. I didn't belong here. I wasn't part of this group. I wasn't thin.

All of my resolutions about loving my body, giving up comparisons, and softening toward myself seemed to have arisen in some other lifetime, perhaps in a sci-fi novel I'd read about some other undergraduate on some other planet, in some other galaxy. In some nice, hopeful world. I tried to listen to the women as they spoke obliquely about their battles with weight and eating, barely able to focus on their words. *How can she be struggling with eating?* I wondered, watching Elin as she used her hands to emphasize her story. *She's so skinny!*

I wasn't in my body; the room felt distant, far away. My mind filled with a static buzz, caught between fear of judgment before a panel of merciless anorexics and trying to remember that the definition of "support group" entailed things like camaraderie, encouragement, and, well, support. The only support I felt at that moment was the little voice inside my head saying, *Get out of here, now!*

Mumbling, I excused myself to use the bathroom, slipped down the hallway and out the door, unnoticed. Trudging mechanically along the paths across campus, the direness of my predicament swept over me. I was a failed anorexic. An anorexic who couldn't starve herself. I couldn't face these other, thinner women, with their skinny arms and unspoken judgments. Seeing myself through their eyes, I was what they feared most: the loss of control, the inability to wield the ferocious mental knife sharp enough to cut away bits of themselves. I was what I feared most.

Back in my room, I flopped face-down on my mattress on the floor, heavy shoes still tied to my feet. I wanted to hold that knife again. And I didn't. I wanted to love myself. And I didn't. I wanted alternately to put as much space as possible between me and my repulsive, angry inner anorexic, and then hold her bony form in my arms, tuck her straggly hair back from her face and tell her she was right. *I promise to listen now*, I wanted to console her. *I promise not to eat anymore.*

But like a lover who endlessly reassures, "It didn't mean anything. I'll never cheat on you again," for the 842nd time, my promises were as hollow as my anorexic's belly. My cheating ways had taken hold for good. I left my inner anorexic to wallow in her imaginary donuts and fiber pills, and packed my bags. I went to Poland.

chapter five

The Wandering Body

Having graduated from Smith with a degree in Russian History, I wanted to teach English to Russians (don't ask me why studying Russian would qualify me for this) before starting law school. But the Berlin Wall had fallen only a few years before, and no unqualified-foreigners-arriving-to-teach-groovy-American-swear-words-to-your-eager-students program had yet gained a foothold in the country previously known as the USSR. So Poland, with its lush fields, passionate underdog history, and new influx of Levi's, Coca-Cola, and stomach-churning eighties music, was to be my home for a year.

Unfortunately, my inner anorexic soon discovered my whereabouts. At the training compound in Warsaw where I arrived with a group of variously aged fellow Americans, we shared meals of cabbage and potatoes, drank tea out of glasses, learned the basics of the Polish language and culture, and were given a crash course in teaching English. One afternoon when we were on our way back to the compound from exploring the Old Town of Warsaw, one of my fellow English teachers, Marcie, started in on herself: "I can't stand my legs.

My belly is so fat. I'm never going to eat again. I'm such a lazy, fat slob." Standing there on the sidewalk next to her, waiting for the tiny primary-colored Polish cars to disperse, my mind froze. I recognized that voice. It was so weird to hear it coming out of Marcie's mouth. My whole idea of Marcie changed as I stood gaping at her petite and plump self, crowned with an adorable face and a playful sense of style: ruffled skirts and bobby socks.

She hated herself. *If she hates herself...are my thighs any thinner than hers? She must think I'm fat too. She's waiting for me to agree and say something awful about my body.* My inner anorexic flexed her fists, cracked her knuckles, and headed my way. *No. NO.* I turned away from Marcie and ran a few steps to catch up with some other friends. *Damn it.* All it took was one woman's voiced self-hatred to press my anorexic's GPS locator and boom, she triangulated my position, donned her black cat suit and steely will, and came after me.

Fortunately, I lost her again on the train from Warsaw to Lodz, where my roommate Laura and I had been assigned to teach. Laura had little to say about her own svelte body that would bring my inner anorexic running to my side. Lodz (spelled with seemingly random lines through the L and Z and over the O, and pronounced *woodge* due to the miracles of Polish pronunciation, as in how much *woodge* can a *woodge*-chuck chuck, if a *woodge*-chuck *couldge* chuck *woodge*?), is famous for its huge Jewish Ghetto during World War II. Lodz means "boat," a reference to the days when several rivers flowed through the city, nearly all of which dried up from overindustrialization and were subsequently replaced by a low-hanging cloud of pollution. With that said, Lodz nonetheless had the most beautiful collection of rose-lined, trimmed-hedge, European-style public parks of any city I've ever lived in, like shiny jewels concealed in a dusty box.

In the flat Laura and I shared, not a single full-length mirror could be found. The climate in Lodz necessitated heavy wool pants and long, bulky skirts for much of the school year, forestalling any possibility of comparing my legs to someone else's, or even of seeing them myself. Much like my time in France, I was on unfamiliar but captivating ground, and in my determination to maintain my vegetarian diet, I ate what I could that wasn't meat. That became my only criteria.

As the snow in the streets turned from gray to brown to black, Laura, a recovering Catholic, decided to give up dairy products for Lent, and since we cooked most of our meals together, I agreed to try it out. We found a tiny closet of a health food store down a narrow cobblestone alleyway that sold tofu and soymilk in boxes behind an ancient wooden counter. The frizzy-haired, bespectacled owner spoke no English, but she eagerly presented vegetarian goodies to tempt us when we arrived on our weekly forays. Nearly every vacant corner of the city hosted a vegetable kiosk, where farmers sold their tightly wound narrow-stemmed broccoli bunches, dusty carrots, dark red beets, ubiquitous cabbages, and surprisingly, bunches of tightly wrapped yellow, fuchsia, and purple flowers. Everybody seemed to carry bouquets, holding them upside down (this mysterious habit, I was told, kept the moisture from leaking out of the stems), leaving me with the impression that half the people I passed on the sidewalk were on their way to a party.

Finding noodles in Poland was easy enough; they carried them at the new supermarket downtown. But nowhere could we find canned spaghetti sauce. It was back to basics: tomatoes from the farmer kiosk and a willingness to experiment over the stove. By accident one evening, I made the most delicious tomato sauce when I left the onions to cook too long and they turned brown and sweet, caramelized—a happy mistake I took care to repeat once I'd tasted the results.

Astonishingly, in a country that considers sausage a vegetable, we found a vegetarian restaurant in the basement of a technical college, where a giant, grim Polish *babka* served a marvelous prix fixe plate of brown rice, roasted vegetables, savory greens, and some kind of tasty baked lentil croquette in the center. Moist, flavorful, so much yummier than the words "baked lentil croquette" could ever suggest. The owner, a short, goofy, wiry guy, fell in love with us, his "Americanski girls," and chatted incessantly to us in Polish, while we nodded avidly, only understanding every third word. One afternoon, seeing us there, he clapped his hands, grabbed a bundle from behind the counter, and sat down at the table with us, as if having waited for this moment. He proceeded to place one flute against each nostril, balance a third between his mouth and his knee, and play a jig. With his hands, his mouth, and his nose. A drone, a melody, and a harmony that sounded almost like an Indian raga. It was pretty good. I was impressed.

Most Poles were skeptical about the vegetarian thing. As spring arrived and the city threw aside its woolen capes for the flowery cotton of spring, a group of female professors at the local university asked me to lead an English conversation group for them. They adopted me as their American daughter/colleague and invited me to dinner and to travel with their families. One sunny afternoon, I visited the flat of Bozena, a biology professor who loved to cook and was determined to master the basics of English. Her frankness and pronoun confusion were endearing, as they so often led to amusing results: "My husband walked the dog today. It stepped in his poop."

Over lunch with her husband and daughter, I oohed and ahhed over the spicy mushroom-stuffed cabbage rolls, hot and sweet blueberry soup served with dollops of sour cream, hunks of roasted pork (well, those I skipped), and thickly sliced bread. Mid-conversation, as if by some previously agreed-upon command, the entire family stood up and left the room. I sat there in bewildered silence, the tiny heater buzzing in the corner, wondering if I'd said something unforgivable or missed the fire alarm. From around the corner in the kitchen, Bozena called to me: "You can eat some meat now. We're not looking."

In Poland, no one was looking. The babushkas wrapped in their wooly shawls on the tram didn't care what I was or wasn't eating. My open-faced teenage students worried more about what their friends were doing after school than what I weighed. Even my inner anorexic couldn't sufficiently regain her footing on the slush-filled streets to worry about what my thighs did or did not look like under my skirt— and I didn't peek either. For the first time in years I experienced relief, a sense that I could eat, not compare myself to others, and not expect my body to be something it was not. A fragile truce, necessary and hopeful. Yet, like Lodz's enormous, haunting, deserted Jewish cemetery that Laura and I sometimes wandered through, there was a dark history still lurking in the back of my mind, one that I would have to turn and face, sooner or later.

In April of that year, my parents called, excited, and rattled off the news over the phone. Cradling the Soviet-era receiver in my hands, I let it sink in: a letter had arrived inviting me to join the first-year law student class next fall. And a PhD program. At the University of California, Berkeley. Years ago I had visited San Francisco, looked out over the Golden Gate Bridge from the Marin Headlands, and thought to myself, *People live here. People drive across this bridge and see this view every day, until they forget how beautiful it is. I want to live here someday. I want to see this skyline so many times my eyes take it all for granted, too.* If I wanted to become a civil rights attorney and save the world, I might as well live someplace astonishingly beautiful.

In August, freshly arrived from Eastern Europe (*Look, a water fountain! You press the button and water comes out. Washing machine, I love you. No more washing jeans in the bathtub!*), I drove my belongings from my parent's house in Ohio out to Berkeley, to start a new career, a new circle of friends, a new life.

It sucked. It only took a few weeks for me to figure out that I hated law school. Even in the darkest days of high school, schoolwork had been my pride and refuge: in the throes of the Salem witch trials, or a Mark Twain novel, losing myself in Puritan Massachusetts or floating down the Mississippi, I forgot I had a body at all. After having loved school my whole life, every blessed minute of learning, there I was, in law school, staring at the writing on the wall. Endless, tedious reading. Learning how to write, as if for the first time. I'd always been told my writing was excellent—until I met my nemesis, the IRAC style of legal writing. Issue, Rule, Analysis, Conclusion: every sentence, every paragraph crammed into a rigid and excruciatingly boring template.

Showing up every day in the dimly-lit lecture halls meant getting Socratized, a tedious question-and-answer process that involves memorizing tiny little footnotes and being orally quizzed by professors who seem to bore even themselves, dissecting long, boring judicial opinions, and regurgitating meaningless holdings like an owl spitting up a pellet of partially digested mouse innards. It eventually became clear that the whole point of the first year of law school was to divest embryonic lawyers of any last remaining vestiges of compassion for others or passion for learning they might have carelessly clung to since elementary school.

Yes, this widow and her orphans will lose their family home, but the ancient scriptures of property law don't support her case, so you shouldn't give a damn. Yes, this large corporation contaminated the river, but the standard of proof isn't met, so the town, its fishermen, and all the sick children will just have to suck it up. This white college kid got probation for his drug charge. This African-American kid—the same age—got 20 years in prison. Meet it all with a shrug. We thought that we were going to law school to argue on behalf of justice, but we found ourselves arguing the finer points of the judicial opinions of wealthy straight white men from as far back as they've been writing down their opinions. We learned that you can use the law to justify any level of outrageous behavior—treat women like chattel, punish elementary school children like adults, and imprison people for the crime of being Japanese. Fairness was not what the law was about. You could leave that quaint little idea out on the curb to molder in the dirt, to get kicked into the gutter and flushed out into the Bay with the rest of the refuse.

In the dank law school basement, I immersed myself in mindlessly numbing law review fact-checking for hours on end, while the gorgeous Sunday afternoon outside the law school's bunker-like walls teased me with its blue sky and crimson leaves.…*Come out to play.* Turning back to the sharp pages of text, I brought my unruly attention to task. Hours later, a desperate black void claimed me for its own as I pored through casebooks in a darkened cubicle in the bowels of the library stacks. The lump in my throat grew heavier each day.

My body complained about the unreasonable hours sitting indoors, but my mind tuned out its endless nagging. Until one morning I found myself lying flat on the floor, barely able to breathe through the pain: my back had gone "out." Like an angry lover, it went out to take care of its own damn self. Out to the store, out to the hot tub, out for a walk, outside somewhere in the sun and fog. Wherever it had gone, it stripped my ability to move until it decided it was ready to come home. After that, my mind reluctantly made more time for my body's need to occasionally visit the gym, stretch, get massages, and go for hikes in the golden East Bay hills. So demanding.

Finally, in my second year, a critical mass of courage and desperation motivated me to find a therapist. A real therapist, not just one who poked her head out occasionally from the pages of my journal. From the first conversations with my potential confidantes on the phone, I laid some ground rules: "No blaming my mother for everything. And no picking me apart." Sample sessions were scheduled with three different therapists: a therapist tasting.

The first therapist I visited sat as far away from me as possible, on the other side of a long, spacious room, and confined her questions to how much alcohol I consumed during the week. "Hello over there!" I felt like calling out to her, "Have you heard anything I've said?" There must have been some transmission problem—she almost had me convinced I should make an AA meeting my next destination before my feet found the exit. I had to reassure myself on the way back to the car that among my many problems, drinking did not appear anywhere near the top of the list.

The second therapist met me in a tiny little office where we sat with our knees almost touching. A few more inches and I would have been sitting in her lap. Eww. The role of mother in my life is already taken, thank you, good-bye.

In the Goldilocks spirit of things, the third therapist was just right. She sat a comfortable distance away, not so far one had to shout, not so close that one could breastfeed. Leigh responded appropriately to my musings, asking the occasional penetrating question. *Much like my own inner therapist.* In order to keep my life and sanity together, I needed a box to put my tears in. I needed Leigh to be that box.

Leigh was the first person to hear at length my frustrations with my body and my ongoing struggles with my inner anorexic. In one conversation, she mentioned that some experts think anorexia is linked to having been molested as a child. *Ah, this must be where professional expertise helps. Is this what my mother feared discovering?*

I'd been visiting Leigh once a week for a year, putting my ambivalence about law school into a convenient therapy box, when I told her about being molested as a kid. Twenty-three years old, and it was the first time I'd told anyone. Looking out at the soggy red leaves beyond Leigh's office window, I told her about when I was seven, spending the day with a group of kids at church. Eight to ten of us kids and a couple of teenage counselors had the run of the whole three-story office building attached to the main sanctuary. We spent the day pulling out the nativity costumes and modeling them for one another's amusement, rummaging through the back cupboards of the basement kitchen, looking for stale crackers and broken cookies forgotten by the Sunday school teachers. Running full speed down the hallways where normally we would be underfoot and scolded for our wildness.

At the end of one of these dim hallways, in the pastor's office, just down the hall from where my aunt worked as church secretary, Denny, my favorite counselor, sat me in his lap, in the same chair our pastor sat to write his sermons. I felt so official and grown up there, gazing at the wide spines of all the heavy books lined up on the shelves. Were we hiding together during a building-wide hide and seek? How did we end up there together, all alone, without the other kids? I had a crush on him, in a little-girl sort of way; he was a big, cute teenager with a charming grin.

When I felt him pull the center of my panties aside and push his finger inside my vagina, to say I was surprised would be an understatement. I don't know how long I sat there, feeling weird and uncomfortable, staring unseeing at the huge books filling the tall shelves beside the chair, before I jumped up and fled down the hallway to look for my friends. I have no memory of anything he said to me before or after, or even whether we laid eyes on each other after that.

Did that little girl have a more playful, flirtatious side that was declared dead and buried as a result of that incident? Perhaps I clamped down on that part of my personality to avoid danger and misinterpretation. Leaning back across the long sofa in Leigh's office, a tissue box clutched in my right hand, I voiced my concerns. As an anorexic, I kept myself small, prepubescent, when my breasts and hips started to come in. Did I starve myself to avoid the attention of men? What about my obligation to other women and girls? I always wondered whether I should seek him out and make sure he didn't molest others, or just chalk it up to his teenage lack of judgment and let it go. Why didn't I tell anyone about it when it happened?

As a knobby-kneed, scraped-elbow girl, I knew what Denny did was wrong, but I didn't know—was it my fault? Would I be punished if I told? Adults were unpredictable. Teachers could paddle you for no reason, or claim you were lying just because they didn't want to know the truth. My parents had never laid a hand on me, but could they handle the truth? I decided not to risk it. *Must be perfect. Must hide anything that isn't perfect.*

A few months after the incident, while waiting for our carpool to arrive in the morning before school and kicking pebbles around the driveway, my Narnia-influenced mind invented a fairytale about how I was a magic princess with a secret jewel hidden inside me. Denny had been sent to try to find it, but he had failed. The secret jewel was still mine, still safe within me. Every time the incident clawed its way to the surface of my awareness, I reminded myself of how I had outsmarted the bad guys and kept the jewel entrusted to me from being stolen. And now that I knew they were after it, they would never get it. Never. My seven-year-old self knew with utter certainty that the story was true. Any shame was submerged under my heroic act. Hence the perfect reason to never tell anyone: *I must never reveal the secret of the jewel inside me.*

What does all this have to do with having an eating disorder? Never before had my body been treated so disrespectfully—for the first time someone else's desire to touch it or manipulate it overrode my own desires and choices. The lack of control jolted me. Much later, fueled by my growing sense that thinness equaled worthiness, I attempted to control people's responses to me, either positive or negative, by rationing what went into my mouth. Then the Parisian concierge taught me that controlling my body didn't add up to control over others' responses at all. I gave up on control altogether.

Another thing I gave up was the law review, the prestigious student-run legal journal that invited me to join after a marathon legal writing weekend. I gave up caring about what I ate, though my inner anorexic still popped up occasionally with her diet tips and thinly veiled disgust. I gave up hoping law school would suddenly become enjoyable. I gave up my PhD program. Wanting something to show for all my trouble, I swam against the powerful tide of overwhelming legal research and exams to arrive at the shore of my law degree, battered, exhausted, and grateful to still have the ability to feel my own heart beating.

The last semester of law school, I signed up for June Jordan's "Poetry for the People" class at UC Berkeley. It was the act of a desperate renegade. At any moment, I expected the student dean from the law school to show up in our auditorium-sized classroom, scope out any AWOL law students, and drag me back to the distant law school building, mid-sentence. That unspoken fear kept me alert and grateful to mingle with undergraduates and write poetry for homework. Maybe that should have been a clue that law wasn't my calling. Out of all the poems we wrote that semester, each student got to choose one to publish and present at our final reading. This was mine:

eating air

i don't know when it was I forgot

myself

it wasn't one instant lipton soup mix

in a hot glass jar break in your hand it was more day

after day of breakfast oj, the cumulative effects of 100%

usrda vitamin c on a young girl's body, growing up and

out imperceptibly

the forgetting started

maybe it was the day I begged my mother to teach me how to

shave my

legs to show me how to draw the sharp pink daisy metal

across

me to look like those girls in my sister's under-bed stack of

seventeens

or the day my friend mike from math class sidled

up to my twelve year old breasts at my locker saying

"you-whore-

you-just-wanna-get-it-behind-the-gym-don't-you"

then scuttered away leaving my face choked with an

empty red silence like hotdogs too long in the microwave

burn your tongue down to your gums and leave you gasping

for air wondering what it was you wanted-to-get but sure

you didn't

maybe it was when I learned to eat plain lettuce

in the lunch room to hear the girls in the bathroom

say "ooh you're so thin" my underwear falling

off but i'd show them how I could still pinch an inch

or how powerful it felt to stick my face into a bag

of chocolate cookies and drink in the intoxicating

odor eyes closed and never   eat   one

maybe it was when I stopped swimming for fear

that invisible imperfections would loom

large at the edges of my suit or maybe when eating or

rather not eating became the definition of what was a good

or bad day when I wished to be either thin   or   dead

I forgot

about

living

I graduated, took and passed (Praise the Lord!) the Bar exam, and got a prime public interest staff attorney position at a small litigation-oriented nonprofit law office. By rights, any brand-new public interest lawyer in my shoes should have been ecstatic. And I was indeed relieved, even happy, for a few days before the general shroud of misery descended once again. Despite my misery, one thing kept me afloat during my stay in Lawyer Land: my sweetheart. Chris is eleven years older than I, three inches shorter (she claims it's only two), and about a hundred times more butch, at least. We met during my second year of law school, shortly after I dropped the law review and joined a radical lesbian political activist group called the Lesbian Avengers. We wore red capes and white go-go boots—not really. But we did plan "actions." Once, we protested a right-wing group that claimed to magically, biblically remove the gay from people's psyches. We arrived at their office with a plague of locusts (crickets, actually—locusts aren't legal in California, but crickets are "pet food") and signs saying "We Are The Apocalypse." Maybe we had our Bible chapters a bit confused, but we didn't claim to be Sunday school teachers. Our logo was a black sparking bomb on a white background—unthinkable in the post–9/11 world, but kitschy in the 90s. Suddenly, I was part of a group where caring about how fat or thin someone was was uncool. No one talked about feeling fat in their jeans or whether they should eat that extra slice of pizza. My inner anorexic would occasionally try to peek her head out the door labeled "THE PAST," but I slammed it closed each time, praying she'd get the hint. Meanwhile I mirrored the self-confidence of the women around me and hoped some of it would stick.

As a stressed-out law student and an overworked teaching assistant for a mind-numbing Democracy and Politics class at UC Berkeley, I got to answer the question "Just how illegal is this action?" for the Avengers. Each Monday evening that spring, Chris and I showed up at an office or basement or classroom in San Francisco's Mission District for the meetings, just to be around other archly funny, politically active lesbian and bi women. During the meeting, I gazed around at all the faces. My heart was a little crushed out on every one of them. Jeans and motorcycle boots helped me embody the confidence I didn't feel as I waited for a sign that one or another of my crushes might be reciprocated. After the meeting ended we all went out to a neighborhood bar, leaving the white male patrons wide-mouthed as a sizable crowd of leather-jacketed womyn's women took over the booths and pinball machines.

Here's a rendering of one of my early conversations with Chris in the neon-lit corner of the bar:

Her: "Can I get you something?"

Me: "No thanks."

Her: "Let me buy you a drink?"

Me: "I have to go home and grade papers."

Her: "How about some water?"

Me: "I'm not thirsty."

Not a very promising beginning, to be sure. But a few minutes later, out on the sidewalk, while getting out my keys, our friend Alicia jogged up to me and chuckled in my ear: "She likes you."

Very seventh grade, I know. Not the way you expect the most significant relationship of your life to start.

Several more awkward moments unfolded before we finally found our stride together. After a couple of dates, Chris invited me over for dinner with her best friends, David, Carol, and Biff. Cradling a lobed philodendron in one arm, a bottle of wine in the other, I arrived early at Chris's "new" house in Oakland, the mostly unfurnished fixer-upper she had recently bought with her savings and a mortgage credit certificate. Following her into the kitchen, I found that, unused to cooking, she had selected some rather complicated and delicious-looking recipes out of a couple of foodie magazines, only to realize she didn't have the basic equipment she needed. I tried to help as best I could, fighting the urge to shoo her away and take over the whole production. We maneuvered around the countertops in a tentative waltz of wanting to touch an arm or a hip, but not wanting to be unwelcomely forward. As I turned to wash some vegetables in the sink, I read the recipe over her shoulder. "It says here to grate the daikon radish. Maybe I can do this part? Where's your grater?"

"Grater?…Um, what does it look like? I don't think I have one of those." She bent close over the cutting board, chopping long strands of green onions. I pulled out a drawer. Empty. I pulled open another. Empty.

She gestured with her knife, "Maybe use the blender instead?"

The tender bed of grated daikon in the full-color picture thus became the tender mush of blended daikon on our plates. But the texture of the radish garnish seemed like much less of a crisis after I lit a dishtowel on fire by setting it down on the stove too close to the oven vent.

"Sorry," I said, slapping the flame out of the charred remains of the cotton towel while Chris looked on in horror. "…for almost burning your new house down," I muttered under my breath. Things were not going well at all.

Once we finally sat down for dinner, we settled in, our eyes playing the same dance of connecting and disconnecting over the small talk and clattering forks that our bodies had played in the kitchen. Her friends left soon after we'd cleared the plates, later telling Chris, "We thought the house was going to burst into flames," as they watched sparks flying from Chris's eyes to mine, and back again to our lips, our throats, until our whole bodies were alight.

I stayed the night, which is the polite way of saying this is not a romance novel. (For excellent depictions of cunnilingus, you'll have to read Radclyffe or Johanna Lindsey.) We cavorted on the futon couch, the only furniture in the whole house aside from the dining room set and, limbs draped over each other, breathed in the light of the waxing gibbous moon as it filtered through the windows. "God, you're so sexy," Chris whispered across the pillow. "I love your body." My mind wanted to argue, but blissful exhaustion silenced me. Early in the darkness of the morning, Chris's dog Ranger realized that I wasn't leaving any time soon, and leapt up into the center of the bed, where she howled her distress to the neighborhood canines. Ranger was right to be concerned. After that night, none of our lives would be the same.

For one thing, Chris cooked as frequently as "pureed daikon radish" shows up in recipes. It was just as well, since I loved to cook as much as she found it a stressful chore. I happily applied myself to making dinners for the two of us. Heaping plates with rice, beans, and vegetables, still following the recipes from my vegetarian co-op days, one evening I handed Chris a plate and sat down with her. She looked at me with surprise.

"This looks delicious, hon, but I'm really not that hungry." I looked at her blankly as she indicated her plate with her hand. "I don't need this much food."

After years of cooking for Tenney House's ravenous twenty-year-old women, various bottomless roommates, and the occasional six-foot-four boyfriend, it took a few minutes for me to understand what Chris meant. *Not hungry, doesn't need this much food. Does that mean she doesn't like it? Does it mean she doesn't want me to cook?* I tried to get my mind around it.

"No, sweetheart, I like it. This is just a lot of food for me."

"How will you know I love you if I don't overfeed you?"

"I'll figure it out somehow."

chapter six

The Big Belly

Despite my unrealized desire to love my body and Chris's assurances that she loved me just the way I was, and despite repressing my self-hatred under the guise of "Real Feminists Don't Hate Their Bodies" and working as a civil rights lawyer, I was still sure my body didn't measure up. As I looked in the mirror while getting ready for work, a deluge of criticism poured out of my brain's faucet: *Am I fat? Should I go on a diet? I'm so sick of this cellulite. Are these pants too tight?* I had to use every ounce of willpower to keep the tap from spilling over and letting the words pass through my lips and into Chris's ears. God forbid she should see my body the way I see it. And worse, that she should catch a glimpse of how very dark the view was from inside the black box in my head.

And how much worse would it be if I managed to get pregnant? Chris and I knew from early on when we got together that we wanted to start a family, though I held off the vigorous ticking of her biological clock's eleven-year head start for a while, getting the ground under my legal feet. But now we were talking about *trying*—which meant not only would I have the usual fat talk mental torture, but I wouldn't be able to see my toes over my belly, either. Or maybe, just maybe, I'd be able to give myself a little break, for the good of a growing baby? Something to aspire to.

Meanwhile, one morning, in front of the closet mirror while trying to get a 360-degree view over my shoulder, the criticism splashed out and threatened to overflow. Chris fished some socks out of the top dresser drawer nearby, unconcerned. Worried about my first solo deposition that would be happening that morning, with the moment insufficiently guarded, I saw the words float out of my mouth and invisibly fill the air between us. I already knew it was a mistake.

"Do these pants make me look fat?"

My gaze fell to the floor. Eye contact would only make it worse.

"Uh…no. Your butt is amazing. I wish I were those pants."

Some corner of my brain smiled, but the rest of me still couldn't look up.

"Are you sure?"

"You're the most beautiful woman in the world."

"Aren't you a little biased?" My eyes finally found hers and rested in their warmth.

"Nope, just lucky."

I sighed and let her cross the few steps between us and wrap her arms around my back and pull me close. My head rested on her shoulder. *If only I could believe her. If only I could see beyond the two dimensions of the mirror and see myself the way she sees me. If only I could feel that love inside and out.*

Just five visits to the sperm donation clinic later, from filling out forms to picking up dry-iced vials of sperm, we found out our little family plan was under way. The clinicians had been so excited when they found out I was still in my twenties, and their optimism was quickly rewarded.

My own hesitant optimism was rewarded as well. When I learned I was pregnant, my two dimensions unfolded to reveal a new hidden dimension—a being growing in me, dependent on me. Someone who was important enough to make me aware of what was going on inside. The desire to listen inwardly grew along with my belly. The changes my body accomplished in just nine months amazed me: shifting from neutral to full-bellied, hairy, big-breasted, achy, and oddly flexible all at the same time. The transformation was much more thorough and amazing even than puberty. I gained weight, deliberately, consciously, for the first time in my life.

After years of concerted scale avoidance, my scale-phobia (and its nemesis/creator, the inner anorexic) took a nine-month, long-overdue vacation. From the moment I looked down at the little pink line on the pregnancy stick, my judgments about my own weight and food seemed to evaporate: *Now I can eat anything I want.* In fact, I gave myself an upward weight goal. Every time Chris and I went in for a pregnancy checkup, I jumped on to the scale eagerly to see how close I'd come to my target weight. Ben and Jerry's mint chocolate cookie ice cream out of the container. Girl Scout cookies. Brie and cheddar and asiago. I indulged mightily, all for the good of my fetus—Sprout, as we affectionately called him.

Even eating everything I craved, I was still hungry. And if my everyday hunger was challenging, pregnancy hunger was a force to be reckoned with. One Wednesday morning during the end of my first trimester, while working on my computer at the law office, I started to feel even more hungry than usual. My little fetus was merely "small plum size," as the pregnancy book described it. I had packed my lunch bag full of snacks to eat throughout the day, which I left in the break room, so that at least the walk down the hallway impeded me from free-feeding on them at my desk. At about 11:30, having already taken two snack breaks that morning, one at ten and another at eleven, I finally hit a stride with the brief I was working on. Still, hunger pangs rose up from my belly.

Just one more paragraph and I'll go get something, tapping away on the keyboard, I bargained with my hunger. *Just let me finish this sentence...a few more words...one more conclusion...*

All of a sudden, I heard a voice in my head, or maybe from my whole body: *NOOO! I'm hungry NOW! Get me something to eat NOW!* It felt like my body had been commandeered by an alien being. As if someone else were running the show and suddenly decided to demonstrate who was truly in control.

Whoa. Command hallucinations from my stomach? You bet that got me out of my seat, down the hallway, into the break room, and cramming a cream cheese celery stick into my mouth. No one had warned me about auditory hallucinations being a side effect of pregnancy.

Let's never do that again. I considered myself fully warned. No more bargaining, no more negotiating. Food first.

Shortly after this incident, I discovered that I needed to top up my lawyerly continuing education hours, which would be all but impossible to accomplish in several months when I expected to be fully immersed in the care of a work-thwarting newborn. Browsing through the catalogue at work one day, I circled with my highlighter a daylong stress-reduction meditation and yoga workshop for lawyers (and their partners!) that would fulfill all the requirements. Grabbing the phone, I dialed Chris to see if she would go with me. Much to my surprise, her answer was, "Why not?"

A few weeks later we found ourselves in a Tibetan temple in Berkeley, my pockets stuffed with gooey peanut butter Power Bars to ward off any incipient hallucinations, sitting cross-legged on cushions, trying to meditate. When we opened our eyes again, the leader, apparently an attorney, meditation teacher, and yoga instructor all rolled into one, talked us through how to breathe and relax while stretching our legs and shoulders in a few yoga poses. With Chris by my side and Sprout in my belly, and the cool winter light shining through the windows, I found I could lean over my leg and breathe without worrying about my weight or wishing myself onto a treadmill. I didn't spend too long wondering where the near-incessant voice of criticism had gone, for fear of accidentally calling her forth. Wherever she'd gone, good riddance. Maybe there was something to this stress-reduction stuff after all? During the nap pose at the end, Chris surreptitiously laid her hand in mine as we dozed under blankets on the carpeted floor.

Months later, on the day I hit my upward target weight, standing on the tall scale at the nurse practitioner's office, Chris and I whooped and hollered and went out to a diner for chocolate malteds. Celebrating being big and round after years of hating myself for every hint of cellulite or fleshy bulge was liberating. I was fat and happy. I liked having a reason to eat, a reason to gain weight, a reason to be happy about my body and what it was doing. "You're gorgeous," Chris told me at least once a day, and her eyes showed how much she meant it. She loved me fat, thin, and everything in between.

One Tuesday evening, parking my car in front of the house and walking up the stairs, I found a big box full of vegetables waiting in front of our door. I shouldn't have been surprised, I had paid for it to show up there, but it felt like a miracle nonetheless. We had subscribed to the CSA (Community Supported Agriculture) at Full Belly Farm a couple of years earlier, receiving a hearty weekly box of sometimes mysterious organic vegetables…what's a kohlrabi, anyway?

A waft of country air drifted up to me as I pulled apart the cardboard flaps. Carrots, kale, spinach, potatoes, fresh green garlic, oranges, and a little bag of the freshest walnuts imaginable. Before even opening the front door, I unfastened the bag of walnuts and popped a few in my mouth. They tasted like walnut candy: tender, delicately crunchy, and almost sweet. Eating one, I imagined the walnut orchard, its vast, soft green lanes, the huge grafted trees spreading their arms in a wide embrace of the sky.

Feeling the first kicks of the baby's tiny feet across my belly, an unfulfilled longing to visit the farm moved through me. Well, not just to visit. We'd visited for their Fall Festival, called the Hoes Down (as in "Put your hoes down and come party!"), staying the night in the almond orchard, waking up to yipping coyotes singing to each other across the valley. One summer we took the tour at the June members' day, walking the riotous rows of snapdragons and bachelor's buttons, and gazing with urgent encouragement over the nodding heads of the yellow tomato flowers as they dreamed of July heat.

I wanted more. My hand drifted down to my belly, where my little Sprout grew, quietly, effortlessly for the moment. We could go to the farm, Sprout and I. I could get my hands in the dirt, eat strawberries right out of the field, and maybe let my hunger relax, surrounded by fresh organic vegetables and fruit trees in all directions. My law job would end in May, and I could go volunteer at the farm for a month, if they'd have me.

I wrote a letter to the partners. They said, "Come."

At Full Belly, my days fell into a blessed routine. Rising early, I greeted the pale sky with steaming tea and toast, then out to the flower fields with the workers to pick the day's blossoms. Late one morning, I stood in the shallow ditch between rows, watching a fuzzy bee alight on the velvety maroon snapdragon I was about to cut. The bee braced herself inside the mouth of the flower and started pumping her little hips like she was gonna ride that baby to Calvary. In and out, in and out. Totally obscene. I turned my eyes away, embarrassed. Then I thought, *Wait, this is not obscene. It's not some triple-X movie at the Mitchell Brothers. It's just a bee humping a flower.* I turned back and watched until my eyes filled with amazement at the flower's erotic dance and the bee's ecstasy. The bee flew away to her next lover.

Once my bucket had filled with long stems of confetti-like flowers, I trudged back along the row, glancing upward as a hawk circled lazily over the main farmhouse. Leaving the bucket at the work shed, my clippers in the scuffed tray, I washed my hands over the enormous tub-size sink and headed for the kitchen to prepare lunch. Lunch at the farm was a miracle. Imagine opening a huge room-size walk-in refrigerator filled with vegetables and being told, "Take whatever you want, more is coming." New potatoes in all colors and sizes, flats of asparagus, huge piles of colorful greens, long carrots with their extravagant tops, the ripest, most tender strawberries, fresh onions and garlic, and striped chioggia beets all pulled me in their own direction. *Pick me!* My task: Make lunch for a dozen farmers and interns. My days at the co-op had prepared me for the scale of the task, but not for the choices laid out before me. Roasted beets? Strawberry shortcake?

The dumpling-shaped baby potatoes called the loudest, so I roasted them with rosemary and garlic, then made greens sautéed with carrots and onions, pan-seared asparagus, mixed-lettuce salad with sundried tomatoes, and coffee cake with fresh strawberries. There was no danger of being hungry here. Pans, pots, dishes, and silverware were gathered from all corners of the farm. I filled Ball jars with lemon verbena–scented water and left them sparkling on the picnic table outside the intern kitchen. Wiping their hands and dusting off jeans and shirts, the farmers and interns arrived in ones and twos, intently discussing an imminent tractor repair, what field to next move the grazing flocks of fluffy sheep to, and how much longer the asparagus would last if the heat kept up.

"You've come to the right place to be pregnant," my intern friend Kate mused from across the table.

"How's that?" I speared another asparagus bite onto my fork.

"It's called Full Belly Farm for a reason," she said, ducking her head as Mike, another intern, mimicked aiming an asparagus spear at her forehead. She grinned at the chorus of chuckles and groans from around the table.

One afternoon, Dru, one of the farmers, laid her hands on my belly as we stood in the central yard of the farm, surrounded by dust clouds, heavy machinery, and tall black walnut trees. Her hands felt cool on my skin through the T-shirt, and she looked up at me, with a soft twinkle in her enormous blue eyes. I felt totally adored and blessed to be standing there with her.

"I love full bellies," she sighed. We both laughed softly. Reluctantly releasing her hands from the shape of the growing being within, she dipped her head to the left and smiled. "You know, Anna's pregnant, too."

Anna, the wife of another farmer/partner, was pregnant with her second child, and as the temperature climbed to over 100 degrees the following day, we stretched our legs down by the creek. I splashed the icy-cool water of Cache Creek over my shoulders and let my fingers sink into the slippery clay bank. Tracing a gray spiral with my fingertip up my leg and around my kneecap, I asked Anna about her experience delivering her baby there at the farm.

"I had Ellis in our house in the middle of the farm. Dru was there, and the midwife. We got comfortable, and they sang to me and massaged me. I felt loved and beautiful. The process of actually giving birth was amazing. They held me and encouraged me, and when he finally arrived we felt so much elation and joy. The whole experience was mystical, wonderful, and long!"

I sighed and leaned back to rest against the creek bank. If only that could be my birth experience. No matter how strong my longing, when it came time to give birth, Chris would be driving us toward a hospital, not away from it into the heart of the valley. My family of doctors would throw a collective fit if I insisted on a home birth, and that was a battle I didn't care enough about winning to start. But I would hold that vision of Anna's birth experience and invite it to support whatever mine would turn out to be. We listened to the low hum of the irrigation pump as it drew water from the creek into the fields.

Joining Anna and her husband, Andrew, for dinner that evening, in their home-cum-farm office, we feasted on pasta with roasted veg-etables and freshly baked bread. As the sun set over the golden hills, leaving watercolor strokes of purple and blue across the horizon, I headed back to my tent, now cool enough to curl up and fall asleep in, to the sound of a million frogs croaking among the rushes.

As the sky turned from pink to lavender, I pulled out my journal and, chewing a bit on the end of the worn pen nub, wrote a few lines to my unborn child:

> I wish I could give birth to you right here at the farm, in
> the yurt, with just a midwife and lots of friends around. In
> reality, though, we'll be driving across the Bay Bridge when
> I start having contractions and pull into the emergency
> room parking lot (hopefully) at San Francisco Kaiser right
> before you pop out. You know what's weird about being
> pregnant? For the first time in my life, I trust my body. My
> body seems to know how to take care of you, form you,

make you grow healthy and strong. Everything about my body is different. My hair is thicker and heavier. My nails grow so fast now. I pee when I sneeze. All the veins in my chest around my breasts and the sides of my belly have popped out like I'm encased in blue webs. I look like Spider Woman! It's bizarre and fun at the same time.

As the last strands of sunlight slid behind the purpling hills, I closed my journal and crawled deep into my sleeping bag, worrying for a moment that the frog chorus in the creek below might keep me awake before falling unconscious.

A few hours later, I woke up under the moonless sky, writhing in pain. My shins! I couldn't straighten my legs...it felt like someone had snuck into the tent and was stabbing my shins with a penknife. My breath came in gasps. I'd walked all over the farm the last few days, after having given up my all usual activities in the first trimester in favor of long exhausted naps. I hurt. I needed to stretch. I needed some exercise. But what exercise would be okay for me now? I was twenty weeks pregnant!

Slowly the pain eased as I tentatively rubbed the length of my shins with my hands. A single word floated up in response to my silent question: *Yoga*. As boring as it seemed, I'd enjoyed my most recent experience with it. Maybe it would be the perfect thing for my body and its little passenger. As the pain eased, I stumbled out of the tent and into the tall grass nearby to pee. Making my way back into my sleeping bag a few moments later, I realized the frogs had fallen quiet, and with only the bright, vague sound of the creek to lull me, I fell back to sleep.

Early in the morning, my eyes nearly caked shut, I followed Dru and Kate down to the grassy corral and open shed where Clover the milk cow lived. After a nuzzled greeting against Clover's bristled, velvety soft cheeks, they settled onto their stools, so close to the cow that they could lean their foreheads on her barrel sides. Using callused, practiced hands on Clover's swollen udders, they sprayed enthusiastic streams of milk with a loud clatter into the metal bucket. Taking in the sounds and smells of brittle straw and animal musk, I watched, transfixed, as Dru explained how to use your fingers to let the milk flow into the teat and then squeeze the milk out into a steady, forceful stream. I took Dru's place and settled in, breathing in Clover's scent and nearness, but my fingers fumbled on the teat, managing only a dribble here and there into the warm foam of the milk below.

"It takes a little practice," Dru gently reassured me, and let me make a few more attempts before I turned my stool back over to her.

Finally, Clover's udders hung empty and limp. The cow seemed to sigh with relief and scraped her hoof on the ground, as if proposing a mosey through the meadow. With an affectionate pat and a whisper into the cow's ear, Dru helped me and Kate hoist the buckets and head back to the farmhouse.

Once I'd returned to Oakland, I still craved my connection to the farm, so I showed up one day in July to help Judith, one of the Full Belly farmers, at the Berkeley Farmers Market. Heirloom tomatoes, in more than twenty different varieties, gold, yellow, green, even deep purple, filled heavy woven baskets, and all kinds of melons lined the bins—orange, yellow, and red watermelons, and delicate orange- and green-fleshed muskmelons. Weighing bags of produce on overhead scales and adding up prices in my head, I chatted with customers about the farm, and munched on raw ears of sweet tricolor corn when things slowed down. Soon, though, my body complained about the long hours standing with Sprout growing bigger day by day, and my time at the market came to an end.

By mid-August not only was standing a chore, but a line of new fur pointed down from my navel to where the baby would come out.

I hoped it wasn't permanent…shaving my belly was not something I expected to get around to once juggling diapers and baby food became daily activities. By the end of August I was eager, desperate, and hopeful that my labor would go smoothly and it would all be over soon. The due date came and went. In early September, my labor started in full force. And the next day Cooper emerged, a healthy 9.5-pound baby boy.

If I had thought Cooper, a.k.a. Sprout, was a hungry instigator in my belly, breastfeeding notched my hunger to a whole new level of constant ravenousness. It kicked in right away, at the hospital. Groggily resting in the hospital bed, I slowly got used to the idea that the little being that had been growing inside me for months now lived outside me, self-contained, in a plastic cart, all wrapped up in his hospital-issue flannels. We had tried breastfeeding, and it seemed like all the plumbing was working, but suddenly this low, achy hunger for milk came over me. My body needed milk, and lots of it, with a deep-down bone-hunger I'd never felt before. The nurse brought me a tiny half-cup carton of milk, even smaller than the ones I knew from elementary school. My mouth flopped open at the sight of the little container; it looked like a snack-time drink for a hobbit child. It might as well have been a single drop for the dent it would make in my thirst. After downing it like a tequila shot, I begged Chris to snoop through the fridge at the nurses' station, which turned up two more identical tiny boxes of milk. After finishing those off, Chris saw the dissatisfaction in my eyes and volunteered to run down to the corner store. She brought back a half gallon of pure milk, mine, all mine, the entirety of which I promptly poured into the water pitcher and drank, only stopping to refill. Suddenly my stomach could expand to hold two quarts of milk, moving into the space where the baby wasn't.

My reflux-suppressed appetite, now augmented by playing the living milk bar to my growing newborn, left me frantically hungry. As in pregnancy, I placed virtually no restrictions on what I ate and how much—Häagen-Dazs ice cream, thumbprint cookies, focaccia bread, whatever. The sleep deprivation must have convinced my inner anorexic to continue her absence, or perhaps my own fogginess dulled her voice beyond recognition. It was easy to ignore my lumpy stomach in the haze of feedings and changings and washings and cleaning spit-up.

It was also easy to ignore Cooper. That is, not ignore him exactly, but not enjoy him either. After the tenth time I caught myself holding his sleepy baby self and thinking, "Is he ready to put down? I need to change the laundry again," I realized how messed up my priorities were. How long would he stay a baby? Was the laundry really more important than enjoying this time with him, his soft hair, his warm, milky scent, his dense weight on my chest? I was a multitasking lawyer. Now I was a multitasking mother. When would I learn to be happy with my child, my body, and my life?

One day at Costco, my law school friend Ani and I sat down to fill up the hole in my stomach made by Cooper's hunger. Ani helped me arrange him on my lap and handed over a piece of pizza for me to munch on. Cooper pulled himself away from the nipple for a moment to check out the warm, foil-covered cheese pizza from the bottom, and Ani, sitting right next to us, got a mini fire hose of breast milk squirting out at her, spraying a half circle across her shirt.

"What?! Oh crap!" I attached Cooper's little mouth back on again and, dropping my pizza on the table, handed Ani a bunch of napkins. "Uh, sorry."

We dissolved into a fit of laughter, of course dislodging Cooper yet again, and spraying more milk all over the table. "Holy crap."

People started to turn and look to see what was so funny. Every time I caught Ani's eyes, we busted out laughing again, and finally only Cooper's mad cries for me to settle down and stop jiggling his lunch got us to calm down. Since when did my breasts start drenching people in public? And when would my body be my own again?

In the mommy and baby exercise class I took Cooper to the following week, we moms practiced yoga and breathing exercises while the babies were entertained by professionals in the next room. For a few moments I could feel my body again. *Feel your pelvic muscles, and draw them up into your belly. Hold your belly and draw it in and up toward your spine. Now move your inner thighs down.* The teacher seemed to think my inner thighs listened to anything I said. She assumed we had a working relationship. I pretended for the moment that she was right, that my thighs listened when I asked them to move toward the floor, and found I could touch them with my clothes on. As we rested on the carpet, she reminded us that what our bodies had done and were doing to grow and take care of our babies was extraordinary. I couldn't help but agree.

"Your body will always be different now. But bring your attention to it, and little by little it will change. 'Drop by drop,' the Buddha said, 'water fills the bucket.'"

Then they brought the babies in, and we held them in our laps and massaged them, pulling and stroking their legs and arms like mama cats with their kittens. Holding Cooper's little finger fists, wrapping his arms around his chest and opening them up again like a tiny cheerleader, I hoped yoga would bring me back to my body. Perhaps the meditative aspects of yoga could make me a better, more patient parent. Perhaps it could make me a better person. Perhaps it would make me a better body, one worthy of love. Or maybe it would help me figure out how to love this body anyway. It was worth a try.

chapter seven

Learning to Love Again

Lying on my back, tired but exhilarated, I look up at the corrugated steel ceiling and iridescent pink halogen lights far above me. I close my eyes to rest at the end of a long, mind-clearing yoga class. "Thank you," I breathe. Maybe I'm thanking myself. Maybe I'm thanking the teacher. Maybe I'm thanking whoever invented yoga, or brought it here to the West, or whatever chain of events and people made it possible for me to be here.

Chris is bathing Cooper and putting him through his sleepy bedtime routine at home. And I haven't thought about food for ninety whole minutes. It feels like a miracle, a breeze of fullness at the end of a hungry day. My whole body feels relaxed and well used, like after a fun romp in bed. The reset button has been pushed on my mind, and for the moment, it's clear, relaxed, and not criticizing my body or anything else. All the sun salutations and downward dogs, and then getting to lie in a puddle on the floor lets my mind chill out, my body flex and stretch, and my heart hum along. I don't know how yoga gets all the parts of me to play nicely, but I have some theories.

Given that my first tentative venture onto a sticky mat in L.A. did not augur a happy reunion with yoga years later, some explanation is in order.

When my back skipped out on me in law school, a kind and matter-of-fact trainer at the vast student gym (no chakras or incense!) gently reintroduced me to a dozen yoga-like stretches (hello, cat-cow) that I brought back to my co-op room to perform among the dust bunnies and textbooks. Later the same movements were echoed in the warm-ups for the women's jiu-jitsu class where Chris and I donned cotton gis and white belts to toss each other around on mats in the evening after work. But when Cooper made his ghostly appearance on the sonogram, we decided there would be no more mid-air falls for this pregnant mama.

Nevertheless, our relaxing yoga session at the Buddhist temple had whetted my appetite to feel the stretch and flex of my muscles again. Yoga studios were popping up on every other block, and following the shin-splints-in-tent incident that I hoped to avoid repeating, it occurred to me that yoga might help me prepare for Cooper's birth. One might suppose I would find and attend a prenatal yoga class, or at least a workshop of some sort? Oh, no. I was way too cheap for that. Yoga classes cost $10 each!

Working as a low-paid public interest lawyer, I was shocked by the sudden burden of paying off my student loans. Chris and I scrimped like crazy. From the "Free Books" box at a neighborhood garage sale we had recently acquired a book on how to cut hair, complete with hilarious early-eighties-style haircuts. Chris bravely let me experiment on her head. If I could learn the basics of hair-cutting from a book, I figured I could learn the basics of an ancient Indian practice from a book as well.

I splurged and bought a brand-new $12 book on prenatal yoga. Since good money was paid for it, I was obligated to use it, and I did—almost every evening before bed. Sometimes I even made Chris do it with me, pregnant or not. I had no idea what I was doing, but I didn't care: I loved it. The first night we did the exercises in the book together, we were staying the weekend at a getaway cabin in Mendocino. Candles, along with the warm incandescent light from the reading lamp, cast long shadows over our bodies as we languidly, laughingly moved through the postures and text. Afterward we lay on the floor, resting, our fingers intertwined. I felt myself soften and relax as if lying again in the Buddhist temple's meditation room, or even under the inner palm trees from that long-ago yoga mat in L.A.

After Cooper was born, I graduated to yoga videos, short twenty-minute sessions with the lithe and long-haired Rodney Yee in glamorous desert locations. I rolled out my yoga mat in front of the TV right before I laid Cooper down for a nap. In about twenty minutes, he'd be awake again, and I would be exhausted, but relaxed. That was the real eye-opener for me. These videos were in the more athletic *vinyasa* style—not the yoga of sitting on your butt, stretching your hamstrings, and listening to vague instructions about directing the colors of your energy. Instead, I followed Rodney's chiseled body through push-ups, crunches, up, down, back, forth, again, lunge, again, lean, stretch, extend…again. I learned to stand on my hands three different ways and had sweat beading up on my forehead. I could barely get through twenty minutes. But once I did, even feeling as if my body had melted onto the mat into a puddle of pinkish ooblek, the rest of the day's diaper changes, crying fits (both baby's and mama's), and drooly play sessions seemed to lose their edginess. This yoga-fed mama could breathe, laugh with, and even enjoy her bow-lipped, curl-naped baby for a moment or more.

And once my body got used to the basic forms of warrior and triangle and downward dog, I was addicted. I recorded Rodney's voice on my tiny tape player and carried it outside with me for a short escape from Cooper's toddling interventions, while Chris watched over him in our little bungalow. Bundled up in three layers of sweat pants and sweaters, my arms stretched up, and my back bowed through clumsy sun salutations in the backyard rain, as if my puffy diligence would convince the sun to come out. Once I had Rodney's voice and sequences in my head, I could head out for the beach and practice the tree pose and downward dog in the sand by the water's edge, seagulls scampering nearby. For those few minutes, I found myself in the dark unknown of my body rather than in my head. I felt my limbs from the inside instead of through my eyes. *This body can sit on its upper arms and lift its feet off the earth!* When I asked my body to stand in tree pose, with one foot lifted to the inside of the leg, it listened to me. And obeyed. Happily. *This body and I can work together. Maybe we're on the same side?* These moments of relief became ephemeral hits of ease I soon began to crave.

What was it about yoga that gripped me so fiercely? For one thing, I could practice by myself, with no one to compare myself to. Even I had the sense not to compare myself to the studly Mr. Yee. The endless critical commentary seemed to subside somewhat with the lack of mirrors or neighbors, and I could just listen to my body from the inside. I felt good afterward—stronger, more supple. Life felt more doable, my body and heart able to fall over, roll around, and stand back up again. The steady, vigorous pacing didn't catch my breath, but deepened it, didn't give me cramps or achiness, but simply a general, delicious soreness that left me feeling more alive. For most of my life, exercise had always felt burdened by guilt, and required forcing my body to move until it screamed for mercy. As a result, I hated running, treadmills, aerobics classes, and Stairmasters, so I figured what most folks called exercise was not for me. Yoga arrived to disprove that theory. Finally, a form of exercise I loved, one that could go with me almost anywhere. Had yoga changed? Had I changed? It didn't matter. I was grateful our paths intersected again.

Around the same time, my inner anorexic seemed to wake up from her pregnancy-induced sleep, stretch her bony arms, and extend her reach back into my unconscious. One morning in the shower I gathered my soapy post-pregnancy belly into my hands and noticed it had shrunk somewhat, but that I still couldn't pull it in against my spine the way I used to. My inner anorexic declared me a failure. *You're fat,* she whispered. *You ruined your belly. If only you stopped eating so much. Ditch this yoga thing and head for the gym to burn some calories. What's wrong with you!?*

Part of me figured she was probably right, but another part of me suspected her antagonism toward yoga had to do with the fact that I didn't need her to force me to do it.

Once the videos could play by themselves in my head, their shortcomings became clear. I could see the instructor, but he couldn't see me. No matter how carefully my back and legs tried to emulate the smooth strength of his body, Rodney couldn't reach through the screen and say, "You're hyperextending your knees," or "Move your shoulders back further and you'll get deeper into the pose," or "Smile, Kimber, you're not here to torture yourself." I needed a teacher.

I had heard my beloved video teacher was local, but beset by scandal, and I didn't want to dive into that mess while trying to figure out how to best take care of myself. I'd heard there were a lot of different kinds of yoga out there, and probably a lot of different teachers, and possibly even the right teacher for me.

Once I started looking, the smorgasbord of yoga classes overwhelmed me, like when you think, *Hey, I need a light bulb and some screws,* and then venture into the vast aisles of a giant home repair warehouse store. A moment of, *Oh crap, what have I gotten myself into?* is inevitable. But I found a little martial arts studio down the street from our house that offered once-a-week yoga classes, and I decided to start there. I walked down the sun-strewn sidewalk on Saturday mornings, yoga mat under my arm, and emerged back into the daylight an hour or two later, a little wobbly and soft-headed, and strolled back home to the possibility of a nap on the couch. What luxury to have yoga nearby.

My teacher, Naomi, a youthful student of Rodney's over at Piedmont Yoga Studio, talked me through my first awkward attempts at handstand against the wall. She helped me feel whether my knee was straight or bent, my shoulders hunched or relaxed, through her touch and feedback on the placement of my body in each pose. One Saturday afternoon she casually dropped me a potent gem of wisdom. "Be patient with yourself," she intoned, while we struggled to move more deeply into a one-legged forward bend.

Huh? Be patient with myself? I'd never heard of that. I'd always been told to be patient—patient waiting to follow my sister to college, patient waiting at the doctor's office, patient with the agonizingly slow line at the grocery store, and with the irritating superciliousness of the clerk at the DMV. I'd admonished myself a million times to be patient with my baby, my son. *Geez, Kimber, why didn't you let him play longer, can't you see he's not ready to leave the park? Why can't dinner wait another half hour?*

Be patient with myself? Surely you jest. Straining forward over my leg, I was pushing myself hard, and I felt those words plop into my heart, like a drop of water in an empty bucket. My mind struggled with the implications for a moment, and then my heart spoke: *Of course, you can't be patient with anyone else until you learn to be patient with yourself.* My eyes felt itchy and teary. I'd always been impatient with myself, always pushing myself, always giving myself a hard time. *Why don't you exercise more? Why did you eat that sundae? No wonder you're such a f...* Could yoga help me stop that?

Much to my dismay, some Saturdays Naomi had other things to do than teach me yoga, like go visit her boyfriend who lived on some tropical island. The nerve. Eager for my yoga fix, and slowly getting used to the much longer class format (my videos were only twenty minutes long—Naomi's classes were ninety!), I looked around for something more. When I mentioned to a group at a party how much I enjoyed yoga, friends often asked me skeptically, eyes narrowing, "You don't do that *hot* yoga, do you?"

Perversely, I wanted to be able to say yes, just to see horror creep over their faces. They made it sound like eating a bug while sky-diving, something dangerous and icky, but exhilarating. I had to find out. After my experiences shivering in the rain of my own backyard, maybe extreme yoga was for me!

Hot yoga, it turned out, was Bikram Yoga, named for its Indian founder, Bikram Choudhury, who developed a fixed series of postures normally performed in a carpeted room warmed to 110 degrees. As if there's anything normal about standing on one foot in 110 degree heat.

Fortunately for my adventurous leanings, a new hot yoga studio had just opened up near downtown Berkeley—a curious yogi could subject herself to unlimited 110-degree exercise for 10 days for $10. Irresistible. They had a packed schedule of classes, from early in the morning until late at night. Happily, the heat didn't bother me so much—smothering at first, and then like the chill of my outdoor practice, it became just another stimulus to tune out.

The classes were crowded, the lighting fluorescent. The teacher stood at the front of the mirrored wall with a headset on and barked out the poses. "You in the purple shorts, lock that standing leg!" *Fabulous*, I thought, staring back into my own eyes, trying to keep my balance in an extended dancer's pose, *now I get to see my thunder thighs reflected back to me from every direction.* But the heat and vigorousness of the practice seemed to quiet the determined critique of my inner anorexic. She was covered in sweat, too. My legs had never been so grateful to collapse onto the floor in savasana. So different from my personal practice with Rodney Yee's voice in the back of my head. So different from the handful of students at the martial arts studio. Still not quite right for me.

What bugged me most about the hot yoga classes wasn't the lack of arm strengthening, which I badly needed, or the lack of variation, which I found boring after a while, but that the studio had a revolving schedule of teachers, so that you never knew who would be barking at you. No one would ever know my name, I would always be "the woman in the purple shorts." The teacher of my dreams would learn my name, and I hers.

After months of cruising different yoga classes—vinyasa, hatha, ashtanga, kundalini—I found my teacher unexpectedly one Friday evening, at Piedmont Yoga Studio in Oakland. I needed some yoga— it was like a recently arrived itch I couldn't stop scratching—and I headed over to a vinyasa class with a teacher I'd never heard of, Katchie. Arriving in the lobby, hiding my shoes in a cubby and enjoying the heated floors, I laid out my mat, plopped down, and watched as a severe, dancer-like woman opened a mysterious musical instrument and invited us to chant with her in Sanskrit. Fortunately, the chant was call and response, and I loved singing anyway, so I happily followed along, only a little bewildered. I thought I knew what to expect from yoga, and here was something entirely new.

Katchie guided us through the poses, encouraging us as we paused and transitioned.

"Do you feel like you're reaching for perfect, and when you finally get it, they move the bar a little higher? Just out of reach, but not quite? Enough to make you keep jumping?"

We were standing firmly in warrior two on our mats, arms reaching out over our legs, and I found myself nodding.

"Give up on perfect. Quit."

Tears appeared beneath my lashes.

"All those perfect people! They're not as happy, tappy, toffee as they want you to think."

What? I laughed into my mat as we rested, foreheads to the floor in child's pose. But she wasn't done.

"Are you? Are you as happy as you want people to think?"

More tears. It was as if she was in my head. And I wanted her to be there. I never wanted her to stop talking, her voice was such a relief, a trustworthy counterpoint, to so many of the voices I was used to controlling, repressing, or giving in to. Fortunately, she spoke throughout class, interspersing the poses with little wafts of wisdom that drifted through as the light faded from the August sky.

Then we lay down for savasana, and I closed my eyes, and she took her instrument out once again—it sounded like a cross between an accordion and an organ—and began to sing. Her voice was not simply beautiful, but heartfelt, with a daring and earnestness in it that reminded me of folkloric Russian peasant women singing for one another as they worked in the fields. I rested into that sound, let it fill me, and it echoed inside me: *This, too.* Yoga can fill this part of me, too. The part of me that loves wisdom and singing and longs for more. Yoga can take all of me. Waking up from savasana in the dim overhead lights, I suspected that I'd found my teacher.

After class, having forgotten to bring anything but credit cards for payment, I discussed with her how to square up. She was not pleased that she would have to wait for me to return from the ATM with cash. Imagine my surprise to realize my teacher was this crabby, vaguely irritated European woman shoving her bags around and looking toward the door impatiently. (Later I found out that I had caught her at a bad moment, in the midst of a painful breakup.) But the essence of her class lingered with me, assuring me that the annoyed woman I looked at now was the surface, that her true voice was the one that had spoken directly to my heart.

I continued to crave that voice. Mostly, my mat and I followed Katchie from studio to studio, but she didn't teach every day, so her classes became interspersed with other, more vigorous classes, ashtanga and intense "vinyasa flow."

Vinyasa flow classes stimulated my need for variety; each session was taught with a unique and creative sequence. They sometimes included poses I'd never done or heard of, and sometimes the teacher would create such a long, complicated series of poses you couldn't remember how it started and you'd laugh, wondering how the teacher could remember where to start when she began again on the second side. The vinyasa teachers often played music as well, told stories, and read poetry. My mind and heart gratefully received whatever wisdom they had to share once my body had been fully engaged and tired out.

Every class felt like a moving meditation; each pose, poetry— Whitman perhaps—written onto the silent lines of my body. *Deepen your breath*, the instructor repeated. *Notice what's happening here. What are you feeling? What are you thinking? Can you bring your attention back to your body and the breath?* I feel surprisingly graceful with one arm over my head and the other resting on my back leg. My thoughts move to whether I'll ever be able to stretch my pinky toes away from their curled brethren. *My thighs are going to fall off if I don't come out of this pose soon. I notice that I'm breathing…and thinking… about my body while fully inhabiting it.* My mat has floated me far away from the faint concepts of dieting and what I'll next eat. At last. We swing our arms down to the mat and return to downward facing dog.

You are not a human having a spiritual experience, the teacher reads aloud, *but a spirit having a human experience.*

Oh dear, I think. *Poor spirit.*

The key to yoga, I slowly learned, was tuning in to your body, actually listening to it. The idea of paying attention to my body after years of starving it, ignoring it, overfeeding it, and forcing it to sit manacled to a library cubicle, was desirable, but fragile and new, like my inner prisoner finally walking free in the world after her decades-long wrongful incarceration. Anything could happen. The uncertainty was terrifying. My body had been something I had to control, discipline, and subdue, and my inner prison guard had been only too happy to comply.

The prisoner-guard relationship, like an old black-and-white TV show with the sound turned off, hadn't bothered me during my pregnancy, and for a while yoga was the new distraction that kept the volume muted. But gradually the subdued farce returned to its usual noisy intensity, spilling over into my yoga practice: the guard struggling to reassert control, and the prisoner/body carrying out her silent resistance by causing the maximum possible discomfort and pain. My body's failure to get into a pose correctly was overt disobedience, which I met by pushing it harder, or by scolding it, sometimes viciously. *What the hell is wrong with me that I can't widen my leg further back? Push harder. Reach. Why can't I come into full splits or get my ankles behind my head? Why won't my body cooperate?*

Though I heard Naomi's soft encouragement, "Be patient with yourself," and Katchie's reminder to give up on perfect in the back of my head, the habit of listening to my pushy voice was so ingrained, I lost my teachers' words somewhere during the first sun salute and tuned in to KPUSH FM, like a spooky old dial radio that always floats back to the same staticky station. *Do it. Harder. Better. Deeper.*

*Faster. More...*I injured myself a lot in classes. My shoulders ached, my knees hurt, my back threatened mutiny.

"What do you want from yoga?" Katchie asked us at the beginning of one evening class. *I want ease,* I thought. *Not more pain.*

At first, I was completely in the dark. I walked out of a class one night with a teacher who was substituting for Katchie, thinking, *What a terrible class, that teacher is awful, I injured myself in that backbend she had us in. I'm never going to her class again.* But it was the same thing the next day with a different teacher, and the day after that with yet another one. Soon it became clear I would run out of teachers long before I ran out of injuries. One night in class with a teacher I'd only taken from a few times, I began to notice my thought process as she progressed us into a series of deepening hip openers. And slowly the dimmer switch turned to bright. As much as I tried to concentrate on my own body and not stretching myself too far, soon enough I found my thoughts drifting away from the breath and my eyes starting to dart around, checking out what other people were doing. The Compar-o-matic revved up, churning out its usual judgments, if not about the size of my thighs, then about how close my chest got to them. *Look, she can get her head all the way to her knee. Just a little farther, and I can get there, too. If I pull harder here, and push harder here...ouch. Stay with it, just a little bit more...*No matter how it felt in my own body, no matter how painful it was, no matter how often the teacher said, "Come out of the pose if this hurts your knees, or back, or shoulder," I'd hang on through the last excruciating breath. *Could every teacher be injuring me?* I wondered. *Was it possible? Or was I injuring myself?*

Finally, the wisdom of Katchie and my other teachers started to sink in. *What am I here for? Why am I doing yoga, and what do I want out of my yoga practice?* I'm *not* here to injure myself. I want ease...but what does that mean? I took up yoga to feel better, but along the way

I'd somehow turned my body into a heavily outmatched punching bag. What I really wanted from yoga was to stop ignoring my body; to jump out of that old habit, and walk a different path. To give my body the loving attention it long deserved, but was never offered.

One morning, after getting Cooper off at school, I sat on the couch under the front window and wondered whether going to my usual yoga class would make the pain in the front of my shoulders better or worse. Hoping to elicit some answers by probing my unconscious, I opened my journal and began to write:

What I want from yoga:

1. Be strong and flexible, like an oak tree crossed with red licorice vines.

2. Offer my body the long-overdue love, kindness, and attention it deserves.

3. Ditch the harsh, pushy, demanding voice (whose voice is that, anyway?).

4. Listen to my body's wisdom (assuming that it's willing to share its genius after what a jerk I've been to it).

The definition of insanity, Katchie said, is doing the same thing over and over and expecting a different result. Class after class, injuring myself again and again, pushing myself harder and harder, I expected a different result. *This time I won't get injured*, I told myself. Ha.

A new tactic was called for: Notice my body, pay attention to it, and back off when it says, "That's enough!"

Could I follow through, or was it too little, too late? I had seriously screwed up my shoulders, both of them, to the extent that throwing my sticky mat away and giving up yoga as quickly as I'd taken it up was not out of the question. But no way was I letting go of yoga. It was the first place I'd slowed down enough to see my thoughts. The first place where I noticed how those same thoughts turn into actions. My thoughts about wanting to be perfect turned into actions that hurt me. My mind and heart needed this practice so badly. Could I find a way to make it work for my body, too?

I stood on my mat in the living room. Move my arms overhead? Ouch. Lower down from plank to the floor? No way. Stretch my arms back or to the side? I gave up. Sitting back on the couch with my journal, a tear rolled down my cheek and pooled on the ivory page, magnifying a short section of line I'd written earlier. I wiped it away with the back of my hand, smearing the word *need*. Yoga had crippled me.

No, I reminded myself, I had crippled me. Each session on my mat made the pain worse, not better. If I wanted to stick with yoga and the gifts it promised, I needed to ask for help. I'd recently learned that Anusara was the name of the type of yoga Katchie mostly studied and taught, along with her previous training in the styles of Jivamukti and Ashtanga. In addition to its spiritual emphasis on intention and community, practicing Anusara involved learning beautiful principles of alignment that could help my body therapeutically, to create more connection rather than alienation, a suitable metaphor for pretty much everything in my life, from my strained muscles to my parenting, from food to the abyss that seemed to separate me from my heart.

"In Pain, Need Relief" I titled the e-mail to Katchie asking for a private session, half wanting her to help me with my shoulder issue, half wishing I could swallow a handful of pain meds, ignore my shoulders, and ask her to show me how to touch my feet to the back of my head while standing on my hands. The pushy voice didn't take days off for sick leave.

A few days later I arrived at the front door of the giant renovated Elizabethan house Katchie shared with some friends and followed her to her rooms, which looked out onto a back deck and grassy yard. Standing among the bookshelves full of yoga tomes and candles, I explained about my shoulders and mentioned a couple of poses I'd like to do better.

She raised a brow at me.

"Stand over here in front of the mirror."

I stood awkwardly where she asked, looking into her dressing mirror.

"What do you see?"

Uh, seriously? I see a body I once loved, then stopped loving, then forgot how to love, and I'm trying to learn to love it again, but now I've really pissed it off and I don't know how to apologize.

"What do you mean?"

"Look at your shoulders. Do you see how they slope down and point forward?

I couldn't see what she meant. *What? Don't everyone's shoulders look that way?*

She made me stand straight and lengthen my torso toward my ears, lifting my whole chest, and then brought my shoulder blades in toward each other, firmly on my back toward my spine.

"It feels weird. Unnatural."

"Does it feel natural to be in pain?"

Her eyes met mine in the mirror.

Yeah, it does. But I don't want it to. Not anymore.

She gazed at me sternly.

"This is where your shoulders should be when you practice."

You've got to be kidding.

Moving through some basic poses, she showed me how to keep my shoulder blades hugging onto my back in the push-up, downward dog, and forward bend repetition of a sun salute. She was right. It did feel better. In fact, with my shoulder blades firmly settled on my back, there was no pain at all.

"Don't just do it when you practice," she said. "Do it when you're in line at the grocery store, when you push your son's stroller, when you're behind the wheel of your car, everywhere, and all the time."

My upper back ached for the first three days. The muscles between my shoulder blades were in unfamiliar territory, unused to holding themselves close to one another along the spine. But the shoulder pain in the front of my arm bones and along my neck, which had been making me so miserable, was nearly gone. Each day the ache between the shoulder blades lessened, and later in the week, standing in line at the grocery store, an unfamiliar sense of ease crept over me: my shoulders hadn't hurt for days, and even my upper back felt fine.

Yoga had hurt me; now it cured me. Or, I had hurt myself, and yoga showed me how to make myself whole again.

Slowly, I eased back into a regular yoga practice with my shoulder blades on my back and pain only an occasional reminder. But the pushy voice floated back to me, barely audible at first, but slowly cranking its volume up to blaring, subwoofers pounding the beat. My shoulders improved, but I still pushed myself, just with better alignment. My injuries slowed in frequency, but gave no signs of letting up. Oddly, if I came to class with a crook in my neck, or an achy lower back, it would disappear by the end of class, only to be replaced by some pain in my knee or hip instead. When, in the name of Kali, Ram, and all 300,000 yogic gods and goddesses, would I stop hurting myself?

Maybe it wasn't as simple as changing the lift of my shoulders. Maybe I needed something more.

In keeping with Anusara's spiritual emphasis, at the beginning of class Katchie liked to remind us to set a personal intention and dedicate our practice to that intention. I often made my intention to benefit others: *May my practice help my sweetheart be happier, may our family be well, may the world be at peace.*

Great, right? But it dawned on me that if my practice was making my body hurt and my mind crabby, and left my heart wondering what the hell was going on, then what good was a selfless intention? My practice wouldn't help anyone if my postclass ritual meant coming home, swallowing a handful of painkillers, and spending the rest of the day lying down because I'd pulled my mid-back again trying to pull my head toward my shins. No stacking five-foot-high towers of blocks with Cooper. No helping Chris lure him into his nightly bubble bath. If I really wanted to be helpful I needed to help myself.

The next Tuesday morning class with Katchie, standing at the top of my mat, my intention made a long-awaited U-turn in the direction of taking care of myself:

I will take care of myself, I will be compassionate toward myself, I will be kind to my body. I will see my body as a partner, not an obstacle to overcome.

This, I vowed, would be my mantra from now on. Until it stuck. Until I learned to put my own oxygen mask on first before assisting others. And yet, before the end of class, I'd strained a groin muscle trying to straighten my leg in some fancy arm balance. *Keep trying.*

Over and over, like prayer beads on a mala, one word strung after the next, I repeated my intention: before class, during class, in each pose, just before I pushed myself beyond my edge and into pain again. *I will take care of myself, I will honor my body.* Finally my will might help me instead of hurt me, might help me value rather than punish myself.

Or not. One Monday night, intention tightly wound around my breath, I injured myself yet again, this time wrenching my lower back in a deep twist. And again the next day, same intention...Both my knees hurt for three days. I was still bossing myself around: Work harder. Don't be lazy. Eat this thing that's good for you. And *don't* eat that fatty thing. Or else. The sweet, loving, positively phrased intention of *I will take care of myself* just didn't have the necessary sassiness to repel the more insistent voice of, *Push it. You went deeper yesterday. You can do it. Go. GO!*

My wussy intention did not cut it. I needed an intention strong enough to do battle with and declare victory over my inner pushiness.

I will NOT hurt myself.

I will NOT push myself.

I will NOT injure myself.

Take that, pushy self.

Whenever I reached my limit in a pose and wanted to push further, I reminded myself of my promise: *I will not hurt myself. I will not push. I will back off and breathe.* And, much to my amazement, it worked.

It took a year.

A year of every practice reminding myself, *I will not hurt myself,* before each pose, *I will not hurt myself,* with each breath, *I will not push myself.* Even then, sometimes I forgot and pushed myself yet again to the point of injury, and had to bring myself back to the same mantra: *I will not hurt myself, I will not push myself, I will not.* Finally, after a year of not pushing myself—and finally not hurting myself—I could turn the mantra around again to something more positive and compassionate: *I will take care of myself.*

At some point I started to wonder, where did this pushy voice come from? It was more than just the usual crowd. My grandfather, a retired Marine colonel, came to mind as a possible suspect. My pushiness definitely had a military edge. A persistent, demonic edge. Katchie once told the story of Buddha in his cave: Buddha was being tormented by the demon Mara, who hovered outside the cave, whispering, hollering, shrieking, appearing in different forms and guises, trying to get a rise out of the former prince. Buddha realized that chasing Mara away wouldn't work, fighting back with the same pyrotechnics wasn't possible, and hiding out and being scared was not an appealing option.

So the next time Buddha heard the demon scratching near the opening to the cave, he yelled out, "Mara, is that you? Come in and have some tea, why don't you? Come in and get warm by the fire. Welcome, Mara, welcome old friend, come in, come in." Could I invite my demon in for tea? Could I ask its name, and perhaps even befriend it?

Sitting on my meditation pillow at home one morning, eyes closed, I contemplated my inner demon. She seemed female, somehow, not my grandfather, but maybe my feminine internalization of him. Her personality took shape first in my mind: insistent, authoritative, judgmental, aggressive, completely unembarrassed, and seemingly lacking any self-awareness at all. Indeed, she seemed to feel entitled, like it was her job to push me harder, to make me work more, to force me to do "better."

Slowly, like an old instant photo developing before my eyes, her features came more into focus. I expected her to be petite, tan, wrinkled, and tightly skinny; I figured I'd be face to face with my inner anorexic at last. Or maybe the beleaguered prison guard, hair messed up and breathing hard. But when she finally came into view, she was huge. A tall, heavy-set woman, graying-blond hair pulled back in a tight bun, little eyes, red blotchy cheeks, seventies-style zip-up sweat suit. Her name was Svetlana—it came to me abruptly—and she was a Russian gymnastics coach.

Holy cow. I don't remember being traumatized by gymnastics as a kid, and Russian culture had always been one of my great loves—or I wouldn't have lived through four years of majoring in it. Why my pushy side suddenly revealed itself to me in the form of Svetlana, I had no clue, but it certainly explained a lot. Turns out that pushing me was Svetlana's job. In my inner world, I was the gymnast who felt she had to starve herself to live up to the coach's standards, to push herself to the point of breaking. She didn't care what I ate. As long as I was working hard, she left the diet monitoring in the brutal hands of the anorexic and the prison guard. As my coach, she wasn't trying to be unkind, it was just a role, and from Svetlana's point of view, she was looking out for my best interests. Who else would push me? How would I ever get the body I wanted? Who else would help me knuckle down and make an awesome life for myself? Without Svetlana to nudge, and nag, and berate me to exercise and achieve, how would I ever get anywhere?

Hidden in the dark, unseen, Svetlana dismissed all that listen-to-your-body crap: "Fuck your inner wisdom and listen to me," she hissed. Oddly, once I'd brought her into the light, to the table, and offered her some metaphorical tea, she seemed content to sit politely, munch away on her cookies, and put any bad feelings aside. As the Buddha story predicted, she wasn't as scary up close, with her age spots and her own challenges and disappointments. I could learn to say, when I heard her sneakers coming up the stairs, when the urge to push myself arose unexpectedly, "Svetlana, is that you?" And take a deep breath and pause and ask myself if I should rest, or press on, or just bring a little more mindfulness to the moment. This could work. It's at least worth a try. May my patience slowly grow, drop by drop, until someday, hopefully, the bucket overflows.

chapter eight

A Menu of Hunger

On my way out of yoga class one Monday morning, happy that I haven't injured myself in weeks, my friend Alex gives me a big hug and asks how life is treating me. Older, handsome, and full of energy, Alex embarked on his yoga path around the same time I did, also under Katchie's inspiration. On the deck outside the studio, we let the April sun warm our backs as he shares that he bumped into a mutual friend, Patrice, at a recent trip to a hot springs resort. Mildly distracted by the idea of Alex and Patrice having a naked chat while hanging out by the hot tubs, I push that thought aside and lean in to hear more.

"Patrice said his latest practice is learning to let go of what he doesn't have." With a smile, Alex goes on, "I decided to let go of wishing I was in a relationship. You can't imagine how freeing it is." His eyes look bright but relaxed, his dimpled smile easeful.

I catch his drift right away.

"It's true, isn't it? We identify with the things we lack. We get attached to our deficiencies and define ourselves by what we don't have: I'm poor, I'm unhappy…"

I'm hungry, my mind whispers.

After parting ways with Alex, I walk down the creviced side-walk, wondering, could I feel fuller by letting go of wanting to feel full? Maybe getting attached to hunger sabotages my efforts to not feel hungry. The wanting causes emptiness, and the absence of wanting creates fullness. I have to let go of wanting fullness in order to feel full. It's like a Zen koan. When is the bowl not empty?

Maybe it's just that fullness and emptiness are a pulsation, like stability and freedom, inhale and exhale, up and down. At times we feel full, at times empty, but no one can expect to experience a con-stant feeling of satisfied fullness. It's like we turn on the air condi-tioner when the temperature reaches 74 degrees, and the heater when it reaches 72, as if we could keep the whole world a constant balmy 73 degrees. Nope, Kimber, life isn't about always maintaining an ideal temperature or emotion or feeling of fullness. Sometimes you sweat, sometimes you shiver; other times you're flexible, then stiff; elated, then despairing.

Yet hunger feels more basic than that. If you're hot, you take off your jacket; if you're wet, you dry off. But I'm hungry so much. If I simply ate when I was hungry, I'd be eating all the time. In order to avoid feeding myself constantly, whenever an achy, hungry feeling comes up it triggers a series of elaborate calculations in my head:

1. How long ago I last ate, *minus*

2. How "good" for me that meal was, *plus*

3. What I haven't eaten today that I believe my body needs, *minus*

4. How much I've exercised, *plus*

5. What am I craving at the time, *minus*

6. What's not in the house, *divided by*

7. How much time will it take to fix.

Sometimes I just give up. Shouldn't eating be simpler than algebra with seven variables? And on top of all that, a measuring tape and a barometer are also required to determine exactly the depth and intensity of any particular moment's hunger, as in "Mmm, I could eat a little something right now," versus "If I don't get something in me right away, I'm going to melt into a puddle on the floor." Or better yet, "Feed me now, or I unleash the crabby bitch!"

My self-regulator is broken. Probably the sledgehammer of starving myself dented it up pretty bad and then the blackout-inducing hypoglycemic lightning bolt sent any intact dials haywire. The mysterious process that would normally tell me, *Hey, you're hungry*, or *Hey, now you're full*, seems to be stuck on Hungry. Admittedly, I'm not hungry every single minute of the day. Every other minute, maybe. There are times when I go for a whole hour without thinking about food or eating. But mostly, when I'm not eating, I think about eating. While eating, my mind is already contemplating the next meal. I'm obsessed.

And of course, what makes obsession even more fun? Feeling guilty about it. Caught up in my self-absorbed hunger, I think of all the people in the world who truly are hungry, who lack access to food or even clean water. Millions...even billions! Come on, Kimber, true hunger is something you've never experienced—being hungry because you don't have access to food. Starving your fifteen-year-old self while surrounded by food is *not* the same thing. Depriving yourself of dessert? Feeling hungry after a big meal? Not even close. Here I am, one of the best-fed humans on the planet, complaining about how I feel hungry all the time! It's ridiculous.

I wonder what aid workers in countries experiencing famines do. They must have their own food supplies. What is it like for them to eat normally, knowing that thousands of people nearby are in danger of starving to death? It must be hard not to want to stuff your pockets full of food and share it all with the next person you see. Every day, the United States of America produces more than three times the number of calories needed to feed every man, woman, and child in this country, but many people all over the world—yes, even people here—are malnourished, and even starving. Suddenly my hunger seems pathetic and small. And inexcusably demanding, like an absurd opinion that doesn't know when to shut up.

The navel-gazing of examining my own hunger and body image: I'm ashamed of it. But there's no shortcut. There's only through it. The longing to be on the other side, the tentative promise of yoga that I might be able to see my flaws with patience and love and engage with the world free of this crippling self-consciousness— that's what keeps me going when the vulnerability feels too much to bear.

Thankfully, I don't think about eating much when I'm on my yoga mat, or when I teach now, but for some reason that doesn't extend to time off the mat. Like last night, when I ate too much after getting home from teaching my Thursday night class. I devoured a big bowl of rice, greens, beans, and veggie sausage before class for dinner, and then came home and ate a bowl of ice cream and more dinner. My stomach was mad at me afterward: icky, bloated, full. Once I leave the studio, I return to the world and all the things that make me anxious—money, Cooper, life—and these anxieties drive my eating. Are we able to afford the mortgage on the house? That question is turning up the flame under my digestive fire tonight. It's lucky I didn't clean out the fridge and the cupboards with my tongue. My mind thinks that by packing in more food, the blood supply will be sucked out of my brain and into my stomach and leave no room for uncomfortable thoughts. Besides, if my mind is filled with angst about overeating, real-life problems get shoved aside. Anxiety eating equals avoidance. And then the inevitable remorse.

Partly, it's also habit. When I walk in the door, the keys drop to the table, the purse on the chair, and my feet lead me straight to the snack cupboard in the kitchen where I set myself to pasture and graze. Apparently I've programmed my body to equate being home with eating. My body doesn't register, "Hey honey, I'm home!" until my stomach gets something to ruminate on. Since living on my yoga mat isn't a possibility, I need a substitute behavior, something that grounds me when I get home, instead of browsing the shelves and hanging out with the door of the fridge wide open, like I'm going to climb inside and eat my way out.

Loitering in the pantry last night, I didn't stop to ask my body how hungry it was. I felt like eating, so I piled more into my already full stomach. Afterward, I thought to myself, *Nothing will cross the threshold of these lips until all that stuff is digested, until my belly is empty again.* Which would probably be a fine idea, except that those very words echo around the broken cement walls and take me further away from listening to my body instead of closer to it. The prison guard picks up his keys and readies the cell. Hello, bingeing and starving cycle. And here I thought you'd lost my trail.

I know from years of experience that the bingeing cycle gets triggered when instead of eating regular, healthy meals, I alternate between depriving myself and indulging myself. First the guard says, *No, you can't eat anything. Take your punishment.* Then I get so hungry

I'm willing to eat anything, and lots of it. The prisoner thumbs her nose at the guard as she slurps down French fries, chocolate bars, ice cream with nuts. *You can't stop me.*

Regular meals are my defense against their exhausting farce. A reasonable amount of healthy food at regular intervals soothes my hunger, leaving the prisoner and her guard in suspended animation, like puppets whose master has left them dangling over the stage.

The "regular" thing is difficult, though. This morning my belly feels full from having overeaten the night before, but I know I'll be hungry later when there won't be time to eat. Should I eat now anyway? *Make time to eat later.* What? *Bring something delicious and healthy along and make time to eat it when you're hungry.* Huh, that's a great idea. Listen to my body's signals, make time to treat my body right. Where did this voice come from? Sounds a lot like my inner therapist. I didn't know we had an appointment. Seems she thinks I'm calling her with these questions. Maybe I am.

I'm going to need to keep her voice of reason on speed dial, just to help me undo the endless litany of dietary guidelines I've carried around in my head for years. Every diet I've ever been on has left its mark: Eat fresh fruit, don't eat fresh fruit, eat whole wheat bread, don't eat bread at all. As a result I have no idea what my body really needs.

One of the problems with so many diets is they make everything sound so simple: Eat this, don't eat that, blah, blah, blah. As if eating were like punching a clock: eight o'clock banana, ten o'clock yogurt, twelve o'clock sandwich, three o'clock apple, tick, tick, tick, BZZZT! What about when it's 4:00 p.m., two hours before leaving work, and your stomach rumbles and the only thing around is the vending machine or the bag of dried-up licorice in the bottom of your desk drawer? What then? There are so many moments like that when there's a tricky transition in my day when I need food, or some food alternative. I want to eat something good for me, but if nothing else is available, the sticky-sweet, peanut butter–nougat, chocolate-drenched candy bar starts calling my name.

The reality is, these tough moments happen all the time. What can I do in these situations that would help me feel better? Maybe eat something with a lot of protein, like nuts or jerky. Or take a short walk and see if I'm still hungry afterward. I could meditate or just sit and take twenty deep breaths. Then if I'm still hungry, eat something. *Or I could listen to my body and try to give it whatever it needs.* There's my inner therapist calling again. Hope she puts me on redial for the next time hunger strikes. Won't be long now.

After the next Monday yoga class, while I'm sliding on my shoes in the hallway, my friend Sally, a nutritionist, reaches past me to grab her sandals. When I tell her about my struggle with hunger, she recommends writing down everything I eat for a week, and then she can have a look at it and make adjustments as needed. It seems so simple. *No problem*, I think. *Great idea!*

Let's see. What did I eat today? When I sit down, pen in hand, to list all I've consumed for the day, my mind goes blank. I freeze up. I push my notebook aside. *I'll start it tomorrow*, I think. Then tomorrow comes, I'm busy, and I forget. Then it's the next day and I'm thinking, *I should have started it today, but instead I'll start it tomorrow, because I already had a big chocolate snack today.* The next day I forget again and the day after that we go out to dinner and I eat too much and no way am I writing down all the crap I just put in my mouth! By then I've procrastinated keeping track of what I eat for a whole week. And then another week. And another week after that. What is up, girlfriend?

Musing over my food-induced writer's block, I remember how carefully I kept track of everything that passed through my lips while anorexic. As a result of creating a calorie encyclopedia in my head, for many years into college and law school, long after the starving year was over and the quadratic equation and the distance between the sun and the earth were forgotten, my inner anorexic still knew exactly how many calories things had—a tablespoon of butter 100, one green apple 80, a slice of whole-wheat toast (sans butter) 78, a cup of air-popped popcorn 30, one ounce of potato chips 180. At the grocery store, I compulsively looked at the caloric values on labels. If a serving had more than 100 calories, I felt guilty about putting it in my cart. Guilt was something I didn't want to push around the grocery store.

Once when I was still a lawyer, wandering around the grocery store one afternoon I caught myself putting a package of cookies back on the shelf because they felt too indulgent. *Look at how much fat those have in them. But cookies are okay to eat sometimes.* I put them back in my cart. *No! You'll just sit down and eat the whole box.* Back on the shelf. *I want some cookies, dammit.* My hand dropped them back in the cart again. My other hand put them back up on the shelf. *Back in the cart. On the shelf.* I tried to avoid the stare of the older woman behind me who was obviously wondering if I might require professional intervention. *Crap, look at me, I'm turning OCD.* Cookies in the cart. I hid them under the bag of spinach. I tried not to feel guilty. Miss Anal-Retentive Calorie-Counter could sit back there in the dark recesses of my mind and endlessly pile cookies back on the shelf. I tried to ignore her obsessive ramblings.

But every once in a while, after eating something at a restaurant, an office party, or in the break room that I knew had tons of calories—a piece of mud pie, or fettuccine alfredo, or a cream puff—my inner anorexic's shrill cries would echo in my head: *stupid, fat, gross, you disgust me*—and I would fall numb, a vague nausea creeping over my body, a heavy itchiness between my inner thighs. I could practically feel them growing bigger. *Hey, Kimber, you're trying not to care about calories anymore, remember? What happened to enjoying yourself, enjoying your food, enjoying your life?* Occasionally my inner anorexic would fall silent and allow me to savor my meal. Other times she would sit there, glaring at me, twitching with fury.

Sitting here, thinking about writing down my food list for the day, I can tell I'm still wearing the glasses of that girl plotting her own demise under the library stairs. The urge to jot down the approximate calories of every item I've eaten, total it at the end of the day, and write down a little chiding remark wells up inside me: *Good job, but you can do better*, or *Lay off the chips next time*, or *You sure screwed yourself today, didn't you, Miss Piggy?*

Even though I'm determined to take off those calorie-colored glasses and put them aside for good, there's also the embarrassment factor: I'm ashamed to reveal to Sally my real food choices. *Oh no, I'll be discovered! I have a terrible diet, terrible eating habits! I'm a bad person!* I suspect this isn't true, but some part of me fears it anyway. If keeping a food diary is going to work, I have to be totally honest with myself and with the world about my food intake. I've got to be humble and willing to start over from ground zero.

What will Sally think of me? But isn't that the reason to meet with her—to take advantage of her expertise? Not to have her tell me that everything I'm doing is right. It's all part of the process of self-exploration, figuring out what I really eat versus what I think I eat. I can do this.

Again I sit down to write. What did I eat today? The urge to lie or omit rears its hyperbolic head, the accompanying urge to change my habits going forward—to avoid eating certain things just so I don't have to write them down—follows close behind. Yup, I change just by observing myself. Like in physics, where the observer changes the behavior of the observed particle, I'm editing my life and my diet as I write it. *Come on, Kimber, a little honesty, please.*

Finally, pen to paper.

- Breakfast: Leftovers from last night's dinner, sautéed greens and veggie bacon. And a big mug of double-bag roasted green tea.

- Lunch: An asiago cheese stick and a salad. Water with lemon. Then I felt kinda full, but hungry at the same time.

- Snack: Half a bag of natural cheese puffs while on my way to pick Cooper up from school. They're natural, right, so they're fine?

- Dinner: Penne pasta with tomato sauce, broccoli, bread.

- Dessert: Ice cream

- Before bed: An orange. I still felt munchy on my way to bed, so I had some crackers.

Looking over my list, my inner anorexic has some opinions she can't help voicing. And my inner therapist must be with another client, because no one seems willing to step up and keep little Miss Anorexia in line. *You ate a lot of bread. I lost count, but it was outrageous. Then cheese puffs? Really? Those calories are a total waste. And ice cream...goes straight to your hips. And crackers right before bed? What, to fuel that marathon you'll be running...in your dreams?*

This is what happens when I keep track of my food. Sure, I get more awareness of what I'm eating, but a massive torrent of judgment follows. Is it worth the vicious circle of self-criticism and destructive behavior, leading to more criticism, more destructive behavior, and more food? I suppose it's an echo of the cycle of injuries that I used to put myself through on my mat.

Part of me wonders if I'm not still after the same thing as my fifteen-year-old self: thinness and fullness at the same time. Have I just picked up where she left off? Have I made no progress at all in the intervening twenty years? I imagine myself fifty years from now, a shrunken granny with a cane wearing a girdle and still sucking in my belly, walking the hallways of my nursing home, comparing myself to my blue-haired roommate (*Look at what skinny chicken legs she has, I wish I had skinny chicken legs!*), still trying to find the perfect diet (*No, ma'am, don't put any of that sugary parfait on my tray. I only eat DIET Jell-O. Got to keep my figure, you know!*), and still hoping to resuscitate my inner anorexic from her food-induced coma (*After all the peanut snacks at Bingo Night, I swear I'll never touch a piece of caramel corn again!*).

Please don't let that be my life. Can I work with my hunger from a more positive, life-affirming place? Perhaps I'm simply deluding myself by putting the lid on my simmering feelings of self-disgust. Falling back into the cycle of self-judgment, deprivation, and ignoring my body's needs isn't where I want to land. Kindness is key. A real change would be to start from the place of loving my body, of feeling connected to my body, of accepting myself just the way I am.

WISH LIST FOR MY BODY

1. Learn, listen, and understand my body's language. You'd think that I'd be a native speaker, born here in this body. But no, I'm gonna need the Rosetta Stone course.

2. Enjoy what I eat, and eat what I enjoy. Guilt is so yesterday.

3. Look in the mirror and see every part of myself—yes, even my thighs and hips—as beautiful.

4. Touch my body with love and appreciation. Can I stretch to love my stretch marks?

It's got to be possible. Remembering back to college, I put myself in the place of Ms. "I-Love-Putting-Lotion-On-Myself-Naked-At-The-Gym," enjoying the warmth of her skin and how her body looked in the mirror. I'm not there yet, but the desire to feel that whole and loved, by my own hands and eyes, emanates from me like a force field. My body wants to feel beautiful all the way to its bones. *Hey, body, you and me, let's enjoy being alive.* I could start with not judging myself when I look in the mirror. Could I just say "hello" to my body instead of launching into an immediate tirade? *Hey there, body, how's it going, what's up with you?* Before I can be kind to my body, maybe aiming for neutrality is a good step. A nonjudgmental attitude toward my body and my food. Since my détente with Svetlana, my yoga mat is a place where I'm able to pay attention and be kinder to myself. I need to bring that gentle but firm attitude toward myself during the other twenty-two and a half hours of the day, too.

It looks like keeping track of every bite I take into my mouth and reporting it to Sally isn't going to work. Not with my tendency to annihilate myself for every little "mistake." There's got to be another way.

Although what I want—fullness—seems sweet but vague, I have a good sense of what I don't want. I don't want some new diet, not from Sally, not from anyone, especially not one that needs to be followed to the letter. If there's a post-traumatic stress disorder for dieting, I've got it.

Just how many diets have I tried? My mom, sister, and I joined Diet Center together just after my thirteenth birthday, with the special meals, fashion shows, and bizarre recipes: egg whites smeared on wheat crackers with cinnamon and saccharine; scrambled eggs cooked in the microwave, minus butter. *Eww.*

For a long time, the low-fat diet was a major contender, but slowly things like salty buttered toast and caramel ice cream found their way back onto my plate. I tried high-carb diets, beans and brown rice, macrobiotic. For a while I tried the alkaline (vegan/raw food/ green vegetables) diet and discovered it gave my inner anorexic a new paradigm to obsess about: *You're not going to eat that potato chip, are you? Think of the effect on your pH! You're going to cook that kale? It's better raw!* I briefly considered the anticandida diet and found that even thinking about it made my head hurt. No cantaloupe? No corn? You've got to be kidding. I also tried not worrying about my diet at all, with mixed results. I've made feeble attempts with a Mediterranean diet and a Japanese diet—mixed outcomes, but the same overall result: still hungry, still not full.

One friend I confided my endless hunger to blamed my mostly vegetarian diet. He quoted Tom Snyder: "If we're not supposed to eat animals, how come they're made out of meat?" Lots of folks who eat meat are convinced pork chops are the secret to fullness. But I've talked to meat eaters who feel hungry all the time, just like me. It will take more than a few carnivorous quips to convince me that my decades-long struggle with hunger can be solved by eating animals.

I can't do this. I have to tell Sally that journaling is not going to work. My eating habits are not an orchard apple tree in need of a little trimming and fertilizer. An apter metaphor—my diet feels more like the Brazil nut tree struggling to survive as a creeping strangler fig weaves its old fibrous web of self-judgment, body dissatisfaction, and misguided self-control around its trunk from top to bottom. Unfortunately, a pair of pruning shears and a bag of compost are kind of beside the point.

Instead of putting my diet into the hands of yet another authority figure, I want to listen to that inner voice, the inner therapist who is my loving, bigger perspective self. The voice of reason and love that wants me to listen to my body's own wisdom and untangle the roots that keep me stationary instead of constantly looking outward for someone to tell me what to feed this embodied spirit.

❀

For my birthday on Saturday, Chris and Cooper and I head to a little raw food restaurant called Café Muse inside the art museum on the university campus. Under the radiantly sunny Berkeley sky, we sit outside, in the shadows of giant modern sculptures, watching a party of children play chase. The food is amazing—fresh and tangy gazpacho and a Thai mushroom salad full of thinly sliced vegetables and tossed with a lime basil dressing. The raw cookies are irresistible: chewy cashews blended with lemon, coconut, and honey. As usual, even after my soup, salad, and cookies, I still feel munchy hungry. It's so frustrating. I've eaten well nutritionally. My belly feels full. But my mouth could still eat more, more, MORE!

An article I picked up yesterday on my way home from the yoga studio suggests I'm not alone in misinterpreting my body's hunger signals. Most people don't know what hunger really feels like. The article recommended thinking about a scale of hunger from one to ten, with ten being Thanksgiving full, and one being I haven't eaten all day, I could eat a horse. Five being neither hungry nor full.

Hmm, this theory assumes that I *have* a state of being neither hungry nor full. To me, not being full equals hunger. It's like I bounce between two and nine on the scale, without ever visiting anything in between. Perhaps my next step is to look for a state when I'm not hungry—that is, not wanting to eat, but not full either. Does such a state exist for me? Do I ever not want to eat? Except for when I'm hanging out with Downward Facing Dog and all its twisty friends, the answer has to be no.

Monday, I binge—eating tons of bread before dinner. The hunger article says that unless you're at three on the hunger meter, you don't need to eat. I am not at three. Not even close. This crusty, half-eaten roll in my hand isn't about feeding my hunger. What is it feeding then? My need for comfort: I *deserve* this roll. Am I really hungry? No, but my mouth wants to chew on something. *Drop the roll and back away slowly.* When I get that mouth-hungry feeling, why not have a glass of water or a cup of tea? Even a whole pot of tea. Sometimes I mistake thirst for hunger.

I get myself a big glass of water and drink it down. Do I still feel hungry? No, not really. Why not have this little chat with my belly *before* eating?

My fullness meter is highest when I'm in the act of putting food into my mouth. This morning while working on the computer at the yoga studio, I was eating corn chips and enjoying them, feeling quite good, full, happy…their crunchy saltiness seemed to relax me, to hit some pleasure center in my brain, calm me down, and mellow me out. Snacks as drug.

After dinner, before bedtime, 10:15 p.m.: I feel pretty full, dinner was yummy, Chris and Cooper and I sit around while Cooper tells stories about his school day. I'm not belly hungry, but my mind still wants something to eat. If a big bag of cheese puffs appeared in front of me, I would chow right through them. Or a muffin or some other kind of bready treat. Even though I'm feeling full and even a little bloaty, a big bowl of popcorn or some other snacky thing sounds like the perfect thing to munch mindlessly until the bottom of the bowl appears. Where does this come from? Why right after dinner? I feel mellow, tired, sleepy, and crave a little reward. *How about a medal? A ribbon? You made it through another day, Kimber. Congratulations.* Sigh. I just want to feel happy and full.

Cooper seems to do this, too. When he gets sleepy at night, even if he's just had his dinner, he says he's hungry and asks Chris to bring something upstairs for him to eat. Usually if she heads downstairs to get it, he's asleep by the time she makes it back up to his room. It's like he wants to hold on to the day a bit longer, take a little more of it in, up the blood sugar a smidgen and stay awake a few more minutes. Perhaps this is what goes on for me as well. Maybe hitting the sack instead of grabbing that extra bite is the best idea.

Some nights I want to go to bed with a warm, heavy stomach. Like a contented kitten, having drunk itself into a milk-induced stupor, cuddled along the length of its mother and siblings. When I'm eating well, and exercising and taking good care of myself, my body feels great, and beautiful, and sexy. And I love to eat, well or otherwise. Perhaps just a little at a time, I could start to wean myself off of eating before bed, or maybe have tea or a glass of milk, or... snuggle with my family.

I could start right now. Heading upstairs, I shut off lights along the way, saying good night to the dog, the cat, and the fridge.

I survived last night without eating anything else. But when my feet hit the mat for my morning yoga practice, I'm ravenous. Which turns out to be ironic, because I picked Fullness as the theme for my practice, repeating to myself, "I am full, I have everything I need." And then in the midst of repeating this mantra, hunger crawls over me like a blanket of army ants. In the midst of attempting to cultivate feeling full in a spiritual way, my body detects tiny hungry feet covering every pore and crevice. The words "I am full" feel shallow, meaningless, even insidious. As if I'm trying to convince myself of something that clearly isn't true; which makes me worry that I'm returning to that anorexic place of planting hurtful concepts in my own mind: *You're fat, you're ugly, you're not hungry, you're just weak*. It takes so little to conjure up my anorexic and her destructive mantras.

Instead of ignoring my physical needs and succumbing to my anorexic's spell, I go into the kitchen and find a peach to eat. Turning my back on Miss Anorexic yet again. A victory of sorts. Sucking the last peach bits from the pit, my energy lifts right away, and I can go on with my sun salutations. Back to my mat, I meditate on "I am full" again, and then I let it morph into a slightly different mantra: "I am everything I need." *Hmm, how does that feel?*

My mind argues with it. Obviously, I am not everything I need on a practical level. Food, shelter, clothing aren't manufactured in this body along with saliva and methane, sweat and poop. However, all the resources needed to meet my needs are here. That's right, everything I need is right here. Hands to shape. Feet to move. A mind to envision. A body to explore. A heart with an enormous capacity for love. *I have everything I need*. A sense of oneness, wholeness settles over my body. I breathe: "I am one, I am whole. I am full." My toes grip the mat and my arms reach for the sky beyond the ceiling. It feels lovely.

It feels too overwhelming to hold on to. Distracted, but still repeating the words in my head, the meaning loses it way on the path to my heart. But my poses unfold and dissolve in the afterglow of that experience of fullness. My practice feels good, even with the sense of having let something precious slip through my fingers.

Wednesday night, we go over to our friends Denise and Pete's house for dinner. I ask them about hunger over fish curry and brown rice, chutneys and fresh buttery flatbread. Their question—"What do you mean by 'hunger'?"—makes me wonder whether what I experience as hunger is the same for other people. When I get a chance to contemplate the question later at home, I sit down with pen and paper to chart the different hungers I'm aware of. It seems that at least nine distinct types of hunger revolve through my body, a kind of solar system of hungry planets.

The first is mouth hunger, that longing of the mouth, when I just want something to chew on and swallow. An entire bowl of popcorn, bag of potato chips, or plate of celery can be demolished with just a mild case of mouth hunger. Mouth hunger seems innocuous, until I'm looking at the bottom of the bag, thinking, *More.*

The second, belly hunger, is real physical hunger, when my stomach growls, which I translate as, *Hey, we're ready to get back to work, send something our way!*

Deep down empty hunger comes after I've managed to distract myself from both mouth and belly hunger for a chunk of time, or after a good long cry. When I feel deep down empty hunger, food better follow, because if I don't eat right away, the alarm sounds, and…

Blood sugar crash hunger kicks in. This is when the SYSTEM FAILURE button starts to flash, the dials go crazy, the voice over the loudspeaker shouts in its monotone: "Meltdown Imminent. Evacuate The Area. Meltdown Imminent. Evacuate. Now." Then I know things are headed downhill fast.

Panic hunger arrives on the heels of blood sugar crash hunger. Stale food is desperately consumed, and the urge to keep eating continues unabated, long after I know I've eaten enough, just to make the scary feeling of hunger go away.

Emotional hunger is subtle, sneaky even—when creeping anxiety induces daydreams about madeleines and chocolate milk, and my feet make a beeline for the nearest café. Sometimes emotional hunger takes the form of a chirpy reward: "I've been so good today, I finished my entire to-do list! I deserve this black and tan sundae, a fill-in-the-blank oozy gooey, whipped cream–laden gold star. I deserve this candy bar I was saving to give my son on a special occasion. This is *my* special occasion." *Heh, heh, heh, mmm.*

Eye hunger is when at a café I spy a new dessert item in the case. *It has caramel and chocolate and fruit! I love caramel and chocolate and fruit! Mmm, so tasty looking, I have to try it.*

Nostalgic hunger, related to eye hunger, can be triggered merely by seeing the words "apple pie" on the menu. *Ah, I remember Grandma made the best pie for Sunday dinner, I wonder if it will taste like hers.*

Spiritual hunger may be the distant, amorphous outlier. Then again, it might be the sun, right at the center, the one that holds all the others in its brilliant thrall. It's a longing for something more, a sense that there's something missing, a desire for some kind of intensity which can sometimes be temporarily met by a really good piece of chocolate. Spiritual hunger can feel a little bit like mouth hunger, with a touch of gnawing belly hunger underneath. Sometimes it's an ache, a soft, almost desperate emptiness in the center of my heart that calls out to life for an answer. When life doesn't respond, food seems the closest alternative. Food brings the world inside, brings Life inside me, makes it part of myself.

❀

Today I fast. Without intending to. Oops. I got thrown off my schedule this morning by waking up late and then helping Cooper find his "missing" homework before Chris took him to school. Of course it wasn't missing, but was in his backpack right where he put it the night before, and naturally we didn't look there until twenty minutes into the search.

Usually on Thursday mornings I get to enjoy my breakfast of eggs and veggies around 7:30 a.m., teach until 11:30, have a banana snack around 12:00, and eat lunch after my noon class at 1:30. But today I eat my eggs, forget my snack, and squeeze in an acupuncture appointment at 1:30, so it's 3:00 p.m. now, and I haven't eaten since breakfast. Wow, that's seven and a half hours of not eating—that's a big deal for me. I rarely go more than two or three hours without eating at least a little snack. Predictably, deep down belly hunger has set in and I can feel panic hunger approaching. My whole body feels shaky, irritable, and exhausted. Throughout the acupuncture appointment, my stomach growled every so often, waking me out of my needle-induced drowsiness on the table. All nine hungry planets are spiraling inward on their orbits and threatening to annihilate me from all sides. Even my elbows and knees are hungry.

When I finally get home, I put a dish of leftovers into the oven, set the timer, and sit down at the kitchen table to wait for them to warm up. My mind wants to wander off into a dark place of blame and hopelessness, but with my last ounce of will, I set it to the task of observing. This is where I am. This is what's happening. Can I notice what's here instead of pushing it away? Every mindful breath on my mat feels like preparation for this moment.

My hands tremble. I hate feeling this way. Incompetent. Bereft. Like if someone asked me to pass the salt I would freak out. Don't ask me to do anything beyond the immediate requirement of just staying alive and sane until lunch is ready. I could cry over the tiniest thing right now, as if my heart were breaking. The roots of my hair feel tired, my toes are ready to crawl away and look for crumbs under the sofa. My mind feels completely off-kilter, fuzzy, and illogical. The shadow of my lean year looms over me. Pretty much every minute of being fifteen felt just like this.

Getting this hungry sucks. It's a combination of yucky feelings all rolled together. Like a wave of loneliness and depression with an extra wallop of shame to knock you off your feet and pull you underwater. As separate entities you could maybe survive each smaller undulation on its own, but all at once it's a powerful rogue wave.

The tendrils of a headache wrap themselves around my forehead. Paranoia starts to creep in, as if the whole world is out to get me. No wonder I try to avoid this state at any cost. All my eating habits are based on avoiding feeling this way. The blood sugar crash leads me toward that old void of depression, becoming a nonfunctional, sobbing, globbery mess.

The timer finally buzzes and at last I sit and quickly gulp down the leftovers of green curry cauliflower and spinach with jasmine rice. They were delicious last night, but now I barely taste anything—my spoon is just filling my mouth's empty space. I eat and eat, without thinking about how any of it tastes. Finally, I look down at the cleaned-off plate, all of its contents filling my belly, and realize my belly still doesn't feel full. My immediate physical hunger has abated, but the anxiety, the shakiness, while gone on a physical level, leaves an emotional impression on my body, a hole that lunch doesn't fill. The desire to stuff myself more to make up for the recent emptiness asserts itself. Dad's words from so many years ago echo in my head: "No fasting."

Everything's okay, you have enough to eat, it's all right, you don't need to gorge. You're eating lunch late. You're not in danger of starving yourself. You're not reverting to old habits. You're okay now. The fatigue lingers and while some of the mental fog slowly lifts, some still seems caught between my ears, like tufts of wool on barbed wire. I need to take better care of myself and not let myself get this strung out on hunger. Two steps forward…three steps back.

The other day when we were at home, Cooper came halfway up the stairs to ask me if he could have some more graham crackers.

"Listen to your belly, honey. What does your belly say?"

Perched on the edge of the step, one arm clutching the railing, he looked down at his stomach and then up at the ceiling, as if listening for a moment.

An enormous, deep, rumbly voice emerged from his little body.

"I need more graham crackers!"

A chuckle burst from my mouth. "Well, better not ignore that voice, huh?"

I'd love for Cooper to develop self-moderation. No one ever told me to listen to my body, to listen to what my stomach needs. To pay attention to the signals that my body is sending. After ignoring those signals for so long, it's hard to interpret them now. Perhaps if Cooper starts to listen now, he won't get stuck on the same hunger roller-coaster that my body's been whiplashed by for years.

I seek comfort and love from food—and offer it as well. Fortunately, as much as Cooper loves candy, he loves asparagus and artichokes too. Everything I make him contains love. But I hope that he is attuned to all the other ways Chris and I express our love for him: telling him we love him every day, watching how he enjoys picking raspberries along the back fence, listening to him explain how he got mad at a friend at school, meeting his need for more time playing at the park, standing under him while he's climbing a tree, and giving him space to move out of the protective circle of our arms when he's ready. The idea I guess is that he internalizes love in these forms and finds that he's able to offer love in these ways to others… and to himself. Maybe learning all these forms of love is what I'm doing with my body, too. Listening to what my body's telling me, watching what my body enjoys (and doesn't), meeting my body's needs for comfort and love with more than just food. A sort of reparenting of this hungry, unloved body. May I be as good a parent to it as I hope to be for Cooper.

I've charted the planets of hunger, found the occasional fullness mark on my hunger meter, and started hearing the quiet, rational voice that reminds me to be gentle on my mat speak hopefully of moderation and eating out of love. Yet at times my hunger still feels like it's smothering me, like the friend whose drama demands all your time and energy and all the space on your couch, night after night. I need some distance from her. A little break. Dealing with her in my head, where I'm learning to work with Svetlana by feeding her tea and cookies, doesn't feel like enough.

Perhaps I can externalize my hunger. Can I pluck her out of my body and take a good look at her? Maybe make her some offerings? Getting out my son's modeling clay, I wrap a bright, vine-green rope of clay around another one of deep violet. As the clay warms and mixes in my hands, slowly the shape of an owl, a round, birdlike goddess with a huge belly emerges. But where her stomach should be solid, tight, and round, there's a gaping hole. Her belly is a wide, tall-sided bowl with a tiny leak at the bottom, so that no matter how much she receives and is offered, it never feels like enough. My fingers pinch a beaked nose for her, and hooded eyes, and round tripod feet for her to stand on.

Her shape is familiar somehow; she reminds me of a resident of the hungry ghost realm, one of the Buddhist realms of existence populated by beings with huge bellies and tiny mouths who can never take in enough nutrients to feel a sense of fulfillment. Poor thing.

I place her on my altar near the tiny statues of Kwan Yin, the goddess of compassion, Saraswati, the goddess of wisdom, and a lavender ceramic goddess figure I made years ago that represents Mother Earth. She looks pretty happy nestled there with her companions. *What do you need?* I ask the hunger goddess.

Get me something to eat, she responds. Of course.

Pulling a box of chocolates off the top of the fridge, I select one with cherries and dark cordial filling and carefully wrap it in foil. Gazing at the candy in the palm of my hand, I realize she probably needs something else she's not asking for. I wander around the house for a moment, then open the back door and pick a sprig of pink jasmine from the trellis outside. She'll like that. What else? Chocolates, flowers, mmm, jewelry. I hunt through my grandmother's stand-up jewelry box that now lives on my own dresser. As a child I would pull out all the drawers to listen to Laura's Theme on the tinkly mechanism, and pile Grandma's beaded costume jewels around my arms and throat. It occurs to me that maybe I'm looking for a gift to satisfy not only my present-day hunger, but my childhood hunger. My mother's and my grandmother's hunger. Even satisfaction for the hunger of all the women before me. No wonder my little goddess is so hungry. I find just the thing: a silver, heart-shaped pendant, a gift from my parents, with two birds intertwining in the center.

I head back to the altar and kneel there, contemplating my new creation. Her largest feature is her swirled green and purple belly, empty, and her cloaked expression could be read as either sinister or regal. Perhaps it depends on how much—or what—she's been fed. *My dear goddess*, I begin. *May you find fullness.* I place the chocolate into her hollow belly. *May you see beauty.* I place the jasmine alongside the chocolate. *May you feel safe and loved.* I nestle the silver heart to rest lightly against the left side of her bowl. Her belly looks full to overflowing. She seems satisfied with this, for the moment.

chapter nine

Hungry for Wisdom

Who is it about being on my yoga mat that makes it the one place I get a true reprieve from hunger? There's something about doing fifty push-ups and downward dogs, handstands and backbends, breathing through my nose the whole time while opening up my hips, twisting and squishing and stretching, that erases the thought of food entirely from my mind. As if my body is eating the poses, one by one, savoring every movement, tasting every breath. Rarely does even a tiny grumble pass through my belly in yoga class. Even lying down at the end, you'd think my relaxed stomach might speak up and grab some attention in the quiet, but it just lays there, silent and content. Satisfied with a whole body meal. Full, but not of food.

That momentary sense of fullness lured me into the world of yoga teaching. Years ago, just a few months into my regular yoga classes with Katchie, she mentioned at the end of an evening session that she would be offering a yoga intensive and teacher training in the spring. My heart leapt. I couldn't wait to do it. During my first class with her, right on the heels of my blissful awareness that yoga could hold all the parts of me—mind, body, and spirit—a further thought had formulated itself in my brain: *I want to help people feel this. I want to teach yoga.* Somewhere, deep inside me, there was a secret inner yoga teacher. Who knew she was back there all along, coexisting with my inner anorexic, Svetlana, the prison guard and his prisoner, and my inner therapist? I guess amidst all the activities of the other cast of characters back there, she had been sitting in meditation, waiting patiently for her moment. She opened her eyes, loosened her feet from lotus position, and stood up, as if saying, *Yes, dear. It's my turn.* I could sense a different sort of hunger. A desire to learn, to share, to teach.

Generally speaking, a brand-new student's desire to become a yoga teacher is frowned upon; they are too green, too immature, too lacking in knowledge and depth to even think about teaching. Some yoga masters won't let students even begin teacher training until they've studied for ten years or more in their particular system. I knew nothing of this. I imagined that learning to teach yoga would be as simple as opening that big file cabinet in the sky labeled "What I Don't Know About Yoga," and systematically moving files and articles and whole books over to the smaller file cabinet in my brain labeled "What I Do Know About Yoga." Unaware of what invisible toes and unspoken rules I might be thoughtlessly trampling upon, like a camera-laden tourist scuffling across an elaborate sand mandala drawn painstakingly on the temple floor, I bumbled into the depths of yoga. My desire overcame any internal or external, known or unknown objections. I would learn, I would practice, I would teach. I joined Katchie's intensive.

We met each weekend in a dark, high-ceilinged studio in San Francisco's Mission District, and focused our minds and bodies on Katchie's words and instructions until our eyes blurred and our muscles turned to quivering slabs of jelly. We learned the poses from the ground up, and worked with elaborate, complicated breathing and cleansing practices. (Katchie demonstrated for us one day how some yogis take a thin tube, thread it up their nose, down their throat, out their mouth, and hold on to both ends, basically flossing the nasal cavity...Uh, do we *have* to do this to be yoga instructors? Second thoughts started knocking. Thankfully, nasal flossing was optional.) We read the Yoga Sutras, practiced various forms of meditation (staring at a candle until my eyes went blurry reminded me of a childhood slumber party séance), and experimented with teaching each other the postures. Though finally clued in to how much I didn't know, my curiosity and desire to learn remained unsated. One of Katchie's teachers, John Friend, was due to arrive soon in San Francisco to offer a week-long teacher training. Having already waded through the cool shallows of yoga and encouraged by the life jacket of alignment that Katchie had introduced me to, I now walked obliviously toward the edge of the invisible drop-off where swimmers plunge in over their heads: I signed up.

The first day of the training found me and about 120 yoga teachers of all levels of experience in a spacious second-floor yoga studio. For the first time, in John's training, I realized that the file cabinet of things I didn't know about yoga was way bigger than I'd imagined. My brain wasn't nearly big enough to hold it all. I would need an office supply store full of file cabinets. I was totally out of my depth.

My intensive teacher training with Katchie, as fascinating as it had been, was the tasty *amuse-bouche* appetizer. Yoga was a feast it would take my whole life to savor. As my arms and legs were outstretched in triangle pose, John walked by me, scrutinized my stance, and asked, "How far away should the feet be from each other?"

I was psyched, I totally knew the answer to this question. "Ankles as far apart as the wrists!" I replied, leaning my head back and squinting up at him.

"Balanced action," he countered, moving down the dense aisle of arms and legs, a vast human forest. "Close enough for stability, wide enough for freedom."

The amount of information we were expected to learn, to master, and to have already mastered was overwhelming. Five principles, seven loops, a hundred poses—now teach this to your partner so they feel the pose in their heart as well. I proved my utter ignorance over and over that day and throughout the week. The more experienced teachers fluidly described and demonstrated the loops and spirals as if they'd been born in Anusara-land and spoke the native tongue. *Draw your thighs back with your willingness to perceive the big picture. Scoop your tailbone down with the intention to step fully into life.* The "Universal Principles of Alignment," as they were called, mushed together before even leaving my mouth; they were not yet written on the lines of my body, etched into each pose, or drawn elegantly across each plane of skin and muscle. But I wanted them inscribed there. I wanted to understand.

Lying on the floor, on my dusty mat, watching the light set beyond the tapestry-covered windows, I let John's words wash over me. All I could do was surrender and listen. Of all the teachings that week, the one I remember most was John's voice emphasizing again and again, "Look first for the good. Look for what's beautiful in the pose, for what's right and perfect. The student you are looking at is perfect already. Anything you have to offer him or her is a refinement of that perfection, a way for your students to more fully express their true nature. It's not about correcting a pose that's wrong. It's about helping what is beautiful express itself more fully."

As teachers, we weren't supposed to offer our students corrections, but adjustments. We were to see what was beautiful and whole in them, and help them see it, too. I sighed into the back of my head resting on the floor. My eyes filled with tears. All the other yogis in the room dropped away, leaving me alone on my mat and looking into the unknown. The only way to authentically see the beauty in my students, and help them see it in themselves, I realized, was to see it in myself. I would never see it in anyone, never truly witness beauty in the world, if I couldn't find it in the mirror and in my own heart. My desire to teach had thrust me headfirst into the dark void of my biggest obstacle. *See your own beauty, Kimber. See it. It's in there, somewhere.* This body, these long fingers, these warm arms, this soft belly, and sensitive breasts, even these thighs…they are beautiful too. Yoga asked me to become that woman in the gym mirror, loving herself the way she was.

Awash in the awareness of my own ignorance and the huge inner task I had set for myself, I signed up for another yoga immersion and teacher training, this one lasting for a full twelve months, at a new Anusara studio in Berkeley. I also started teaching a few students here and there, whoever would let me; then substitute teaching; and finally, teaching an hour-long class at a women's gym in San Francisco, near the ocean, where the round-trip commute was longer than the class. *Be patient with yourself,* I heard myself repeating to my students. *Notice any tendency to push yourself beyond what makes sense for you.* I sincerely hoped none of them had an inner Svetlana…but if they did, I hoped my words might help ward off whatever cousin of hers might inhabit their inner worlds. The teachings felt fresh and immediate as I watched the women in my class eagerly lengthen over their legs. As the reminders left my lips, their wise residue sank into another deeper level of my own awareness. I'd heard you never fully learn something until you have to teach it; sure enough, my learning and teaching amplified each other, carrying me and my practice along their sinuous wave. I loved at last having my own class, students who knew me, who liked me, who came to practice yoga despite the long mirrors at the front of the classroom, students who came because they related to my teaching.

The weekends of the yearlong training were sometimes grueling: two eight-hour sessions each weekend we met. "What!? You have teacher trainings on Mother's Day *and* Halloween?" Chris howled after examining our schedule. "Don't they expect yoga teachers to have families?" Following that outburst I quietly neglected to tell her what we'd just learned: according to some classical understandings of the Yoga Sutras, yogis were also expected to be celibate. I sensed that her faltering support would not kindly receive that revelation, aside from the fact that this yoga teacher had no intention of following a strict definition of that particular observance.

Our teachers, Jimmy and Ruthie, put us through long paces of *asana* (the Sanskrit term for yoga poses), anatomy lessons (featuring Mr. Wiggly, the plastic bone-and-muscle skeleton wearing a red skull cap, wheeled out to demonstrate the correct placement of the arm bone into the shoulder socket, and so on), and teaching each other basic poses in front of the class. Each weekend I found myself tumbled in the troughs of the waves of teaching and study at least as often as I enjoyed riding the crests.

One spring Saturday we learned about *samskaras*, the deep ruts or habits that we fall into and find it hard to get out of. Over the course of our lives (or even over the course of lifetimes, if you believe in that sort of thing), we develop patterns of behavior that we act on over and over again, despite our desire to change. Even when we maneuver our way up the craggy walls and halfway over the edge, our samskaras (easy to remember by thinking "same scars") tend to be so slippery and persistent, we slide right back down to the bottom again. *Well, that explains a lot about why my desire to love myself is continually thwarted by my habit of self-hatred. It's a deep gorge I keep climbing out of, only to fall back in again.* Consistent yoga practice, we were told, was one way to level off the steepness of our samskaras by helping us notice them, and how they affect our lives. Slowly, over time, the habit of acting on our samskaras would be replaced by the habit of noticing them, smoothing out the rough edges, so that each time we fall back in, it's a little easier to climb out again, until they simply become a gouge in the earth that we can step over without a backward glance.

Samskaras might be a disturbing concept for some, but to me it all made so much sense, how the samskara of being unhappy with my body dug deep into my early life; how it hadn't started with me; and how, if I wasn't mindful, it might not end with me either. The positive habit of my yoga practice and the understanding it promised were helping me see my old habits of hunger and self-criticism, and hopefully would show me how to not fall into them over and over again.

My favorite part of the weekend was when Carlos Pomeda, our philosophy teacher, sat before us, our notebooks and blankets scattered across the floor, and carefully explained the history and origins of yoga. He lulled us with stories of gods and goddesses, sages and yogis, as the shadows lifted and rose across the floor, meeting the evening light.

"Everything is made of the same stuff," he said. "Everything in the universe is divine consciousness." Then, with his soft Spanish accent, he led us in a guided meditation to put into practice the concept we had just learned. *Ham-sa. I am that,* I breathed.

Opening my eyes at the end and looking into his radiant face and sweet, open smile, I found it easy to believe that the divine is in everything. *The divine is in all things,* he intoned, *the divine embodies itself as you.* Of all the ideas I'd come across in yoga, this one resonated most deeply with me. The divine has embodied itself as me. The divine is within me, within all beings, within all things, everywhere. The divine, the beauty is here, too.

From the trash pile of abandoned memories emerged the reminder that I'd once had an experience of what Carlos was talking about. At twelve, my first inkling of the universe embodied as me arose, of all places, in my seventh-grade physical sciences class. Doc Holiday, our teacher, stood in front of the classroom explaining the law of conservation of mass and energy, the first law of thermodynamics. No mass is ever lost, no mass is ever gained. No energy is ever created, no energy is ever destroyed. I looked down at my hands, spread my fingers out in front of me, and suddenly caught a glimpse of what he really meant. The energy that runs through my hands, the atoms that make up my bones, the life force that moves in me has always been part of the universe and always will be. For a moment, my imagination perceived the Big Bang congealing itself into this sun, this planet, this body, this me, and visible energy rising up from my hands and sweeping across the galaxy to the center of the Milky Way. I felt dizzy for a moment. My breath caught in my throat. I looked up, at the back of my classmates' heads, thinking, *Whoa. Did anyone else see that?* The universe is me, always has been, always will be. I didn't see anyone else's face revealing the same dazed feeling that fogged my brain. I think I walked into walls for the rest of the day.

From that day on some corner of me always knew that I was part of the energy of the universe. But often that little corner got dusty and full of cobwebs, rarely visited or remembered, like a sealed-off fireplace. Carlos's words had pulled aside the bricks and burned away the dust, leaving space for a bright fire I could tend and feed.

Back in the yoga studio, appreciating how profoundly Carlos's teaching had resonated with me, I realized that his yoga teachings had placed that experience of oneness with the universe (just another name for the divine, supreme consciousness, nature, or whatever you pray, sing, or talk to) in the world of yoga. Finally I'd found a tradition that could put words to my experience. Apparently the spiritual equivalent of the first law of thermodynamics had been understood by yogis for thousands of years. I wondered if Carlos might be able to put some other parts of my life into context as well. Like my hunger for fullness.

✸

In some places, September is known as early fall. In the Bay Area, it's the warmest time of year, clear and beautiful and definitely *summer*, no matter what the calendar says. In September of 2004, I finally got up the courage to offer Carlos and his wife, Suesi, private yoga sessions in exchange for philosophy consultations, to see if he could help me address my hunger from a yogic point of view. I arranged to meet him at his house in Berkeley. Standing at the front door, reaching for the bell, my hand shook, as if I had stopped by a movie star's house to ask for an autograph. But as the door swung back to reveal Carlos's smiling face, to my relief, he welcomed me warmly and ushered me inside. As he led the way upstairs, I realized that I had imagined Carlos and Suesi living in some kind of meditation cave, filled with pillows, incense holders, piles of dusty books, and a direct phone line to the divine on a low desk in the center of the room. To my surprise and relief, their home was simple, elegantly modern, and would have looked great in a home magazine spread.

Carlos offered me a seat in his kitchen, and placed a hot cup of herbal tea in front of me. Nervous and excited to finally get the chance to pick Carlos's brain about hunger and yoga and my spiritual path, I pulled out my notebook and pen. We started with the basics. What does it mean, I asked him, to be hungry, from a yogic point of view? In Sanskrit, Carlos began, the word *bhuj* means both eater and experiencer, connecting the idea that we experience something through eating it. Like babies who put everything in their mouths, we explore the world, we taste the world, we decide if it's good, and then we take it in, chew it up, swallow it, and let our bodies assimilate it. The world literally becomes us through the process of eating. We eat as part of our search for fulfillment, becoming one with the world by bringing it inside ourselves. I sipped my tea, bringing a small taste of the world into my body.

Carlos continued, telling me that his guru believed that hunger is connected to the desire for liberation—it's good to always be a little hungry. Some hunger is a result of truly not having enough, or a fear that there won't be enough, so hunger serves to make sure your needs are met. It's important, Carlos considered, to understand the purpose that my problem of being hungry serves. Certainly my experience of hunger has motivated me to learn how to connect my body, mind, and heart more fully.

So hunger is a good thing? I tried to get my mind around the idea. Instead of thinking of hunger as this terrible thing I have to ward off, defeat, or give in to utterly, I could think of it as something that's helping me, encouraging me, reminding me of my desire to understand myself and the world more deeply?

Just so, said Carlos. In the Yoga Sutras, the sage Patanjali suggests that if you want to rid yourself of a bad habit, cultivate its opposite. Instead of seeing hunger as a negative thing, see it as a positive thing. Instead of dwelling on hunger, contemplate its opposite: fullness. *Purna*, or *purnata*, he explained, is both fullness in eating, and also the idea of perfection, wholeness, the entire universe complete unto itself, you wholly and fully yourself. In fact, he suggested, when you notice hunger, let it be a reminder to remember what is full in your life.

This could really work, I thought, leaning back into the driver's seat and heading home. I can commit to being mindful about what parts of the world I choose to bring into me, make part of me. When

157

I feel hungry, I can pause, and remind myself of all the aspects of my life that are full and abundant. When I eat, I can remind myself not to eat out of hunger, but to eat to create fullness. Let each bite be a reminder of my desire to be full, my desire to be present with the fullness that is already all around me.

The next day I went to see a doctor at Kaiser. Why not get the Western medical view on what's causing my hunger? The yogic approach would take time and consistency. What if hunger was a sign that something was really wrong, or just a little wrong, something that could be easily fixed by a prescription? Wouldn't it be great if I could just take a pill? Ta-da! No more hunger. Sitting in the sterile room, a tiny little cell in a huge honeycombed building, I waited for the doctor and looked over the Body Mass Index chart. According to the BMI, I appeared to be in the "high-normal" range.

A young, busy doctor hurried into the room and listened briefly to my complaint. She told me that when someone feels hungry all the time, she recommends looking for high thyroid levels and checking the cholesterol and sugar levels in the blood. She asked me a couple of questions and looked over my file.

"You are incredibly healthy," she said, shutting the file with a businesslike flourish and peering at me from behind her glasses. "I wouldn't worry about it."

She peeled a handwritten lab note off the file folder and passed it to me. Blood work. I would have to wait a couple of weeks to get the results, but she was certain they'd come back fine.

Why should I worry about hunger, if my body's healthy? But I'm sick of being hungry all the time. Okay, fine, I'm not hungry all the time. Just mostly. My hunger seems to be waning a tiny bit in the face of my mindfulness. Maybe I should go home and give my hunger goddess an offering of chocolate glazed donuts. That should satisfy her. I laid my arm out for the phlebotomist and turned my eyes away. A wave of impatience rushed over me. When will my search for fullness be over? When I give up trying to lose weight and be perfect and decide to enjoy this body the way it is? When I'm spiritually fulfilled? When I'm exercising three hours a day, seven days a week? When I'm dead? Ach! *Let's not get carried away, Kimber. Enjoying the body you have right now sounds like a good idea.*

There was that voice of reason again. But my inner chorus of negativity still wanted to negotiate its eternal improvement plan, starting where my feet touched the earth and demolishing anything inessential, all the way up to where my head met the sky.

Heading for the parking garage, doubts floated to the surface. If I found the secret to never feeling hungry, and in doing so lost weight, would I be selling out? Does wanting to lose weight mean I've turned my back on all those other big girls in the world who don't want to have to fill their minds with self-hating diet advice? The inner anorexic, Svetlana, and the prison guard held the delicious, skinny carrot in front of me. *Wouldn't you love to never feel self-conscious in your body, feel like you could wear anything? When you're thin, the whole world will gaze at you and say, "Wow, she looks great, she's really got her shit together."*

No. My mind pushed their lure away. *They're wrong.* Being thin doesn't automatically translate into being confident and feeling great. The most miserable period of my life was when I was thinnest and starving myself. Being fat doesn't mean someone feels crappy, either. Doesn't mean *I* have to feel crappy.

Driving home, my mind floated back to the other day when Cooper asked me why he's so big (he's tall for his age), and I told him in a high squeaky voice, "It's because we love you so much." I kissed his head and neck and tickled the soft curls at his nape. "Love makes you bigger!" He shrugged and laughed and ran off. He was big when he was born: 9.5 pounds. He's always been big. I started out at 9.5 pounds, too.

As my fingers jangled the key in the front door, I wondered, am I just fighting the tide? Am I meant to be big? The Serenity Prayer floats to mind: *May I have the serenity to accept the things I cannot change, the courage to change the things I can, and the wisdom to know the difference.* Is my weight something I can't change, or something I can? Do I have the wisdom to know the difference? If I can't be an ideal weight without sacrificing my mental well-being, then my weight is something I cannot change, something I have to find the courage to accept. I always tell my students, "Don't sacrifice your inner well-being for the outer form," when I see them pushing themselves too hard in a pose. Funny how I share with them the very teachings I need to hear over and over. It's not just that I need to see the beauty. My inner well-being needs to come first, too.

For a moment on the couch, I leaned back and closed my eyes. Acceptance was a hard door to open, and I wasn't even sure I wanted to open it. In my imagination, the door marked Acceptance had Svetlana, my inner anorexic, and the prison guard's boots and bodies pushing on one side to keep it closed. My inner therapist and inner yoga teacher strained on the other, determined to push their way through. Which side would I throw my weight on?

At my next meeting with Carlos I stood on the porch, waiting for him to answer the bell, my feet grounded, my body more relaxed. I laughed at myself, realizing how nervous I must have been last week if my calm was noticeable now. He answered the door with a smile and led me up the stairs to the kitchen. Pausing and breathing for a moment, I admired the wind chimes suspended over the inviting balcony off the kitchen and said yes to a cup of ginger tea. I laid out my notebook and pen on the wooden table.

"After last week, I realized I've been thinking about my hunger as a barely restrained desire to eat everything, to grab onto the world and make it a part of myself," I began. "Which of course violates one of the ethical restraints in the Yoga Sutras, you know, aparigraha."

Aparigraha, one of the qualities that yogis are expected to cultivate, translates variously as greedlessness or nongrasping, or in my mind, not coveting your neighbor's Twinkie, or size-6 body, or size-6 body on Twinkies.

"If I could cultivate nongrasping, maybe I could apply it to food, no longer grasping onto every edible thing nearby. Then I could feel full."

Carlos smiled, sipped at his tea, and in his most gentle, wise, spiritual teacher manner informed me that I had it all backwards.

"Nongrasping is the natural and effortless result of already feeling blissful, content, full."

Huh? To feel full, I have to already be full? How convenient. My inner anorexic arched a smug eyebrow. She was not impressed.

My disbelief must have reached him telepathically. "If you want to cultivate nongrasping, start with the highest. Cultivate fullness first."

As he continued to explain, his words started to make sense: Don't focus on disciplining or depriving yourself, it only creates an atmosphere of scarcity and self-judgment. You might as well hang a sign around your neck that says, "I'm naughty, I'm weak, I'm bad." This is not yogic, and not the fast track to fullness. Nonattachment arises from a center of contentment, strength, and fullness. Our Western mindset interprets *aparigraha* as "It is bad to want things," but in the yoga tradition, things themselves are not intrinsically good or bad. Good things are those that help you attain a higher state of consciousness, bad things are those that make it harder. So if deprivation takes you further away from fullness, find something instead that brings you closer.

Scribbling down his words, I tried to glean meaning from them and then stopped and chewed on the top of the pen, before pulling it out of the corner of my mouth and setting it self-consciously on the notepad. "But when I go to my favorite Indian restaurant to eat lunch at the buffet, I have to stop myself from going back for seconds, because if I'm not strict with myself, I'll eat more than my body needs and end up with a stomachache."

"That's wonderful," Carlos responded, crossing his legs alongside the table. "You're being kind, compassionate to yourself. You eat and enjoy what you need. You're honoring your body by not letting yourself overeat and end up in pain."

Oh. The word *guru* in Sanskrit can mean "the one who removes the darkness, and lets the light shine through." Although Carlos does not describe himself as a guru, I felt as if he had lifted his hand across the kitchen table and pulled the string on a light bulb I didn't even know was hanging over my head. I could reframe my behavior. Instead of, *I can only have one portion because I have to control myself, I'm like a ravenous tiger that has to be carefully handled and restrained,* my approach becomes: *I eat one portion because I am devoted to honoring myself, taking care of this beautiful body, just as it is. I eat enough and not too much out of love for my body and myself.* Loving restraint instead of fearful deprivation.

A sense of relief flooded through me as the afternoon light poured through the wide kitchen window. All this time my attempts at self-discipline brought up the fear that I would summon my inner anorexic from her exile, to wreak havoc on my growing sense of well-being. Carlos showed me how to sidestep her bony arms entirely. I didn't need to embrace her or exile her. I didn't need to control myself at all. There is space in between "not enough" and "too much," his words assured me. Perhaps that space could become my home, a place where self-love could grow. Self-devotion instead of self-discipline.

Leaving, I sprang down the steps of Carlos's house and out to the sunny sidewalk. I could put his ideas and my insights to work right away. My old habits around food wouldn't all disappear in one day. But a brand-new sense of empowerment around eating excited me. Saying yes or no to food out of love—rather than out of obligation or punishment—seemed possible, echoing my new but growing inner voice. I could stop at four cookies out of love for myself, *because I felt full*. Or even stop at three or two or one.

But as I got into the car to drive home, my elation dimmed somewhat. Will this work? Huge portions of my brain are trained to give myself a hard time, to treat myself like a straitjacketed wacko. Teaching myself that I deserve to love and take care of myself as I am—I could spend the rest of my life working on just this one piece of the puzzle.

One of my favorite poems by Galway Kinnell starts out with this reminder:

The bud

stands for all things,

even for those things that don't flower,

for everything flowers, from within, of self-blessing;

though sometimes it is necessary

to reteach a thing its loveliness,

to put a hand on its brow

of the flower

and retell it in words and in touch

it is lovely

until it flowers again from within, of self-blessing.

I turned the car onto the highway, musing. All the blood work I'd gotten a couple weeks ago had turned out fine. My body was perfectly healthy. There was no medical reason for my hunger; nor could a lab analyze why, despite all my self-awareness, I still avoided looking at my thighs in the mirror. I wanted to love my thighs just the way they were. *Why is that so hard?* Just the other day I was standing in the closet, looking at myself in the full-length door mirror, naked. There I was, a little pale, my pink places showing. Overall I could see where yoga had defined the muscles in my chest and arms. I could look at everything without too much trouble until I got to my thighs and butt. Had so little changed since the first time I tried this in college? Was there anything I liked about them? Maybe if I stood at an angle, I wouldn't be able to see how they pooch out at the sides so much, how poofy they are. Nope, I could still see it. Maybe it's the lighting. Come on Kimber, try. Try *harder*.

So now instead of pushing myself into a forward bend, I'm pushing myself to love myself? If Svetlana doesn't have exercise to bully me with, it seems she'll grab whatever's nearby. Maybe I could just back off and take a deep breath. Give myself some space. What am I comparing myself to, anyway? A line of walking mannequins on the catwalk in my head? Looking at my thighs, my mind automatically brought up snapshots of what my thighs are supposed to look like—some composite photoshopped, airbrushed supermodel's thighs that have been burned into my retina after a lifetime in American society. She has perfect thighs, smooth and unblemished, with that stripe down the side like a race car, thighs that effortlessly transition into her butt without a bulge, wrinkle, or stretch mark. Where did this come from?

Sitting in the traffic on I-80 gave me the chance to ponder the question thoroughly. With a sense of horror, I remembered that I'd done this to myself, participated willingly in imprinting the negative of "The Perfect Thighs" on my brain. As an anorexic fifteen-year-old, one day I made a poster-sized collage from fashion magazines of acceptably thin thighs and butts in tiny bikinis, playing with beach balls in the surf. Sitting in a pile of teen magazines, I carefully cut out the skinniest hips (often omitting their heads entirely), pasted them onto the thick sheet of paper, and added "encouraging" remarks in thick black marker: "If you want to look like this, you can't eat that!" I hung it up in my closet where it could remind me of my less-than-perfect thighs every morning while putting on clothes before school. Nothing like starting the day with a large dose of self-disparagement. If I felt tempted when my friends were eating ice cream or candy or donuts, I could remind myself of my heart's desire: apparently a decapitated swimsuit spread in the latest teen magazine.

The traffic slowed even more, as if deliberately letting me stew in my realization. Another memory floated back, hadn't I seen that collage more recently? Oh yeah. Once while visiting my parents' house during law school, I walked into my mother's closet only to be confronted by my homemade motivational poster hanging prominently inside the door. I gasped. "What is this doing here?"

There it was, the painful, accusing reminder of my efforts to cut pieces of myself away. Airbrushed thighs and tiny butts jumbled together as the only goal worth pursuing. Mom laughed, and didn't glance up to see the look of nausea that crossed my face.

"Oh, I found it a while back. I thought it would inspire me to stick with my diet." Like a bad spell, the poster had retained its magic, still serving the same perverse purpose its creator intended. A strange sort of hand-me-up.

Finally the traffic let up when I merged onto our highway exit. Pulling myself back from the past was a relief. A few minutes later I turned into the shadowed driveway and shut off the engine. As an anorexic teen, all I wanted was to look thin, at whatever cost to my self-esteem and well-being. And in the years that followed, I held on to that narrow ideal, bankrupting myself with checks written for higher and higher amounts of self-hatred. No more. Beauty I wanted, but a beauty that flows from the inside out. I wanted to cultivate inner kindness, love, mindfulness toward myself and others first, and have that inner beauty overflow into my outer form. No more striving for the outer appearance of beauty while being an impoverished mess inside. Could I forgive myself—and my mom—for how deeply we've dug this samskara together? I let out a long sob and leaned my head against the steering wheel. Could I put myself back together from the inside out?

I struggled for the rest of the week with how to think about beauty. It occurred to me that I was afraid that if I let go of being hard on myself, I would slowly turn into a giant, hairy gorilla. My inner anorexic had returned, sending me *National Geographic* photos of furry, lumpy primates, with "THIS IS YOU" scrawled across them in red marker. *I'm a lawyer. Can I get a restraining order against part of my own brain? That bitch is stalking me. She needs to spend more time dealing with her own issues and less time thinking up ways to torture me.*

The next week found me and Carlos perched in our usual spots on the kitchen chairs, fragrant tea cupped in our palms. I asked him to help me think through the differences between inner and outer beauty and learn how to connect the two.

Carlos leaned back thoughtfully and answered, "You can culti-vate the practice of suspending judgment. Walk through the world as though seeing things for the first time. This helps develop an appreciation of beauty and allows the heart to become very receptive."

In the ancient language of Sanskrit, he explained, there are many different words for beauty. *Rup* is the outward appearance of beauty, but can also mean the beauty that comes from the inner form. *Sunda* means bright, shining beauty, the expression of the self from inside out; it can also mean beautiful goddess. *Sri* is radiant light, divine beauty, and another name for the goddess of abundance, Lakshmi.

Carlos looked out at the square of framed blue sky behind the kitchen table.

"So much in our lives is superficial," he mused, "and we don't take the time to stop and see things in a deeper way. It's often diffi-cult for people to see from the heart. We tend to live life on the surface and never go deeper."

He turned back to me, laying his hands palms up in his lap.

"Our usual mode is to pursue outward forms of beauty at the expense of inner forms. So we end up trying to derive our sense of satisfaction in life from superficial things. We must not base our self-worth on exterior forms. Remember not to judge yourself by how others see you."

I stopped my frantic scribbling of notes for a moment to look up at him. *Easier said than done,* I thought. Yes, he's right, and I've known this truth for a long time. But knowing the truth is one thing. Living it is something else.

Of course, I needed to take it a step further. To not judge myself through the eyes of my inner anorexic. She's wrong. I don't need to be perfect to be beautiful.

The traffic while leaving his house that day was thankfully lighter. Driving along the highway by the Bay, I could see the sunlight playing on the water and the rounded mountains in the distance. I could see and appreciate the radiance of beauty in nature. Who looks for perfection or symmetry in the ocean? It doesn't need our ideas about what it is or should be…it's the ocean, for chrissake. When I'm out at Muir Beach, right on the edge of the Pacific, and see the tumbling waves and the craggy rocks and the windswept trees, I enjoy the asymmetries, the imperfections, the changes, even the chaos—nature is perfect in all of that. The truth is, I, like everyone else, am beautiful in my imperfections, with all my chaos, with all my asymmetries. The impossibly perfect and artificial ideal is not compatible with life. I am part of nature. Beautiful just as I am. Shining, radiant, divine, from the inside out. Can I embrace a concept of beauty that encompasses my whole self, even my inner anorexic? When she throws ugliness at me, can I reflect back to her beauty and love instead? *You're beautiful. I'm shooting love rays at you, skinny girl. Take that.*

It's ambitious. But it makes me smile to think it's possible.

Just two days after my session with Carlos, driving home from the yoga studio, I saw his wife, Suesi, at the bus stop, so I pulled over and gave her a ride home. She asked me about Cooper and about how we decided to have a baby. I gave her the whole story, starting right at the beginning: how I had been a public interest lawyer, with dental insurance for the first time in my life. My wisdom teeth needed to be removed, and after many years of deferring what every dentist had told me would be necessary sooner or later, I finally decided to have them taken out before they took me out. Suesi looked at me expectantly, as if settling in for a good story, so I continued.

On my initial visit with Dr. B., the oral surgeon, the first thing I saw when I walked into the waiting room was a huge bouquet of enormous purple roses. They were too beautiful to be fake, too perfect to be real, just too extraordinary either way to be sitting in the reception area of a doctor's office. They seemed more suited to a life-size fairy castle, with little birds twittering around them and a string quartet playing quietly nearby. Looking at them more closely, I realized they were, in fact, real, more than two dozen lavender roses, gloriously in bloom, densely gathered in a big glass vase.

When the receptionist called me up to the desk, I couldn't help myself. "The flowers are gorgeous, where are they from?"

She didn't even look up. "Oh, they're from a patient. We get stuff like that all the time."

That should have been my first clue. What kind of doctor inspires that level of gratitude?

Dr. B. was a perfectly normal, affable professional during my initial appointment, everything you'd hope for in someone you're going to be unconscious with while he probes in your mouth with sharp instruments. I left planning to return in two weeks, fully expecting to end up with huge chipmunk cheeks, woozy from the mixture of pain and painkillers. The day of the surgery, filled with some trepidation but reasonably calm, I took my seat in the operating chair and closed my eyes as mellow rock music played in the background.

I woke up, seemingly only seconds after my eyes had closed, groggy, mouth cottony, asking, "When are you going to start the surgery?"

"We're all finished now," the assistant whispered with a half-smile. "Let me help you into the recovery area."

As I regained consciousness in the half-darkness of the recovery room, I remember feeling complete and total bliss. *I'm so happy*, I thought looking up into the dim light. *I love this, I love my life.* Sigh.

"I feel great."

Oops, did I say that out loud? Oh, well.

The assistant chuckled. "I'll go get your partner to wait with you until you're ready to leave."

Within moments Chris appeared at my side in her familiar denim shirt and jeans.

"I love you so much," I said. "You're so beautiful, you make me so happy, I'm so happy, I love everyone. I love our lives. Everything is so wonderful."

Chris was bemused and laughed along with my ramblings. Blissed-out is not the state you expect your sweetie to be in after oral surgery.

At some point Chris helped me up and out into the car. I barely remember the ride home. We stopped at the drugstore to get a heavy-duty painkiller prescription for me. I was dazed, looking at the world with new eyes. I sat there in the car, looking out the window at nothing in particular, thinking, *I love Chris so much. I love our life. Whatever makes her happy, I want her to have more of in her life. Why am I so worried about being the best lawyer in the world? Why do I care so much about pleasing my boss? I don't really care about being a great lawyer…I don't care about being a lawyer at all…I want my life to be about loving Chris and making all our dreams possible together. If she wants us to go ahead and start a family, we should do it. I don't want my life to be about struggling to be the best at something my whole heart isn't in. I want our lives to be about fulfilling our dreams.*

Amazingly, this train of thought lasted for two or three days, long after the effects of whatever drugs he'd given me should have worn off. Most of what I said and did that weekend I can't even remember. I had a whole phone conversation with a friend that my brain deleted moments after it happened. All I remember is being in complete bliss: a total release of my emotional inhibitions, a letting go of things I'd been worried and stressed about, and a feeling of oneness, happiness, that overwhelmed every other event, thought, and emotion. Pain must have taken over where my wisdom teeth had just vacated, but it didn't stick in my memory. I rested and rode my little wave of bliss. A sense of the overall beneficence of the universe and myself as part of that overarching goodness bathed my heart and mind. It felt familiar and yet brand new all over again.

Within one year of this revelatory experience, I had quit my job and was in my second trimester of pregnancy. A couple of years after my son came on the scene, I was well on my way to becoming a yoga instructor, and looking for that same bliss in my relationship with my body, mind, and heart.

The whole story came out in the course of the ten or so blocks between where I had picked Suesi up and where I dropped her at her doorstep. Suesi listened appreciatively and laughed.

"In the ashram we'd call that a *shaktipat* experience, that feeling of pure bliss, recognizing for the first time who you truly are. Everything looks brand new. And your heart fills with love."

I had heard people talk about *shaktipat* and, without knowing anything about it, had always felt that their experience seemed familiar. Now I knew why. The irony of having my life changed by having my "wisdom" teeth removed has been pointed out to me more than once. Perhaps their removal unblocked my inner wisdom and opened a path to bliss in my heart, a path that's hard to find in the midst of dirty dishes and dust bunnies, but one that leads me back to my yoga mat over and over.

Part of me wondered if my desire to find fullness was the desire to have that feeling of bliss continuously. Although if that were the case, I would have requested my medical records, found out what he'd given me, and become one of those patients who bounces from doctor to doctor, looking for a fix. Either that or I wouldn't have any teeth left. The word *ananda* in Sanskrit is translated as "bliss" or even "divine joy"—a deep abiding happiness in knowing one's true nature, which is bliss. I sensed at the time that the drugs only unblocked the flow of inner joy that was already a part of me, that I could access at any time. Indeed, through my yoga practice I found that it was true; small moments of joy arose lying on my mat or resting on my cushion when I sensed the truth that my very nature, the very nature of all beings, is bliss. If this joy is my true nature, fullness is also my true nature, that is, I am fully, wholly, perfectly myself right now, and always have been. Why does fullness feel so elusive?

What I want is a transformation—a transformation of the way I relate to food, to my body, to the world. Food is right at the interface between the world and ourselves. It's that part we choose to bring inside us, to make part of us, to fuel us, our actions, our thoughts, until we return back to the world as dust and heat—the world we've never been separate from all along. What would it be like to look at food as part of the world that I choose to become? Not what my anorexic thinks I should or shouldn't eat, or even what my inner prisoner thinks looks tasty. Instead, I can look at what food is offered and ask, "Is this something that my body wants to become part of me?" Profound, yet very simple.

As human beings who have choices and preferences, we have to decide what our lives are going to be made of. And then bring those things into our lives, into our mouths, into our hearts, into our very being. Fullness, I'm calling you. Come be with me.

chapter ten

Out with the Old

One Monday morning found me cleaning out the closet in my parents' local vacation condo, just a few miles from our home. Not that I ever take the time to clean out my own closets. But we had guests who were coming to stay for a month. I figured they'd need a place to put their things, other than in the tiny corner between my mom's piles of empty shopping bags and my dad's stacks of cedar-scented shirts. I wanted our guests to be able to inhabit the space, make it their own. I tried not to judge, but who hangs their acid-washed jeans from the eighties in the closet of their second home? Seriously. And do all these shoes really fit? And then I realized: I still have a pair of acid-washed jeans somewhere in my closet (they're purple, from eighth grade), and no, all the shoes in my closet do not fit. If you ever want to confirm your genetic lineage, dismantle your parents' closet. I predict that scientists will someday discover the packrat gene with its specific list of what your chromosomes have programmed you to never discard.

I cleaned, cleared out debris, organized, and straightened, all to make room for a different fullness to come in. The closet slowly exhaled my parents' stuff, so it could inhale someone else's. Just like us humans...to inhale, we exhale completely first, creating emptiness, a vacuum, and then we fill that space once again with the breath. Then fullness and emptiness become an interplay—a vacillation, a vibration. My parents' detritus washes up, then is sucked out, our guests' flotsam will float in and be carried out once again, tidy in rolling boxes. Admittedly, I hate to think of anything filling up the space I've so carefully created, but that is the whole point.

I've been feeling the desire to do a cleanse myself, not of my closet but of my body. In order to feel full, maybe I need to clean out the debris first. My longing to transform my relationship with food feels trapped inside a flaky skin I've grown out of; I want to slough off the old and find what's new—and me—inside. Snakes rub up against rocks and trees to loosen their skin. I'm ready, I think, to rub up against my own assumptions about what foods my body can't live without, to find beneath them what foods my body most wants to make part of its yoga-doing, kid-schlepping, Chris-loving life.

For her part, Chris thinks the whole idea of a cleanse is ridiculous ("Um, isn't that what your colon is for?"), but she rolls her eyes a lot whenever the topic of yoga comes up, or the topic of cleanses, so a yogic cleanse should rightly send her eyes spinning into the back of her head like demonic tops.

The trick for me is finding the right cleanse—I'm not willing to starve myself. I already know the effects on my mind (self-domination) and on my body (sheer panic). The idea of a calorie-restricting cleanse makes Chris a little worried about me, given my history, so that option gets cut loose like a ballast bag off a hot air balloon. My sweetie would prefer that I kept my eating experimentation down to a minimum, but my mind is already set on its course, and a little bump called "No Starving Cleanses" isn't going to stop me.

Fortunately for me (maybe not so much for Chris), the other day I picked up a flyer at one of my yoga studios about a cleanse with a local Ayurvedic consultant, Mark Altar. It appears to involve actual food. An eating cleanse, what a great idea!

Ayurveda is Indian medicine, which focuses more on preventing disease and treating imbalances in the body than on curing sickness. According to Ayurveda, food is medicine, and you determine what foods are best for you based on your specific body and personality type, called your *dosha* or constitution. There are three basic constitutions: *Vata*, or air, people tend to be skinny, their feet not always touching the ground, prone to anxiety and fear. *Pitta*, or fire, folks tend to be ambitious, muscle-y, prone to anger. And then *kapha*, or water/earth, types tend to be laid-back, a little on the round side, and prone to depression, but also contentment.

You used to have to visit an Ayurvedic doctor to find out what your dosha was, but nowadays there's the Internet. I surfed around for a while last night taking a bunch of "What's Your Dosha?" quizzes. Some of the questions they ask seem totally random. One starts out with what kind of weather you dislike the most, asks how you respond in a crisis, and ends up inquiring about whether or not you remember your dreams. Some of them give contradictory answers, but mostly they point me in the same general direction: kapha, with a leaning toward pitta. Earthy with a kick. Sounds like me. Sounds like just what I was afraid of.

The self-evaluation quizzes are hard, because I don't necessarily trust my own assessment, especially when it comes to body image. Am I muscular or thick-bodied? I think I'm both. But if I have to choose, I'd choose thick-bodied because that's how I perceive myself, whether it's how others perceive me or not. I perceive myself as big— maybe I always will. I perceived myself as big even at my skinniest. There are things about me which seem more objectively kapha—dark hair, soft eyes, soft but thick skin—and I do think my essential nature is kapha: steady, calm, rooted, happy. But what about how ambitious I am? That seems very pitta, the overachiever, becoming a lawyer, my struggle with impatience and my desire to be perfect. The feeling of always being hungry.

I'm pretty sure my inner anorexic is pure pitta.

❀

The cleanse with Mark starts the next weekend. I decide to go ahead and try it out. It's not like boot camp or getting drafted into the army—it's my choice. A short, seven-day Ayurvedic cleanse that involves lots of whole fresh foods, soups, and teas, and yoga practice. Basically, we eat a citrus smoothie for breakfast, a nutritious curried soup/stew called kitchari for lunch and dinner, and can eat whatever fresh fruits and vegetables we want as snacks in between. Our group of twelve cohorts can also eat almonds soaked overnight in water as a snack, and Mark wants us to drink something called Superfood mixed with apple juice, too. I open the jar of Superfood. It's a dark green powder you mix into juice to make a swamp beverage. Sounds iffy. During our orientation meeting last week, Mark said, "I know it looks a little intense, but I want you all to try this." Sounded to me like he suspected we'd spew out the first musty sip. Will it be super-good or super-nasty?

The excitement over trying something new and nervousness about being hungry in the midst of it are competing for my complete attention. Yesterday while sitting at the computer, I wrote Mark an e-mail with some questions about the cleanse, as I grazed on holiday truffles.

"Hi Mark, I looked over the cleanse and it sounds great. [Insert chocolate-covered caramel here.] I'm so glad you're doing a cleanse like this right after the holidays. [Insert almond coconut truffle here, *mmff.*] The issue I'm dealing with around eating is that I perceive myself as hungry all the time. [Insert toffee here, *crunch, crunch.*]"

Just thinking about purifying my body makes me want to plow through a box of chocolates. Instead of waiting for the feeling of deprivation to kick off a cycle of bingeing, my cravings proactively kick in, before the cleanse even starts. Go team! Some skepticism over how this week is going to go lurks among the crumpled paper cups and truffle crumbs.

So that the cleanse doesn't turn out to be a total disaster of me gorging myself into a delirium in front of the fridge, or decimating yet another box of chocolates, I'm going to need to take some extra precautions. Or, let me rephrase that—I'll need to take some steps to take extra good care of myself, so that I feel nurtured by what I'm doing rather than deprived. *Remember what Carlos taught you, Kimber-love.* This body is not a hungry tiger who needs to be chained or sedated. It's a baby bird. Needing care and feeding and gentleness. *Do the cleanse out of love for yourself. Not because you're trying to fix something that's broken.*

Also on my schedule: meditation, relaxation, and napping. All the leftover sweets from the holidays will have to be tossed in the compost (does that stuff biodegrade?) and replaced with some decent snacks and treats instead. Pears and raspberries. Almonds, celery, fennel, raw sunflower seeds, sundried tomatoes, and peaches.

Tomorrow The Cleanse begins. It takes on some extra gravitas when I say it in a low vibrato, like I'll be heading into my arteries with a pair of rubber gloves, hip boots, and a pressurized water sprayer: "Out of the way, lives are at stake here, folks." Anything gooey and icky and stuck will dissolve in the face of my super cleansing powers.

My friend Jasmine, who's also doing The Cleanse, meets me at the nearby overpriced natural food store to gather all the stuff we need—basmati rice and mung beans, whole turmeric (it looks like ginger root with sunburn), pure ghee, lots of vegetables and fruit, and something called asafetida to add to the curry spices. You'd never find most of this stuff at the regular grocery store. "Ass-a-fu-*what?*"

In the spice aisle, I locate asafetida right between the arrowroot powder and dried basil. It practically has a warning label: "Use this rich, powerful-smelling spice in small amounts." In other words, don't let its stench turn you off. And we're supposed to eat this? Seriously, a spice with the word "fetid" in it doesn't sound all that promising. Apparently it's also known as Devil's Dung, clearly named by someone who loved it so much he wanted to keep it all for himself. Another nickname, paradoxically, is the Food of the Gods.

Pulling down the bottle and peeking over my shoulder to make sure no one's watching, I unscrew the lid, peel back the paper seal, close my eyes, and sniff, expecting the worst. Stinky feet? Farts? Dog breath? My eyes open wide....Garlic! It smells delicious, like warm, buttery garlic bread. Sure, I can cook with this. Asafetida. Yum. I grab a bottle for Jasmine, too. I can't wait to tell her.

I find her near the cold case where the ghee lives. Putting a jar of ghee (clarified butter) with the word PURE across it in big letters into my cart, I tell Jasmine, "I feel purer already."

She laughs. "But you're already pure!" She turns down the aisle to look for the mung beans.

That's right, I'm pure already. Perfect already. Beautiful already. I keep forgetting. Hopefully The Cleanse emerges from the desire to explore what's possible for me around eating rather than yet another sneaky way of trying to win "Miss Gotta Be Perfect at Something." My motivations may not be entirely trustworthy. But I do trust my growing impulse to care about my body and listen to its needs. That will have to be enough for the moment.

One of the hardest parts of The Cleanse will be eating the same thing every day. The good news is curry happens to be one of my favorite things to eat, so eating curried soup twice a day sounds pretty awesome. The best part is that if the kitchari fails to meet expectations, it will be over in just seven days. I can do anything for seven days, especially if it doesn't involve being hungry.

The thing I'm most looking forward to about The Cleanse has nothing to do with eating. Every morning, Mark wants us to do self-*abhyanga*, or self-massage with sesame oil. Here's what you do: thoroughly rub down your entire body, from head to toe and everything in between, with warmed raw organic sesame oil. My reaction surprises me: it sounds decadent. Delicious. Delightful. Sounds like I'll be spending lots of time smelling like a warm sesame cookie.

The first time I'd heard about self-abhyanga was in Carlos's yoga philosophy class, when he described it as one of his daily practices. He also mentioned that self-massage was wonderful to do along with a healing mantra, *Om Namah Shivaya*: I honor the divine within myself. In my mind's eye, I see the woman at the gym, applying lotion to her body as if she believed her body was divine. Here's my chance to try it again, a little more healed, a little more optimistic, a little more loving. With no mirror. And a lot more intention. I want to love myself. I want to take care of myself. I want my whole life, even my thighs, to become a reflection of that love.

Daily Schedule for The Cleanse:

sesame oil massage

shower

tea

yoga

citrus smoothie

teach or meditate (depending on the day)

kitchari soup (with ghee) for lunch

meditate or teach

pick up Cooper

kitchari soup for dinner

teach again (if I have an evening class)

read and early bedtime

Day One

Mmm. The sesame oil massage is amazing. In my sleepy state, I pour handfuls of warm oil into my hands and rub them all over my body. My critical mind isn't quite awake yet, so I get to enjoy the feeling of touching and warming my body without getting all "Judgie Judgerson" about it. My skin soaks up the oil like it's been dying for the attention.

Already on the first day I get anxious about getting all the food ready in time. Cook this, mix that, chop this other thing…oh my God, what time is it, will I finish before I have to go teach? I'm supposed to be relaxing and cleansing my system and instead I'm getting stressed out about doing everything right.

The good news is, the kitchari is delicious, better than I expected. True, it might get boring by the end of the week. But there's no reason to get ahead of myself. And surprise! The Superfood drink is fabulous. It's a tiny bit weird and arguably nasty, but I love it. It's sweet, it's green. It's hippie Kool-Aid.

Day Two

The self-massage is rocking my world. I'm especially relishing it as "necessary" to my daily routine. It's like I needed someone else's voice of authority to give myself permission to touch my body all over and whisper sweet things to myself. It's good for me. And it's every bit as luscious as it sounds. Touching my body this way feels easier than it's ever felt before. I can't look in the mirror while doing it, but progress is being made: I'm enjoying touching my body! Even my thighs are getting some sweet, long-needed touch.

Still, my hunger continues unabated—it doesn't seem to matter whether I'm eating "good" food or "bad." I'm supplementing the kitchari meals with fresh fruit, which amazingly is having the effect of grounding me—normally I rely on bread and chocolate for feeling less spacey and more present. The soaked almonds are a treat. They get all round and fresh and chewy in the water, like nutty grapes.

Day Three

Wow, last night The Cleanse finally got me. I fell exhausted into bed at about eight o'clock and didn't wake up till 6:00 a.m. Cooper wanted to play at the park after school, so we did, and then he had a friend over to play. By 7:00 p.m. I was ready to fall over. Sleeping that hard felt great. Still hungry all the time, though. Maybe I should mention it to Mark.

Day Four

At 3:30 p.m. today, in the middle of running errands, I parked the car under a shady tree by the curb and called Mark to talk about how it's going.

"I'm doing pretty well, but feeling as hungry as ever."

"When you go back to your normal diet, increase your protein intake. Try seitan (wheat gluten), tofu, beans, eggs, and fish. Protein is really important for feeling full. Eat it for breakfast and lunch both. But for dinner, eat more lightly, it will help you sleep better."

Protein, right. Double the soaked almonds. Possibly my hunger will succumb to a regular influx of more protein. Back to basics.

Day Five

I'm sick of kitchari now. And swamp juice. And soaked almonds. Thank God there's just one more day.

Day Six

Today we were supposed to just drink liquids, juice, and broth. Just relax and meditate, stay home and contemplate our kitchari-filled guts. I couldn't do it. It's Saturday, and I wake up to a clear blue sky and the strong urge to go to the park and fly a kite with Cooper. Food, real food, is necessary for that undertaking. Tomorrow, day seven, we're supposed to ease our way back toward normal eating again. Rebel that I am, I ease my way back into normal eating today, having a couple of eggs for breakfast and an orange. Then Cooper and I chase his frog kite up and down the clover-green hills of a park overlooking the Bay before driving home for lunch. It's possible the liquids-only fast scared me off—part of my hungry history, I guess. But no way can I regret spending the morning with my little boy.

I learned a lot from The Cleanse. I don't need chocolate to get by. Or caffeine. Or sugar, or even bread. It didn't kill me to eat only whole foods and kitchari for a week. No blood sugar crash, no yelling at Cooper or getting crabby with Chris—at least not any more than usual. I didn't starve or feel deprived, knowing it was my free choice to take care of myself this way. I felt fine and, amazingly, not any hungrier than usual. Even better, my inner anorexic and her cohorts seemed to be off in Vegas for the week and forgot to send me even a postcard.

These feel like small, positive steps. They didn't quite add up to my imagination's hopes—that I would slither out of my food-related samskaras and emerge a sleek and powerful serpent, leaving my old dried-up habits behind. Small is real, though. And maybe enough of a foothold (tailhold?) to wind my way out of my ruts later on.

And the self-massage is wonderful. And healing. After smoothing oil all over my body for seven days, it's started to feel natural and normal and sweet to touch my body this way. My hands feel eager to reassure my body, and my skin drinks up the oil like it's been starved of attention and affection. No surprise there. As long as I stay out of range of any nearby mirrors, my body feels cherished for a few minutes in the bathroom each morning. What do they call a good habit you want, if the bad ones are samskaras? "Practice" sounds so tenuous, impermanent. Discipline? That sounds harsh. Maybe it's a ritual. A ritual of self-care and devotion. Like how I show up on my yoga mat every day. Whatever it's called, this fresh-pressed habit of loving self-massage, I want to do it every day for the rest of my life.

Wow, what a day. I just spent all day driving around, dropping off boxes of fresh organic vegetables from Full Belly Farm all over the beautiful East Bay hills, and feeling completely blissed out. Joy welled up inside me so strongly, but it felt ephemeral, like a huge iridescent soap bubble; I was almost afraid to breathe. Tears sprang into my eyes, and I wondered for a moment, *Is it safe to drive like this? Should I pull over? If I pull over, will it go away?* I realized I was starting to worry about losing the bliss more than I was enjoying it, so I tried to just relax and breathe it in: the feeling of expansive peace, that everything is wonderful and beautiful. A wish that every being might experience this same moment, this same feeling, this same love.

Wow, where did that come from? I just finished up The Cleanse last week, was it that? Is it the yoga? The teaching? The daily warm sesame oil massages? Something in the water? My heart feels as if the universe reached inside my chest and reminded me with a gentle and heavy caress that despite all the messiness, there is good in me and in life and in the world. It's amazing to feel so deeply happy and deeply sad. To feel anything deeply. I feel so lucky, so blessed. I can still feel the residue of bliss in my body a little. It lingers, even now. Like the opposite of a hangover. A blissover.

It's been six years since I had that same intensity of feeling coming out of the dentist's office. It's wonderful to feel it again, without drugs this time. I knew. I knew it was in there all along. Part of me, not artificial, but real. Something inside knew this path of yoga would lead me back there, to this feeling. And here it is. *Om Namah Shivaya.*

I noticed a few other interesting changes after The Cleanse. While shopping at the big local warehouse store today, I nibbled on some of the offered samples. The hummus was okay, but the crackers, sugary yogurt, chocolate milk, and energy bars were kind of yucky. My taste buds had changed. All the samples tasted artificial, like eating stuff that's been stored too long alongside the heavy cleaning fluids. Mmm, bleach-flavored cheese! Ammonia-scented cereal!

My cravings are different. Instead of automatically reaching for the bread and chocolate, I reach for fruit. When I got home today, I spied some wild arugula in the side yard and pulled a leaf off to chew on. It tasted so good! Made me want to get down on my knees and graze on it right there in the yard. What would the neighbors think?

Eating a bigger breakfast seems to help me get through the day pretty well. Eggs and veggies for breakfast are a nice protein-rich combination. Mixing some cooked polenta into the eggs is nice—it gives them more body, and expands more in my stomach. This morning I cooked up three sliced mushrooms and eight spears of asparagus, with some polenta, all sautéed in butter; then added two eggs, and served it all with some warm puttanesca sauce on top. It was a work of art. Filling, nutritious. I enjoyed every bite. But more, my body is clearly enjoying the delicious fuel I'm sending it, what I'm choosing to make part of me.

For two months after The Cleanse, everything went well. But right at this moment I'm on a tear. All the good habits I tried to cultivate went on vacation somewhere without me! Take me with you! I had a reasonable breakfast, and then took Katchie's class this morning. I ate a big helping of rice and veggies for lunch, and then a whole bunch of dried mangos, and then a chunk of bread—*Okay, now stop! Full now. Pull up! Give way, yield, halt, whoa! Can I just catch my breath a second, pause and think?*

Riding home on BART from San Francisco, I scan my brain and my body. Why am I suddenly feeling so ravenous? Am I stressed out? Anxious? Unsettled somehow? PMSing? I can't figure it out. I need to just take a few breaths. Perhaps meditation will help.

On the blue upholstered seat under the transit map, my hands rest in my lap, eyes closed, and I try to meditate with the hum and rumble of the train all around me. *Just feel the sensations of hunger. Notice them, observe them, don't judge them.* Ugh. I hate this. I feel hungry. I want to eat. I'm tired of being hungry all the time. *Go back to the breath. Notice the thoughts, don't hold on to them. Hold whatever arises without judging it. Just give it some space.* I feel empty, empty! I want to feel full, full! *Okay. Fair enough. Keep breathing.*

I don't know if the meditation helped. I still feel hungry, but slightly less desperate. Back in the car, I slurp down my green swamp drink, and that tides me over for about another hour, until anxiety about getting to class on time to teach gooses the hunger back full force. Once home, the hunger gods are still clamoring. I eat three pieces of bread while making dinner. After dinner, I eat a bowl of cardamom ice cream with pistachios. Just now I'm drinking a rice milk tea.

After the ice cream tonight, I felt the overwhelming urge to refill my bowl and eat it all over again. Looking down into my empty bowl, I remember eating that whole half gallon of mint chocolate chip ice cream as a kid and writhing on the floor in pain afterward. I can still feel that urge. The desire to machine-eat to the bottom of the carton is still there, even though I know it will hurt later. I love ice cream, how it tastes, how it feels in my mouth, the crunchiness of the nuts, the creamy coldness. That's what heaven would be for me: being able to eat endless amounts of ice cream without any consequences. But the end of that particular story on this plane of existence called "Real Life" is a stomachache I don't want, need, or have time for. I put the empty dish in the sink and get ready for bed.

After the total loss of my post-cleanse peace of mind, I'll settle for this small victory, which in its way shows I care enough to not hurt myself. A setback here or there doesn't undo all of my mindfulness and inner knowledge. No way. Not unless I let it. What I don't do is as important to my ritual of self-care as what I do do.

Mark is doing another cleanse this spring, so I sign up again, hoping to recommit myself to my new habits around eating. I think I can let go of it being The Cleanse now, and have it just be a cleanse. Like taking my stomach on a retreat. Just a way of checking in and remembering what my body really needs. And what it doesn't.

The only thing I'm dreading about this cleanse is that we're supposed to drink ghee. The rationale is that certain toxins in the body are only fat-soluble, so you pack the large intestine full of fat and let the toxins seep out into the fat, to be flushed out with the castor oil laxative treatment at the end of the week. Yes, sipping on delicious melted butter…adding a little bit more every day. Yuck. Talk about fuel for my inner anorexic's fire! I might as well pour it right into the flames. A little stirring in the back of my brain—*do you know how many calories are in that?*—tells me that my inner anorexic may not be headed to Vegas this time around.

Day One

The melted ghee isn't as bad as I thought. Not something I plan to add to my daily routine, or something I'd recommend to a friend, or even something I'd willingly admit to doing myself, but fine nonetheless. In our yoga class this morning, Mark described pitta digestion: you know you're a pitta when if you don't get a bite to eat, you bite someone's head off. You have a stomach made of iron, and you want your meals on time. Practicing patience, he said, is what helps cool pitta anger.

That's me! He's talking about me!

Ever since my teenage diagnosis of hypoglycemia, my unconscious habit has been to always have food with me and to eat, hungry or not, so that biting someone's head off becomes less likely. If it gets to that point, it's often too late—hunger-induced madness descends and lots of feelings can be hurt before I'm able to eat something and chill out. Chris knows this about me. If I snap at her, one of the first things she asks is, "Have you eaten anything lately?" Which sometimes results in a snarly "No!" and a tantrum-y stomp into the kitchen for a quick blood sugar stabilizer. But if the answer is "Yes!"—she knows I'm really mad.

Mark nailed it. Learning to be more patient with myself. How many times will I have to hear that lesson?

Apparently I have a kapha body and a pitta mind. A big, comfy body and an ambitious mind that's always wishing its body were smaller. That fits.

The worst thing about today is a pounding in my head that just won't let up. Sigh. It won't last forever.

Day Two

Oof. Yesterday was kind of terrible thanks to the eight-hour-long headache that didn't go away until I took a couple of Advil at 11:30 p.m. I don't know what was going on. It's unusual for me to have a headache that lasts for more than fifteen minutes.

Drinking ghee in the morning hasn't made me throw up yet—hooray—but my brain feels mentally dead afterward. My body feels sluggish, too. We're supposed to drink two tablespoons of melted ghee on the first day, four on the second, six on the third: you get the picture.

In consultation with my inner anorexic, she promises to leave me alone if I don't drink more than two tablespoons of ghee a day. This is a ginormous compromise for her, She-Who-Favors-Dry-Toast-And-Plain-Vinegar-Salad-Dressing. I'm in the compromising mood, because honestly, drinking ghee is disgusting and I'd rather not do it, but I also don't want to be a prisoner to my hangups around fat. I'm going to consider my willingness to drink any ghee at all a sign of progress.

Day Three

Eating the kitchari wasn't bad yesterday, especially since I was so busy. I didn't get too hungry. Drinking the big wad of fat in the a.m.

probably helped. But the lack of mental clarity is annoying. My bowels feel stopped up, too. Yet, to my surprise, I was able to stay in a very patient, even-keeled mood for the whole of a very long day.

The first cleanse was for the gallbladder and required the morning smoothie; this second one is a colon cleanse, which apparently requires the morning ghee beverage instead. I want to tell Mark how dirty my gallbladder feels. It needs cleansing more than my colon. I swear my gallbladder told me how bloated and gnarly it was feeling just yesterday.

I just can't subject myself to thirty tablespoons of butter in one week. Package it in chocolate cake, or brownies, or whipped cream—well, yum. But drinking butter for its medicinal properties? As if. Yet here I am, sipping it down every day. It's more likely that the Internet is run by gerbil power.

Day Four

I spoke to Mark today, pestering him about being hungry, like it was his fault. *I'm hungry! Can't you do anything about it?* He recommended a few different herbs to me and suggested paying attention to chewing my food, lengthening the time it takes to eat every single meal.

"Every meal should be based around satisfaction and have dense nutritional benefits. When you feel full, it should be invigorating, not depleting."

Everything points in the same direction. Carlos, my yoga practice, my inner therapist, now the cleanses. Slow down, enjoy, and eat until invigorating fullness sets in. Yet another good habit I seem to only intermittently embrace. How many beneficial self-care rituals can I implement at once before my old demons get fed up and join forces to corral me back into my usual samskaras?

Day Five

It's a beautiful day to be alive, hanging out with Cooper and his friend at the local science museum with a stunning view of the Bay. The sky is huge and blue. I'm at the top of the world.

Despite the rough start, this cleanse has gone way easier than the first one. Everything seemed so weird then; kitchari and hippie Kool-Aid were exotic and unknown. Could anyone survive a week without the four major food groups: chocolate, caffeine, bread, and sugar? Doubtful. This time it's all familiar, except for drinking butter. Instead of "The Cleanse," it feels like I'm just being a little more mindful about what I eat. And I'm actually...wait for it...slightly less hungry than usual. Hallelujah!

Day Six

Today for breakfast I reluctantly eat my kitchari, which tasted great at the beginning of the week but now is boredom in a bowl. Cooper's cereal box is still on the table, and my eyes, drawn to the Nutritional Facts on the back, start to read. My mind follows. Soon the last bite of kitchari finds its way into my mouth and I've barely tasted any of it.

Despite my efforts to be more attentive at meals, this happens all the time. Sometimes I'll sit down to a delicious meal I've prepared and eat it while reading the food section of the paper! Or while reading a cookbook. Then later, after making the meal in the cookbook, I'll sit down to eat it and read about some other meal *at the same time*. Reading about food while I'm eating and not tasting the food in my mouth. Insanity.

My desperate need for distraction is annoying. Isn't eating important enough to give it my full attention? After looking forward to my meal, the minute my butt is in the chair, I look for something to distract myself from the food that's right in front of me. I start reading or talking to someone and then before the flavors have even registered on my taste buds, I look down to find my plate is empty! Who ate all my food? No wonder my hunger won't move along.

Why not just eat the meal in front of me? Why is it so difficult to be in the present moment? Instead of thinking about a meal that exists only on paper, I could enjoy savoring every bite, every morsel laid out for my enjoyment. What else requires my mindful attention? Oh yeah. Yoga. Meditation. I need to treat eating more like a meditation and less like something I do on automatic pilot. Taste every bite. Listen to my body as I savor and enjoy. If I make the effort to not read or do anything else while I'm eating, would fullness come more often, sooner? Would it linger a while? Perhaps. One bite at a time.

After teaching my 10:00 a.m. class, I ditch the kitchari in favor of a visit to one of my favorite restaurants, a macrobiotic-vegan-Tibetan-chef-blessed organic kitchen. They only serve one thing: a plate of roasted veggies, some tofu or bean protein, a scoop of rice and millet, fresh greens, and steamed kale leaves. It's always delicious. I eat slowly, enjoying every bite. Admittedly it's easier to eat mindfully here, alone, while Cooper is at school and Chris is at the office. At home in the evening, being mindful about eating is not the first or the last thing that occurs to me. Even when I have lunch with a friend, it's hard to focus on my food, because naturally my focus is on their love life or work problem or yet-to-be-accomplished dream. Come on. How rude is it to say, "Mmm, never mind about your broken heart, these sweet potatoes are roasted to perfection!"?

But by myself I can hone my attention-paying skills, and maybe some of that extra mindfulness will eventually spill over into the rest of my meals, too. Savoring every bite, I find myself pushing the plate away before the beans and kale are finished. I could eat the rest. Part of me would like to eat the rest, to prolong the experience of eating, chewing, tasting, swallowing, the feeling of filling myself up a little longer. But isn't it more about what my body needs rather than what my mind wants, sloughing off the punishments of my inner prison guard and the ill-advised rewards of his alter ego, my indulgent prisoner? My mind and its misguided occupants need to take a back seat, and let the body drive a while.

The tentative good news: my inner anorexic has been rather quiet after voicing her first buttery objections. I think she's losing her edge.

❁

Lifelong habits, those old samskaras, die hard, but since the cleanse ended, I've been better about eating slowly and deliberately, as Mark suggested. Even on busy days driving around, I've made time to sit down—and not in front of the steering wheel, but at a park or under a tree—and eat mindfully. Sitting down, creating the most relaxing space possible, and quietly enjoying the meal seems to help the rest of the day flow more smoothly.

Another bonus: enjoying my meals has naturally awakened my feelings of gratitude toward everything on my plate. The other day at my favorite Indian restaurant, with the plate in front of me filled with curried vegetables and rice, I closed my eyes and envisioned all the plants and spices coming from all different directions, touched by many different hands to create the meal before me. And from that nourishing drawing in of energy, onto the plate and into my body, the meal expands further, fueling the energy of my life to reach out and touch people all around me in concentric circles, reaching back out in every direction. This one beautiful meal connects me to the whole world, and to my whole life. Every meal I've ever eaten I could have enjoyed in this way, but only now have I slowed down enough to perceive what's been there all along, right in front of my nose.

chapter eleven

My Own Best Friend

One Friday afternoon in late spring, while I stand in the cool, lofty lobby of Cooper's Montessori school, waiting for him to say his polite good-byes to his teachers, David, the father of one of his little friends, says, "I've got to tell you what Emily told me the other day: 'My body is my best friend.'"

"She said that? That's wonderful!" *My body is my best friend. Good for her!*

In the car, I help Cooper fasten his seat belt, musing, *I certainly don't think of my body as my best friend. Barely an acquaintance, really. More like a relative I hardly care to know, the annoying great-aunt who shows up at every event, taking pictures and drawing attention to herself and leaving lipstick smudges on everyone's cheek.*

I want to think of my body as my best friend, and at times I'm getting closer. My body and I are starting to warm up to each other, have a few laughs, some good times. A frolic on the grass. An inside joke. A good, solid handstand. A sigh, followed by a reassuring pat. There's some tentative trust-building between us.

Surely with my intelligence and all the resources at my disposal, I can learn to be a better friend to myself. I want fullness, but not simply toward the end of figuring out how to end my hunger. I want a fullness that helps me cultivate trust toward my body, my heart, my mind, and my whole self. Did I ever feel the way Emily does, that my body was my best friend? Before holding in my hand that shocking photo of my belly taken on our vacation in Florida, I don't remember caring about whether my butt was square or round or what size jeans I wore. (Who had time to worry about stupid stuff like that when there were fireflies?! And sparklers!) But it never once occurred to me as a six-year-old, in my yellow canvas overalls and scuffed up sneakers, that I could see my body as a beloved and scrappy companion for all my adventures, worthy of keeping my deepest secrets and sharing its own with me.

I hope it's not too late to start trying.

After all I've learned from the cleanses, all I've learned about hunger, last night I ate two donuts out of the bag that Chris and Cooper brought home. *What's wrong with me?* The donuts weren't even for me, they weren't for anyone, just extras my little family hadn't consumed yet. The worst part is donuts aren't even in the top-ten list of my favorite junk food! They leave a weird coating and sickening sweetness all over my mouth, which can only be temporarily relieved by...eating another one. I knew while eating them that my body wouldn't feel good later. Donuts might make some people cheerful, but they turn me crabby. My blood sugar level crashes and I feel like the living dead for the rest of the evening. And then of course there's the aftermath, the mental trip I put on myself: *What the hell is wrong with you, Kimber, you just had to eat those donuts, didn't you? Not one, but TWO. Two donuts. All that fried up, corn-syrupy goodness, killing*

brain cells in its wake! My inner anorexic has started to resemble a horror-flick monster that keeps popping up just when you're sure it's dead for good, waiting just long enough to lull you into complacency, then POW.

This is not friendly.

Remember, Kimber, this takes time. Setbacks happen. Nonjudgment, friendliness, seeing the good, it all takes time and practice. Here's that inner voice that sounds like she knows what she's talking about.

Yes please, more.

Lately while driving around doing errands, to make the time in the car more relaxing and nourishing for me, I've been listening to spiritual philosophy CDs, with teachers like Jack Kornfield, Eckhart Tolle, and Douglas Brooks. Nothing like being reminded to breathe, be patient, and see the beauty in all things, when someone's just nearly missed a collision with you by pulling into your lane without looking. I think these teachers have made me a better driver. At least my horn gets used a lot less.

On Monday, while driving between the grocery store and the bank, I listen to Pema Chödrön's CD about *maitri*, the practice of loving-kindness. Pema is an American Buddhist teacher. This is the simplest way to describe her, because actually she's an American who became a Tibetan Buddhist in the Shambhala tradition and heads an abbey in Canada. But if I call her an American Tibetan Shambhala Buddhist Canadian teacher, it makes her seem like a multiethnic sectarian. I suspect her tiny frame might collapse under the weight of all those labels.

Maitri (*metta* in some traditions) means loving-kindness, and Pema says it's the practice of becoming best friends with oneself. My mind needs this practice. Badly. At this point I'd settle for just being a kind stranger to myself.

Pema's teaching offers me a few specific steps to apply self-compassion (and put into action what Carlos encouraged me to try out) over the wounds my inner critics inflict. When I'm being harsh and judgmental with myself, I can:

1. Calm down.

2. Notice the fact that I'm criticizing myself.

3. Breathe.

4. ...And try not to react.

I'm practicing being my own best friend—would my best friend torture me over what I eat? Would my best friend mock me, roll her eyes, and point out I'm fighting a losing battle—better to just forget about the whole thing and eat another round of donuts glazed with self-hatred?

Okay, maybe if my best friend was Cruella DeVille.

For heaven's sake, can't I just be nice to myself? What's wrong with me?

Crap, there I go again. Can't I go even two seconds without criticizing?

Okay, calm down.

I'm acting like a jerk.

Ugh. Still critical.

I'm not...being friendly. There. Okay, breathe.

Now don't react to it.

Right. How does one do that exactly?

Pema says: Notice the feeling of being self-critical. What does it feel like, what's its color and texture?

I pause and feel for it. The energetic source of my self-criticism feels like a very small place, a little pinhole, with a lot of frustration and anger spewing out of it. It feels orange-hot, impatient, fiery. Like an oozing blister. An infected pimple. Gross.

What else?

As I sit with my blister of self-criticism, I notice that it isn't new, it's old and putrid. And I go to that hot, angry place all the time—that fierce pitta energy I identified during the cleanse—and not just around eating, but around everything: how I look, how I talk, what I accomplish in life, whether people like me, lots of things. And as uncomfortable and awful as it feels, that festering blister is deeply familiar. It feels like a room I know and hate: the horrible orange-felted wallpaper and the sticky vinyl chairs. I've spent so much time here, its stained, dirty carpet almost feels like home.

I don't want to live in this place. I don't even want to visit.

The next step, says Pema, is to breathe in this hot, uncomfortable feeling, to offer myself compassion for the stuckness, the impatience, the pain of listening to my self-criticism. And then to breathe out a sense of coolness, love, relief, to myself and to all others who experience these same searing feelings. I keep breathing, and keep offering coolness, spaciousness as relief for the fiery tightness in my heart.

I'm amazed, but it does feel good. I can feel a softening, a sense of release, a tiny shift in my heart, as if the blister is being bathed by a cool breeze, a soothing touch, a bandage to start the healing. Here it is, another possibility: instead of reacting to or believing the judgments of my inner critic, I can learn to hold the underlying energy of that criticism, and offer it relief, right at the source from which it arises.

But we're not done yet. Pema says *maitri* doesn't involve simply being nicey-nice to yourself, or even just sitting with difficult feelings, but requires clear seeing, a total honesty with yourself. Honesty without brutality, without cruelty, not falling over to the side of putting yourself down (*I totally suck*) or tipping in the opposite direction of boosting yourself up (*I'm better than you are*), just a gentle, persistent, clear seeing of yourself.

By witnessing my own habits clearly, without so much judgment impeding my view, perhaps I can notice what's happening before triggering the cycle of self-blame and reactivity, of criticism and punishment. No more bingeing, no more starving. Then maybe, with an observant, kind awareness of my own eating patterns, I can slowly steer the boat in the direction I want, in the direction of greater mindfulness, and straight on toward Fullness.

Listening to Pema in the quiet solitude of my car while scooting around curves and over hills opens a breathing space around my heart. She utterly lacks arrogance and is happy to poke fun at herself. And she never underestimates how deeply humbling the experience of trying to love oneself truly is. To be one's own best friend—maybe that's the hardest thing to undertake of all. To be my own best friend, to listen to my own musings, to observe them compassionately, without judgment, to find it within my heart to love myself over and over again, in every moment and every breath... whoa, could I do that?

At home, I cut off a few strawberry tops to give to Cooper's mouse, Suki. He wanted a hamster, but at the pet store each of the hamsters the clerk dropped into his hand bit him. Now he hates hamsters. When the clerk suggested a mouse, Chris shrugged her shoulders, "Why not?" and a mere few seconds after being dropped into Cooper's hand, the mouse pooped a tiny brown pellet into his palm. He's a five-year-old boy. It was love at first poop. Poop has its fans.

Presented with a juicy strawberry, Suki acts like the red parts are poison and nibbles off every green bit she can find. Which works great for me, cause I think the green parts are, well, not poison exactly, but not edible either. I place the strawberry tops into a little bowl in her cage and shut the door. She uncurls from her nest beneath the mesh wheel, and peeks her whiskery nose out to see what treats might await.

When I want to hold her, I place my hand at the open entrance of her cage with a single peanut in my palm, possibly the only food she likes better than strawberry tops. And then she begins what I call her Mammalian Safety Dance. She tentatively approaches my hand, then stops an inch away and sniffs the air. Spooked and tempted, she turns and runs back to her hidey hole. She comes back and sniffs the merest edge of my fingers, then spins and heads home. Meanwhile I stand there as still as possible and breathe. Each time she gets close, my heart prickles with excitement. *She trusts me.* But if I twitch, flinch, or speak out of impatience, the whole thing starts over. Most times, she continues this dance of approach and retreat until she finds herself in the middle of my palm, happily gnawing her oily peanut.

Perhaps I'm caught in my own Mammalian Safety Dance. My old patterns are like a nest lined with comfy, smelly things that need to be left behind. I'll get the peanut eventually. But meanwhile there are lots of encouraging steps forward and heartbreaking ones back again.

❀

It's Friday and during the noon yoga class, while my students are resting in savasana, I notice one has scars across each of her wrists. Not from widthwise cuts, but lengthwise cuts, the way you cut your wrists when you're not simply trying to get the world's attention, but you really intend to see the face of God. With her pale-pink palms facing toward the ceiling, those old wounds—usually concealed by clothing or movement—stare upward, vulnerable yet intact. It's not the first time I've noticed such scars on a student.

What is it like to wear your attempt to kill yourself right out there on your skin? I catch myself feeling sorry for her, for her former self that would take a blade to her own flesh; and at the same time, I'm happy that she is here, healed or healing, honoring her body and aliveness in a yoga class.

And then I remember. I don't have visible scars, but I tried to kill myself, too. Not consciously, not in a single moment, not in the bathtub struggling with a razor blade. But slowly, systematically, every day subtracting a little bit more from my body, my being. Where are my scars? Just under my skin, invisible but always present.

Maybe the warm oil massage has started to heal them. A little bit at a time. My inner anorexic still pipes up sometimes to complain about my appearance and my lack of willpower, and rants at me to never eat again. The crazy lady at the bus stop. On a good day, I notice her, nod, smile, and go on my way, letting her rantings drift and merge into the ambient noise. I barely even lose my stride. Other days she digs in deeper. *I know you can hear me, Chubs. I'm always watching you. I know where you live. I know how to get you.*

And every once in a while she does get me. At certain moments, a little anorexic shock wave washes over me: the awareness that I am not skinny, that some people would consider me fat, that I'm not the size and shape of the ideal woman in this society. Just the other day, I was feeling pretty good, walking down the sidewalk, and in the window of the bookstore my feet were headed for I caught an unflattering glimpse of my hips. *Eww. I look fat.*

Sigh. Not again. The next few moments of my thoughts unspiral before me, like the loop of a sweater that gets caught on the door handle, and the yarn unravels as if in slow motion, and there's no putting it back.

It starts with the usual refrain: *I hate my thighs.* Closely followed by, *I need to go on a diet.* Right on the heels of, *I need to exercise more.*

Then, predictably as clockwork, *Why have I been cursed with such big legs? Does the universe hate me?*

The next thought is a little fuzzy at first...oh, there it is, coming into focus: *Maybe I should save up for liposuction.*

Inside the store, everyone browsing for books seems to have skinnier legs than I do. The cookies and bagels in the café pastry case taunt me. *Fat-ty! Fat-ty! Bet you wanna eat us! You can't, you can't, 'cause you got a fat ass!* Yeah, yeah. I've been through this a million times. The magic button gets pressed in my head and the whole Rube Goldberg machine starts up and that old smelly egg of self-hatred rolls down the ramp and cracks open into the frying pan.

Here is a chance, I realize, to practice *maitri.*

What would my best friend say?

She would tell me there are lots of perfectly sensible reasons why the window's reflection set off all of my alarm bells:

1. The window is distorted.

2. The lighting is bad.

3. Maybe I'm about to get my period, and I'm a little bloated.

4. Maybe I'm about to get my period, and I had a self-critical mood swing.

She wouldn't leave it at that. She'd sit me down in one of the burgundy leather café chairs, look me in the eye, and sternly remind me:

1. You are not a model or an actress.

2. Your livelihood does not depend on being skinny or hungry.

3. You don't want to spend lots of time obsessing over food or your appearance.

4. You are the size of an average American woman.

5. You are lucky to have such a healthy, able body.

6. You are free to love your body as it is.

7. Your body is worth loving.

She would make me repeat the last three to myself. Then she would tell me to say them out loud. Then she would tell me that's not loud enough! Sassier! Brassier! All the other patrons would pause, mid-sip on their lattes, and swivel to watch the two of us shrieking like banshees. We'd shout, "My body is worth loving!" together until the steel I-beamed ceiling rang with our voices and our peals of laughter. Tripping over each other, we'd run outside just at the moment the floor clerk decided to try to herd us toward the door.

I like this woman.

She should stick around.

My inner best friend apparently has other things to do the following Wednesday, when I go in for a GYN checkup at Kaiser. Most days I live up to my resolution to turn away from the scale at the doctor's office. If I don't look at the number, my weight can't affect my mood or how my day goes. My well-being, my healing heart, and how I perceive my whole self are more important.

Today I step on the scale and ask myself, "Do I look or do I turn away?" Taking a deep breath, I look. Mistake. The readout declares I weigh two pounds more than what my driver's license says. That's eighteen pounds more than what I weighed three years ago, the last time I remember stepping on the scale. I knew I had gained some weight, but almost twenty pounds?

Outwardly I remain calm, but inwardly I am freaking out. And I watch myself freak out. My anorexic reaction. Like an anaphylactic reaction, but different. If only EpiPens came boosted with extra *maitri*. I could inject an emergency dose of loving-kindness straight into my thigh and be done with it.

My inner dialogue becomes a tennis match between my inner anorexic and my inner best friend, who finally shows up at the last minute, skidding around the corner trying to fit on her left shoe while juggling her racket. I'm so relieved to see her that I forget to be annoyed that she's late. I lean forward from the sidelines of the court, watching and hoping.

I'm going on a diet. I need to stop eating so much. (*Whack!*)

(Having successfully pulled on both shoes, my inner best friend bobs on her feet for a moment, takes a deep breath, and swings.)

What you need is to chill out. Your weight is just a number, it's no big deal. (*Thock!*)

What have I already eaten today? I could start my diet now. (*Swack!*)

Geez, Kimber, give yourself a break, you feel fine. Until you saw the number on the scale you were okay with how you look. Who cares what the stupid scale says? It doesn't run your life anymore, remember? (*Whoomp!*)

That's it, I'm skipping lunch entirely. And only a salad for dinner. (*Poomf!*)

Don't be ridiculous, you're going to go on a diet because of what one scale said? You don't even believe in diets. You're fine the way you are. (*Whock!*)

But I'm fat, just look at me! (*Shoof!* She lobs the ball into the air.)

You're not fat, and even if you were, so what? You're beautiful. You're enjoying life. You have so much to be grateful for. Chill out.

(*Smash!* Her diet-obsessed opponent extends her racket across the court to reach the ball and misses. We have a winner!)

The entire match transpires in my head while driving home from the doctor's office. Many years ago the anorexic side would have won completely; I wanted her to win, to have the last word and every word after that. But today my inner best friend won—thank God—the side that notices that I still sometimes freak out about my weight and says, *Hey, just noticing, isn't that funny—how you still freak out sometimes, even after all this work you're doing to be happy with yourself just the way you are?*

No need to despair about it. No big deal. The impulse to freak out is there, but instead of acting on that impulse, I can tune in to the underlying energy: the urgent, restless feeling that I'm not okay and that hordes of emergency personnel and the UN Security Council can't fix what's wrong. Pema calls it a fundamental uneasiness. Flawed, I feel the urge to do everything in my power to hide the imperfection, slathering makeup over the pimple. So what if I'm "flawed"? Being flawed isn't a problem. No one has to fix it. I am perfectly imperfect: a living being, not a cut diamond.

To paraphrase the great Zen master Suzuki Roshi: "You are perfect just the way you are. And you could use a little improvement." This is a huge relief. I'm already perfect—being flawed is perfect. And if big shifts (loving myself) and little refinements (eating to take care of myself, not deprive myself) help make my life even better, that's great, no problem. Bye-bye judgmental mind and all your cohorts. Rather than harshing on myself, I can offer honesty and friendliness. Let's start from the place of being "whole" and "deserving" rather than "imperfect" and "unworthy."

I know all this in my head. Getting my heart to believe it takes some time.

Despite the decisive victory of my best friend on the tennis court, for a few days after my encounter with the scale at the doctor's office, my anorexic reaction has left a nasty hangover. Before the visit I'd noticed that my pants were a little tighter, but they're all yoga pants, how can you tell? It's weird—before seeing the number on the scale I'd actually been enjoying how my body looks and feels. Even my big butt, which I glance at in the mirror as I head out for the grocery store. For a moment my inner anorexic smirks and I can't stop myself from asking the question—"Does my butt look fat in these pants?"—but it takes on a whole different feel when I try saying it in a sexy voice my best friend might use, admiring its width and breadth. "Yeah, mm-hmm, looking good!" My contemplations and companions follow me into the car and we head off to the store.

Love the body I'm in. That really is it. I look down at my hands and further down the steering wheel to my legs while stopped at the light. Love this body no matter what it looks like. I can't let other disappointments in my life express themselves as dissatisfaction with my body. Instead, be friendly to it, nonjudgmental, compassionate. Celebrate its abilities, its beauty, just as it is. See it as perfect right now, not needing it to be something different.

Perfection, I muse while waiting for a parking spot at the natural grocery store, is not about living up to some unattainable ideal, trying to fit into some cookie-cutter outer form. Carlos's voice echoes in the back of my head: *Perfection is the fullness of your own experience. Perfection is fullness.* But what does that mean? To be present, to feel the fragile aliveness of my body, just as it is, right now, all of its desires, all of its intelligence working to digest food in my belly, moving oxygen into my cells and carbon dioxide out, healing injuries I'm not even aware of, feeding my brain at this very moment. Can I accept myself in this very profound way? Not simply tolerate my body, but embrace and celebrate it? My patience is rewarded as a shopper pulls her car out in front of me and I maneuver into her space. Turning off the engine, I sigh and pause a moment before getting out of the car. The sky is that perfect, cool, spacious northern California blue today. My body walks through it, parting the curtain of air that shuts behind me as I head into the store with all the other bodies around me.

Every part of my body is precious. Cellulite is beautiful. At least that's what Chris claims about my butt. From my forays to hot tubs and pools, I know it's true that even thin women have cellulite and stretch marks: it's just part of being embodied. I don't have to wish them away. They are part of my whole self, my full participation in the experience of being a human earthling. How lucky to have had a life in which I've been fed well enough to earn a smattering of stretch marks. Take that, Miss Anorexic.

Pushing the rattling yellow cart into the produce section, I see the bodies around me. Some fat, some thin, lots in between. Looking at people's body sizes, I can't predict whether they'll be smiling or frowning, frustrated or relaxed. The heavy woman in front of me seems ecstatic about the stacks of peaches and nectarines, while the narrow-framed man on the other side of the aisle grumbles into the piles of oranges. *Of course.* Body size is not a predictor of mood or temperament. If I was miserable and felt ugly when thin and anorexic, why can't I be happy and feel beautiful the way my body is right now? The shape and size of my body don't have to be determining factors in my happiness.

As I check items off my list, my mind drifts back to a story Pema Chödrön tells about a Tibetan monk named Atisha who longed for and enjoyed difficulties, to the point of bringing his irritating tea boy with him on his travels, so that he would never be without problems to overcome. Atisha welcomed difficult situations and the drama-inducing unpleasant emotions that accompanied them (long before the advent of reality TV) because they turned the spotlight on where he was still reactive, where he could learn to breathe and respond instead of acting out. The yucky, awful feelings most of us avoid, Atisha invited to the table as honored guests who pointed him to where he could open his heart further in how he treated others. Placing my last item, a bag of organic walnuts, on the pile of groceries in the cart, I head for the registers.

Learning to relish difficulties! Is that possible? If Buddhists use difficult emotions to deepen their inner knowledge, to develop the ability to be happy and centered, even in the midst of experiences most of us would run screaming from, my work is cut out for me. *Yes.* If the Dalai Lama can be happy exiled from his country, can't I be happy inside this body, in whatever form and shape it takes, no matter what my weight is, or what my outward appearance is like? *Yup.* When I'm feeling ugly or fat? *Offer compassion for all those who struggle with their weight, or with feelings of disgust toward their body. Offer compassion to yourself, too.* It's the holy grail of positive body image: the ability to be truly happy no matter what anyone else thinks of me, even myself!

Atisha is a Buddhist superhero. Turning difficulties into something marvelous to nourish the soul. To me, this transformation is no less miraculous than turning water into wine. If you can look forward to difficulties, you never have anything to dread. If difficulties are good, nothing is bad, everything life presents is just one more freaking growth opportunity. Loading the last of the groceries into the trunk, I open the driver's door and settle into the seat. Time to head home.

Wait, if difficulties are good, they aren't really difficulties any more. They are, let's see…blessiculties? Diffitunities? Probolutions? Maybe my annoying hunger is the gateway to finally embracing my body, my eating, my whole self.

On Monday evening, I'm driving up to Spirit Rock in Marin County to meditate with Buddhist teacher Jack Kornfield and hear him speak. He gives the sweetest, most heartfelt dharma talks in the world. The trip takes me across the beautiful Richmond–San Rafael Bridge, past San Quentin State Prison, through the winding hills. Enjoying the drive, excited to see Jack, I notice an empty feeling growing in my belly. Hunger. *Hi there, old friend.* I pause and check in. What kind of hunger is this? All's quiet. Ah, just an early sign— not an emergency. Don't worry, we'll have a little snack when we get there. My belly seems willing to wait.

My anorexic hangover has lifted. But it won't be the last time she turns mean and drunk on me. What's the strategy for the next time the dieting-will-relieve-all-my-self-hatred button gets pushed, when there's some scale that traps me in its claws, or when some part of my body looms up in another reflection? My old strategies—deny the feeling, defeat it, ignore it, starve it—don't work anymore. Actually, they never worked. Time for a new approach. In honor of Buddha, I'll call it:

THE MIDDLE WAY STRATEGY

1. Notice the reaction and its strong emotions, and the drastic and predictable solutions they propose. *Let's starve ourselves to death! That's foolproof!*

2. Take a few deep breaths. Always a good idea, no matter what the problem.

3. Listen to the inner voices. Without getting caught up in them.

4. Respond with friendliness toward yourself and the whole situation.

I'm about ten minutes away from my destination. No time like the present to give it a test run.

Hey, Kimber, you're worried that you've gained some weight. What does that mean to you? That familiar voice sounds like my inner therapist, who apparently has been listening to Pema even more closely than the rest of me.

I feel a little bit out of control.

Aha. Do you really need to be in control? How much control is enough?

That's a wise reminder. Control is overrated.

How are you aside from this? What do you really want?

The truth is—escaping for a moment my thick and sticky layer of self-criticism—I'm feeling fine, happy, good about my body. I probably don't need to do anything at all. I could do a little course correction, as if my tire went off onto the gravel shoulder and I pull the steering wheel gently back onto the road. I don't have to violently swerve into a sudden, skidding U-turn and possibly end up in a heap at the bottom of the hill, earth and sky reversed. Each moment offers the opportunity to embrace myself anew. My weight gain is not a criticism or even a call to action. Perhaps it can be simply a gentle reminder to bring my awareness to what and how I eat. Enjoy my food, notice when I'm full, and push the plate away when I'm done. Continue paying attention, expect the occasional setback, and let my inner well-being be my guide.

That feels better. At last, an appropriate response, not critical or judgmental, but real and loving. The sky isn't falling because of some numbers on a scale. My response can be respectful and aligned with what I truly want for myself: more love, more friendliness.

Pulling into the parking lot at Spirit Rock, I grab my secondhand meditation pillow and almond butter sandwich. For a few minutes I pause on a wooden bench under the redwoods to give my stomach its promised snack and then make my way up to the meditation hall. The wide room is low-ceilinged and crowded, but holds a gentle feeling of community. I wave to a couple of familiar faces, give a hug here and there, and set my cushion down on the floor near the front. We meditate for some long minutes, and when the deep, smooth ring of the bell opens my eyes, I see Jack's warm face at the front of the room. He begins his dharma talk, sharing inspiring stories and quotes, beautifully reminding us of how to step fully into life. Jack's words flow through me and something catches on my heart. "Without compassion," he says, "it's easy to give in to hopeless despair." We close with a brief chant and stream back out into the evening air.

Heading home, I realize compassion is my life buoy right now. It's what I'm clinging to, to keep myself from drowning in the old whirlpool of self-disgust. Compassion keeps telling me, *You're okay. You're okay.* And my compassion is growing, for myself and for all women like me who want to love their bodies, but don't know how.

From the driver's seat I watch the moon rise over the East Bay hills, so reminiscent of reclining nudes, the earth resting in its fullness and beauty, unashamed. Women in our culture sometimes hold a sense that there is some part of our body that it would be unforgivable to reveal. For some women it's their belly, for some their legs, for me my hips, butt, and thighs. Revealing this part to the world would be terrible, something shameful and vulnerable. It's as if we project whatever mean, unforgivable secrets we have lurking within our hearts onto our bodies. So often the unforgivable secret is nothing more, and nothing less, than our perceived imperfection. We conceal those parts of ourselves we fear, those parts that we think are ugly, that we never want anyone to see, that we don't even want to look at in our quietest moments.

Tremendous amounts of courage are required for us to look at our bodies and our hearts, and to be open to what we find there. To pull up the shades on the darkness within, the ways in which we're afraid we've failed ourselves and others. To pull away the illusion of ideal beauty and see the full aliveness within our own flesh, no matter what shape, size, or color.

It's hard when so many of us are steeped in the images of gorgeous, primped, airbrushed women, and awash in expectations of how we should act, think, and be in the world. Why not look at ourselves in a friendly way, to see our bodies as a manifestation of our whole, amazing selves? My wish: may we learn to touch the tenderness of the heart, acknowledging the difficulty of holding space for ourselves to be exactly what we are. By holding ourselves with love, we can finally say, as Cooper's little friend Emily did, "My body is my best friend."

Wow. At last I arrive home and walk up the brightly lit stairs to let myself in the front door. Hopefully Chris is still awake and willing to listen. My whole perspective has changed from when I left for Spirit Rock a few hours ago. It's amazing what an extended meditation—and a long drive—can do.

chapter twelve

Hips to Love

In the grocery store line the next evening, I examine the cover of the *National Enquirer*, splashed with photos of fat and thin movie stars with titles along the lines of: "Who's Gross and Who's Scary: The Obese and the Anorexic." Are those the choices? My heart aches for the actresses portrayed between the leering pages. It must be awful to see unflattering pictures of yourself while waiting in line at the grocery store, or walking past a newsstand on the sidewalk. One actress has ballooned to 300 pounds, her former body and face nearly unrecognizable beneath yards of billowing clothes and flesh. Another is dangerously thin, her stomach practically sticking out like a starving child's. Ribs poking out in all directions. Nobody can say *she's* fat! It's that old whispered challenge: *I dare you to call me fat! Watch as I disappear before your eyes.* I can see from the picture that she still has those little skin pouches in her armpits where her arms connect to her torso. That undoubtedly annoys her to no end. Those little poochy creases gave my anorexic hissy fits all those years ago. Now I have bigger things to worry about.

Standing in front of the mirror in the closet, getting ready for bed, my inner best friend has yet to emerge. What's taking her so long? I catch a glimpse of my thighs as I pull off my yoga pants. I turn sideways, backward, looking over my shoulder.

Gazing at my reflection in the mirror, my mind starts: Why couldn't I have been born into a family of narrow-thighed, small-butted women? Why does my family tree have big hips, generous thighs, and giant feet to balance it all on?

Then I remember that most women's thighs don't measure favorably against airbrushed ones, possibly even the real thighs of the models themselves. The next story quickly follows: Big women just aren't "in" right now. Bending one knee across the other, arching my back, and throwing one arm over my head, it looks to me like my body would have been an excellent model for Rubens's *Sleeping Angelica*. Not so excellent, on the other hand, for a Calvin Klein ad. It's not my fault the fashion world holds up Twiggy-like, surgically enhanced women as the only desirable body type. Poor me, born in the wrong era.

Another thought arises, eminently reasonable: I could dump the stories entirely, and radically take responsibility for allowing the image of the perfect thighs to arise every time I look in the mirror and see my own naked haunches. No one is gripping a page torn from a magazine and shaking it in my face, yelling at me that I have to look like a 100-pound fifteen-year-old. *The only bully here is me.*

I will not hurt myself. No longer.

I close my eyes and try to start over. I look again into the mirror. Yup, there they are. Hi, thighs.

Without consciously comparing them to anyone else's thighs, I observe that they are big, womanly, especially on the inside, all the way down to the knees, where they pooch out and bump into each other. They're muscle-y but there's plenty of fleshiness all around, and my butt gets kind of square where it hangs down a little on the sides. Plus there are stretch marks lining up like little rivers criss-crossing the continents of East Thigh and West Thigh, flowing through the rolling hills of dimpled skin, all the way down to the backs of my knees. So it goes.

The idea that I could look in the mirror and think happy thoughts about my thighs seems far-fetched, though perhaps not as distant as my first attempt, all those years ago in the dorm shower stall. Without the mirror, in the morning, I am able to rub oil into my legs and think nice thoughts: *Beautiful legs, beautiful skin, drink up this oil, this goodness.* But the moment I step in front of a mirror, like now, with my mind sleepy and irritable, my kindness toward my body feels fake, as if I'm pretending the oil is some sort of magical oint-ment that will transform my legs into a perfect size 2 or my negative feelings into happy ones.

Compassion and loving-kindness seem far away. *Try the steps.* Notice my reaction. *Check.* A few deep breaths. *Check.* Hear the inner voices without believing them. *Sort of.* Respond with kindness. One more deep breath.

Hey, thighs. Sorry about all the editorializing. You must be tired from our busy day, too. The last thing you need is someone giving you a hard time right now. Let's go to bed.

With relief, I pull my pajama bottoms over my thighs and hips, and snuggle into bed next to Chris, who is mostly oblivious to my inner obsessions. Letting my head fall into the pillow, my imagina-tion conjures up the big beautiful woman in the fast food restaurant when my capacity for self-hatred was fledging. Surrounded by her family, enjoying an evening out, she didn't give a shit about what I or anyone else thought of her. She was loved and lovable and gorgeous. I wish that my ability to see her beauty and worthiness meant that I could see my own, too.

Yet I realize my desire for fullness has morphed. From wanting to be happy and skinny and never hungry I've moved in the direction of wanting to be happy with this body I've got and dealing with hunger and fullness from inside my belly rather than from what's in the mirror or on my plate. I feel close. And so far away. Sailors who haven't glimpsed land in months say the distance once they've spotted land seems to stretch interminably long as they approach. I get the feeling sometimes I'm staring at the Island of Fullness in my dingy...and rowing myself farther out to sea all the while.

I know being skinnier won't make me happier. I know it. But do I believe it?

❀

I wake up in the morning feeling a teeny bit frustrated with myself. Actually I'm totally fed up with my own bullshit. Packing Cooper's lunch for school, my mind screams down the raceway, multiple judgments vying to be the first at the finish line. Here I am, pretending to be so compassionate with my body, so careful and concerned about honoring it and eating well, and I still go around chowing down on all kinds of things that don't make me feel good, being critical and ashamed of my body, and wishing I was born as skinny as a rail. *This has to end.* As I tousle Cooper's hair and hand him his lunch box, Chris scoops him up and whisks him off to school. It's my day off. Great. Just me and the Daytona 500 Speedway of Criticism squealing laps around my head.

A change of scenery might help. The dog and I decide to take a walk up in the East Bay hills, at the Sibley Regional Volcanic Preserve. Kobu—our big red pound puppy, half golden retriever, half fluffy collie—nervously sniffs through the grass, and stays close. Wide open spaces make him anxious, but he's willing to indulge my need for some outdoor time. I scuff along looking for wildflowers and trying to be present with the fact that it's cooler out today than I anticipated, and having no jacket, I have to deal with dense layers of goose bumps on my arms or go home. I decide to accept the goose bumps and walk a little faster. My mind circles back to its earlier frustrations, but they feel a little more spacious now, held by the wide sky above us. I remember one of the main Buddhist teachings: "Accept Reality."

As if "Reality" is a package, a box that arrives on my doorstep, and when the guy with the computer thingy asks me to sign for it, I'm like, "Not today. I can't accept this. Return it to sender and don't ever show your face around here again." I slam the door, double bolt it, and consider moving. And despite my fury, the same delivery guy comes back the next day and the day after that, and follows me no matter where I move, Kansas or Guatemala. At last, when the relentless courier tracks me down in my camouflaged outpost in the jungle, arriving at my door, machete in hand, big mosquito bites on his forehead, and a cheerful "I found you!" on his lips, it dawns on me: *Babe…it's Reality knocking and it's not ever going away.*

The "Reality" is: I will never have the perfect thighs I've always dreamed of. Never will I awaken one morning to find my wrinkles, cellulite, and flabbiness magically gone forever.

Nonetheless, once the box is inside the door, I willfully pretend that it doesn't exist, or that some black hole will miraculously open up and suck it into another dimension. Against all evidence to the contrary, I fully expect that my box of Reality will dissolve itself into a faint mixture of dust bunnies and cobwebs. But each morning when I get up, it's still there, accumulating a pile of unread mail on top, patiently waiting for me to acknowledge its existence.

Kobu and I follow the dusty path along a row of heavy redwoods, and then he races ahead, looking for cows along the wide fire road. All along, I've wanted to be naturally skinny. Not anorexic, not having-to-starve-myself skinny. One of those four percent of women who are effortlessly, forever thin, it's in their genes, la-di-da, they can't help it. More gelato, please! I suffer, the Buddha would say, because what I want is to be thin and able to eat anything, but when I tentatively open that box labeled Reality, what I find inside are voluptuous, womanly hips and the stately thighs on which to carry them.

My choice is to accept this reality or deny it. I tried denial, I tried suffering, I tried starving myself. Could I try out acceptance? Of all of me, hips, thighs, and (gasp!) my butt? Open up the box, look inside, and finally embrace what's in there once and for all?

It's a task of mythological proportion: The Labors of Kimber. I might as well volunteer to help Sisyphus out with his task of rolling his boulder up the hill of the damned. Sure, placing my shoulder under the boulder of self-acceptance and pushing it uphill for a while isn't a huge deal. But I know before we reach the top, it's destined to mysteriously slip from my grip and thunder down again, bouncing past trees and tufted brush. Hopefully, I can jump out of the way before it squashes me entirely.

Day after day, I want to ask Sisyphus, does the boulder get smaller? After years of grinding it against the heavy bulk of mountain, does it smooth out, pare down to its bare essence of rock? Does it get so small, you can pick it up, hold its cool heaviness in your hand, and throw it to the top of the mountain? Then watch it bounce its way back down again, just for fun? Can I get good at self-acceptance? Could it become easy?

Kobu and I arrive at the base of the crater that the Sibley Regional Volcanic Preserve proudly maintains as its centerpiece. Looking up at the edge of the steep, grassy slope, I wonder what it would be like to run straight up it. Or push something up it. Exhausting, I imagine. And exhilarating, perhaps. At the bottom of the crater is a looping spiral of dirt and stones, the Mazzariello Labyrinth, named after the local psychic and sculptor who created it some years ago.

One step at a time, the labyrinth leads me toward its center, then away from it, until I finally wonder, will I ever reach the center? Did the artist create some mad, frustrating optical illusion where the journeyer keeps thinking they're making progress, but they're not? At last, my feet arrive at the center bulb and I circle slowly, gazing at the surrounding slopes. Of course, I think, progress doesn't happen linearly. Even when I'm impatient, I'm still on the path of learning to love myself. Even when it seems like I've doubled back and gotten nowhere, the progress happens, just by putting one foot in front of the other. The *process* is the progress. Slow, annoying progress sometimes, but progress nonetheless. I'll get to the center one way or the other. Someday.

Kobu's found a sunny patch of dirt to relax in, and I settle onto a wide stone nearby, feeling a bit warmer and a teeny bit less judgmental. Tracing my hands along the curve of my thighs, I take a deep breath. Here's the reality: If these womanly hips and stately thighs are the worst thing I experience in life, I'm pretty damn lucky. No marching ten miles through the desert to get clean water for my family. No wondering where my next meal will come from. Instead, my life overflows with the vast blessings of middle-classness in a first-world country and unimaginable luxuries like hot water and refrigeration at my fingertips. Not to mention beautiful hikes a few miles from my front door. I push the toe of my dusty shoe through the swaying grass as Kobu snuffles at the brush nearby. I have full use of all my limbs. And chocolate. And coffee. And warm socks. So what if big hips are my draw? The size of my hips is not the determining factor in my happiness.

As Kobu and I make our way back to the parking lot, I realize my next step along the path is acceptance: until I accept that I have the Big Hip card and it's staying in my hand, I can't figure out how to turn it to my advantage.

With the challenge of trying out acceptance on my mind, I call up my friend Dari, an energy worker and intuitive who was in my first yoga training with Katchie. My friendship with Dari is an excellent example of how much I've broadened my horizons since leaving the Midwest. Willowy, with big blue eyes and freckles and a huge smile that sparkles like tiny sunlit waves, Dari could be the sister of my first yoga teacher back in L.A.: chakras, incense, and an unalterable, matter-of-fact belief in all things unseen.

I'm in an experimental mindset. If the unseen forces at work in our lives have any insights into how I can come to love and accept my hips and thighs, my heart is willing to listen.

With plenty of time to spare as I'm driving to Dari's place, I get off in downtown San Francisco and make my way through the Castro District, my version of the scenic route. On the radio I hear an interview with Eve Ensler, the founder of *The Vagina Monologues*. The sky, the sunlight, the license plate of the car in front of me, all disappear to a tiny point as the radio waves carry her words to my eardrums:

"Women have a choice: to be good or to be great. Good women are little, cooperative, pretty, nice. They are neat, smooth, and don't stick out in funny places. Visible fat rolls are definitely a no-no. Great women are just themselves."

Waking back up to the red taillights in front of my bumper, it's as if Eve Ensler has reached out of the dashboard and clipped me upside the head. "Just be yourself, Kimber. Just be great." I imagine her extricating herself from the glove box and plopping herself into the seat next to me, where she continues her assessment of my life.

Lifting her feet up to the dashboard, Eve runs her fingers through her spiky hair, rolls down the window, and lets the breeze wash over her.

"Girlfriend, you've wasted too much time trying to be good. You can spend the rest of your life trying to be quiet, polite, tidy, attractively wrapped...like a fucking mannequin...carefully not offending anyone by, you know, being alive, and what will you have at the end?" She sticks her tongue out at me and laughs. "You'll still get old, you'll still die, and you'll be there on your deathbed, wondering to yourself, *What the hell did I do with my life? When was the fun part supposed to happen? When do I finally get to be who I want to be?*"

She leans out the window and yells "Woo-hoo!" to a crowd of women on the corner, adorned in bright pink T-shirts, hats, and feathers, and carrying antiwar posters and banners. She reaches for the door handle.

"Just let me out here," she says. "I've got some folks to catch up with! See ya later, kiddo."

My mouth hangs open. The breeze from the window settles on my arms. I steer onto the highway, my mind reeling. Eve is right, of course. She's pointed out a possibility I haven't yet conceived: is there some fabulous diva waiting to come out from inside me, after I fully embrace my luscious thighs once and for all? She's in there with the anorexic, the prison guard, Svetlana, my inner therapist, and everyone else. Looks like my inner best friend has another glamorous, take-no-prisoners side to her, which I suspect won't stay under wraps any longer. Sweet.

Shaking off my reverie, I pull my car up to Dari's apartment in the Richmond District, just a few blocks from Ocean Beach. Fresh-faced and beaming, she welcomes me in, shows me around the wood-paneled rooms, and sits me down with a rustic mug of tea. I decide to keep my yet-unprocessed interlude with Eve to myself, but share with her my latest hunch that my body is protecting my hips energetically by keeping more weight on them, like putting extra insulation around a hot wire. Also left unshared—the uncontrolled sparking and frayed connections from my girlhood's charged traumas from the hands of men on my body. Hope flares up that she can help me ground and rechannel the electricity I'm so tired of burning my fingers on.

Looking at me through the sage-infused steam rising from her cup, she smiles and says without missing a beat, "Let me do your numbers for you."

My numbers? I'm momentarily confused. What, like my bra and waist measurements? No, my "numbers," she explains, are my birth date added together to get a basic number that corresponds to a Tarot card. I'm skeptical, but willing to play along. I write down my birth date for her. She adds up the numbers, consults a book at her elbow, and looks up at me with a satisfied grin.

"See," she points at the page, "your number is three…your card is the Empress, the Mother Earth card." She shows me a beautiful pastel watercolor illustration of a queen luxuriously clothed in a long robe, scepter in hand, relaxing on her throne, with a far-off look in her eye. "She represents love with wisdom, effortless abundance, a strong connection to the earth." Dari taps on the card with a long finger and eyes me thoughtfully. "The Empress embodies leadership, and teaches the wisdom of love. Her biggest challenge is to support and nurture herself as well as others."

As her words sink in, my heart feels bewildered but pleased. I'm perfectly happy to identify with Mother Earth, whatever the circumstances. But a queen?

She raises a brow over the twinkle in her eye and says, "You need your hips to sit on and survey your kingdom. Enjoy them!"

I burst out laughing, tears filling my eyes. Wow. That's a totally different take. I need my hips. I need them to be big and comfortable. Like a throne. Like a voluptuous mama goddess draped over a divan couch, surveying her subjects, eating peeled grapes, being fanned by nubile...okay, maybe that's taking it a little far. Especially given that I hate to let anyone "do" anything for me. I'll hardly let Chris bring me a glass of water.

Maybe my hips represent the more feminine parts of myself I'm reluctant to embrace. Maybe I can sit back and enjoy life a little more. Maybe...I can start to see my hips as powerful, desirable, even good. Our session complete, we chat for a moment longer, and Dari sends me off at the door with a hug and a package of energy-cleansing bath salts.

Stepping off her porch and into the afternoon sun, I realize the Pacific Ocean is only a few blocks away. On a gorgeous day. A chance to enjoy myself, here and now.

Sitting on the beach, I watch the ocean curl and crash, let my hands drift down to touch the sand and water, and feel how the imprints my feet make fills up with each wave, which in turn drains back into the foam, without effort or resistance.

Drawing half-circles in the sand with my toes, the irony of the situation dawns on me slowly. Despite my total disbelief, Dari's insights were just what I needed. Be a great woman: emphasis on the great, emphasis on the woman. Commit to embrace the parts of myself that are powerful and emphatic and feminine. I've been such a hypocrite. While hating and denouncing that part of our culture that rejects shapely hips, generous thighs, and soft bellies and has for so many years exclusively embraced an artificially skinny, boyish ideal, in my own body, in my own mind, I'm still acting out my inner resistance to curves and shapeliness. The sand doesn't resist the ocean. Why should I resist? It's a perfect day, and the wind and the tumble of the ocean resonate along the fine hairs on my skin and all the way into my belly.

At home sitting down with my journal (part of me has begun to think these musings might be raw material for a book…someday), I'm ready to try out this acceptance thing. If I'm going to look inside the Reality box, pull aside the tissue paper and find some way to embrace the womanly aspects there, I might as well treat my hips like a gift, like the present I've always wanted. Time for a list:

WHAT'S GREAT ABOUT MY HIPS/THIGHS/BUTT?

1. They support me when I'm resting.

2. They make a sturdy, soft cushion to sit on.

3. They give me stability in my yoga practice and for sitting in meditation.

4. They're warm and soft.

5. They make a nice, stable, comfy nest for lovemaking.

6. They're curvy and nice to look at.

7. They almost never hurt or get in the way—they effort-lessly support me throughout my life.

Wow, seven things. Before today, I didn't realize there were seven things to love about my hips. Apparently my hips deserve some serious gratitude and acceptance. More than they've been getting, certainly. And I forgot one of the most important jobs my hips have done for me: they helped me make and carry an adorable baby! That makes eight.

I'm clear on the reasons to celebrate and love my hips, so now what? How to demonstrate my growing respect and love for my hips? I chew on the pen for a moment.

Number one: Get or find some really feminine, hip-shaped thing to put on my altar, and learn to love it. Meditate on the beauty and power of the feminine in the world and in me.

Number two: Create more freedom for my hips—let them express themselves more, show off a little more, dance more, let them have more fun. Learn to hula hoop. Wear skirts. Let them out for romps in the park. Now this I can get excited about.

It's Thursday afternoon and I'm sitting in Redwood Regional Park in the Oakland Hills, where summer camp is about to let out. Having arrived a half hour early to enjoy the fresh air and sun, I welcome these few minutes to write and gather my thoughts. Ever since my imaginary conversation with Eve, I've been questioning where my loyalties really lie. Am I still buying into my inner anorexic's single-minded reasoning, the prison guard's threats, and Svetlana's cookie-soothed pushiness? What would Eve tell me? That I should step up, be part of a movement to provide women with an alternative view of a happy, strong, not-thin woman, teaching yoga, loving life. Am I that woman?

Today I saw a bumper sticker that said "Change the way you see, not the way you look." It had a drawing of a lovely, voluptuous woman next to it. Changing the way I see is exactly right. Give up my teenage fantasy of being a model, or even of looking like a model, and settle in to relish my ice cream and yoga, my chocolate and hiking, and everything in between. Enjoy life.

When I was six, my father presented my sister and me with identical pink jewelry boxes, the kind that when you lift the lid the little plastic ballerina pops up and dances in front of the mirror, twirling to the tinkly music. Hard to say how many hours my little girl self spent winding and rewinding the box, head in her hands, watching the ballerina's seemingly endless pirouettes. As the ballerina spun, my mind followed…*I'll be thin and popular, and maybe even famous, perhaps even wealthy, admired far and wide for my beauty.* I've heard men sometimes hit their midlife crisis when they suddenly realize they're never going to be rock-and-roll superstars. My personalized, feminine version is no less laughably heartbreaking: the secret fantasy of being a runway supermodel still lurks in my unconscious, reluctantly succumbing to its slow and inevitable death. It's time to finally shut the lid on that jewelry box, and donate it to the Goodwill. Someone else is welcome to it.

The hilarious part is that, rationally speaking, I have no desire to be a supermodel. It sounds inordinately boring to be watched, photographed, and appreciated only for how youthful and sexy you are—and on top of that, having to stay that skinny and worry all the time about losing one's looks. I'd hate it. Being preoccupied with my appearance (even more so than I am already) is not my idea of a good time.

My mind is chock full of myths about what it means to be thin or fat. Thinness gets equated with being weak, feeling less able to take care of myself. Part of me definitely associates being big with being tough, able, and smart, the type of person no one messes with. Thinness means superficiality, ditziness, weakness, and helplessness. And from my time as an anorexic, thin also equals depression. Time to shine some sunlight on all these dank assumptions.

Myths About Being Thin/Fat

1. If you're thin, more people love you.

2. If you're fat, you're harder to love/fall in love with/stay in love with.

3. If you're thin, more people think you're sexy.

4. If you're fat, you hardly ever have sex and no one will think you're sexy.

5. If you're thin, you feel sexy and loved all the time.

6. If you're fat, you feel ugly and unloved all the time.

7. If you're thin, your life is together, you have nothing to worry about.

8. If you're fat, your life is a mess, you're out of control.

9. If you're thin, you have to be taken care of/protected/ helped by other people.

10. If you're fat, you can take care of your own damn self.

Wow, it's scary, the stuff that lives in my head. If these myths were true, thin people would be sex and love addicts who never have to lift a finger and never spend an evening alone, and fat people would have no relationships and be simultaneously messy and able to take care of themselves just fine, thank you.

All these myths are patently absurd. It's easy to bring to mind miserable thin people who never feel loved and whose lives are out of control...for example, me while starving myself. It's also clear that there are lots of happy not-thin people who are well loved and confident. Again, me—now. Well, sort of. On a good day. I set down my notebook and enjoy the slanting sunlight on my face. The sound of voices and shuffling feet tumble down the woodchip path.

A dusty, weary Cooper appears with his backpack, looking for me. His first words as he approaches: "Do you have a snack?"

"Yes I do, baby. How was your day?"

chapter thirteen

Mind-Full

Tonight for dinner, I made myself a yummy fresh collard green roll—a salad burrito you hold in your hand, full of carrots, peppers, sprouts, tofu, and spicy dressing, all wrapped in a collard green. The first one was so tasty, I made myself another and ate it sitting on one of the little chairs at Cooper's art table, watching out the window as he played with the neighbor kids in the lengthening fall shadows on the driveway next door. Wednesday night Chris attends a poetry class in San Francisco, so Cooper and I are on our own. A bean-and-cheese burrito waits for Cooper when he's ready to come in from chasing the basketball around with his friends.

As I rinse my plate in the kitchen, I see through the window over the sink that the fig tree's fruit is ready for picking. The perfect dessert. As I head out with a colander into the garden, the dog by my side, I contemplate how my eating habits have revealed themselves slowly, the way you get to know what an animal likes to eat when you've lived with it for a long time. Kobu happily begs for pizza crusts but ignores raw chicken. If you forget to feed him dinner, first he tilts his head and looks at you mournfully, then he comes and tries to sit all seventy-five pounds of himself in your lap. If he had thumbs, he would spend every free moment we weren't looking raiding the cheese drawer in the fridge.

My body doesn't care for raw chicken either, and pizza crusts are a toss up. I feel bad when all I've had to eat all day is cake. Yuck. When my body gets to decide what it wants to eat, it craves mostly vegetables and any good food that makes it stand up and say, "Yeah, baby!"

But what is "good" food? Nutritious, health-promoting, organic, unrefined, unprocessed? Doesn't "good," with its righteous overtones, imply that there's "bad" food to compare it to? How I can be less judgmental about food (and myself) when it's all about good and bad? What about the organic whole wheat, unrefined sugar, fair-trade chocolate brownie? Is that "good" or "bad"?

When someone says, "I've been eating a lot of crap lately," they don't mean they've been eating bowls of what the bunny leaves on the floor of his cage. Not actual crap. What they mean is, "I ate too many chocolate-covered pork rinds," or deep-fried Snickers bars, or some denizen of that realm of hell reserved for "bad food." Once, "bad" food might have meant the donuts had mold on them or the chips were stale. Nah. Today "bad" food means, "I don't even want to think about how many calories those fried olives had. I can feel the fat slathering itself onto my hips from the inside out."

Bad food doesn't mean that the birthday cake wasn't intensely delicious. And it doesn't mean that the Girl Scout cookies turned into mercenaries on the way down my esophagus and are now fighting their way out. It means the food was morally bad. Something I shouldn't have eaten and will now have to punish myself for. If you eat bad food, you're bad. Bad in, bad out.

How many times have I heard friends say, "I've been bad today"? Not that they stole the neighbor's roses and then ran over the mail carrier with the minivan. Not, "Oh, honey, you wouldn't believe how bad I've been today! I lay in bed all morning making crank phone calls and then, *then*, I showed up to work in my pajamas, walked right into my boss's office, and gave her a photocopy of my butt! So *bad!*"

Nope. When my friends say they've been bad, they mean they ate three, count 'em, *three* brownies *and* half a bag of chips. Or even one brownie, and they thought about eating a bag of chips. And maybe they skipped their workout and their skinny jeans don't fit them anymore and they've given up hope of ever wearing a bikini again. Bad.

Why is that "bad"? Why do we take on the misplaced qualifiers of the food we eat? No more writing "BAD" on my forehead with the metaphorical Sharpie, simply because I've put this or that into my body. I want to eat and enjoy some radically yummy chocolate when it happens to intersect my path in life instead of using it as an opportunity to berate myself. Making certain foods off-limits creates a taboo, transforming them into a sinful indulgence, something even more desirable. Moralizing about food turns eating just a square of chocolate in front of the family into sneaking downstairs later to finish the whole bar while standing barefoot on the cold tile floor.

When my inner anorexic was at the height of her power, a piece of bread or a half teaspoon of olive oil—or, God forbid, both— resulted in a tightening of the hairshirt/belt another notch or two until tears came to my eyes. Punishment equals a really bad idea.

Burdening food with judgments doesn't work for me anymore. Eating should not be an exercise in self-hatred. Food doesn't inherently have a moral component. Sure, there are some things that are healthier than others. So what? I can eat mostly healthy things, fewer not-as-healthy things, and let go of the moral implications.

I hereby resolve to rescue eating from the hell realm of punishment and reward and lead it into the light of conscious awareness of this body's physical and emotional needs, a true feeding of the self. My anorexic self—that skinny little girl determined to vanish away to nothing—has already loosened her hold on me. Can she let me embrace my whole self, my body in whatever form it is in, my heart with all its tenderness, my spirit with its longing for wholeness? My mind knows the balance I seek is out there somewhere. Or, more likely, *in here* somewhere.

Several nights later, a Chris-less Wednesday night, Cooper and I eat yogurts together after dinner and I set my empty cup on the table while he's barely a third of the way through.

"Wow," he says, eyes wide. "You eat really fast."

He's right. Earlier in the day, I watched him stick a big wad of Indian flatbread into his mouth, and I said, "Take little bites, honey. Take your time, enjoy it." I guess we're watching out for each other that way.

My parents have been around this week, which is great. They take Cooper after school while I'm teaching and then we get out the card decks to play euchre in the evenings, teasing each other and laughing a lot.

Unfortunately, when my parents are around, my intention to eat more mindfully pretty much goes out the window. Maybe it's old habits from childhood. My mom and dad would spend an hour or more making dinner and then the whole meal would be consumed in less than fifteen minutes. Every night we sat down, said a moment's grace, and turned our attention to our plates, quickly, efficiently, no nonsense. One bite after the next, on to seconds, on to dessert. No resting in between bites, no thinking too much about the process of eating at all. A couple of questions about how your day was and that's it. Everything cleared from the table and into the dishwasher.

One Thanksgiving when I was a kid, my mom spent days preparing for our extended family to come, making dozens of delicious dishes, including tiny little bite-size pecan pies from scratch. She got up at the crack of dawn on Thanksgiving morning to put on the finishing touches: crispy onions on the green bean casserole, Cool Whip spread on the ice cream pumpkin pie, chilled olives and carrots and celery laid out in rows for hors d'oeuvres. Then the guests filled the house, piled their plates high with a hundred hours' worth of food, and the entire meal was finished in about twenty minutes, including the seemingly endless prayer my lay preacher grandfather led us in while the food cooled (or warmed) to room temperature before our hungry lips.

The concept of fast food was invented for my family. When we were kids, both my parents worked full time, spending long hours at their adjoining offices, so when they came home for dinner, we immediately piled back into the car and headed out to a restaurant like Wendy's or Long John Silver's, or our favorite local cafeteria, the Cambridge Inn. Pizza Hut was out of the question—too slow—and Bill Knapp's, a sit-down country-style restaurant, was a special treat where we might occasionally spend an extra five minutes on a Friday night. Once at the fish restaurant, I swallowed one of my baby teeth, which had fallen out while biting into some corn on the cob. I couldn't find it anywhere. I wasn't chewing my food carefully enough to notice a tooth mixed amidst the buttery kernels in my mouth. Hmm.

If we happened to go to a sit-down restaurant with a waiter and everything, we ordered our desserts at the same time as our meal, and Dad asked for the check the minute the entrées arrived at the table. One evening, he bawled out a waitress at a twenties-era family

232

restaurant for not putting the dessert orders in soon enough. They were ice cream desserts! Was she really supposed to set our sundaes aside to melt next to the heat lamps while we finished our burgers?

These folks obviously didn't know the Simpkins. We could eat everything on the table in ten minutes or less. Fries, sodas, burgers, salads, everything gone. Before the ice cream can even think about melting.

In the last several years, my parents have mellowed considerably, and they're now able to sit back and relax during the meal, enjoying the process of eating, the atmosphere, and the company. No doubt it helps that we mostly see them during holidays and vacations.

Maybe it's an American thing, to treat a meal like one more thing to get done, rather than an end in and of itself. Not for enjoyment, but purely serving a function. But why rush dinner? If not for that rest mark at the end of the day, if not for a little bit of time to spend with family or friends, what are we living for? If all we do is jump from one moment to the next, wishing this moment was done already, then even our leisure time starts to look like a marathon: "When *this* is over, I can start working on *that*."

Last Thanksgiving, my sister Jen and I made an effort to change our family's habits around eating big meals. Instead of serving Thanksgiving buffet-style, we decided to serve it in courses, a little bit at a time, giving everyone the chance to relax and enjoy each dish. Best of all, we didn't need to have everything ready to be set on the table at once, and the meal took a full two hours to eat (not including dessert)! We got to enjoy the roasted vegetables in cornucopia croissant rolls, the butternut squash soup, and each dish with all its separate flavors. The major downside: tons of dishes. But the long conversations at the table and the relaxed atmosphere made it worthwhile, even my parents and extended family seemed to enjoy it. Jen and I agreed we'd do it this way every year.

Thursday morning. During breakfast, I try an experiment. No books, no newspaper, no magazine, no assembly instructions. Just me and my breakfast. Savory brown rice, some avocado, and an egg fried in olive oil. A meal meditation. Bite, chew, mmm, swallow. Next bite. It's hard to think only about eating. Just eat, I remind myself. The brown rice is warm, and chewy, and the tiniest bit sweet. All week in my yoga classes, I've been working with the theme of being present where you are. So here I am, with my breakfast, just eating. Why is it hard to be present here? I'm used to entertaining myself while I eat, by talking, listening, reading, walking around, even driving. Is it just habit, or am I avoiding having to pay attention while I'm eating? Mmm. This avocado is delicious, so creamy. The egg is cooked just right. But this morning something is different. I'm enjoying my breakfast quite a bit, every bite. When I finally get to the last bite, there's no, *Hey, who ate my breakfast?* Just, *Yum, that was good. My belly feels...full.*

After teaching a morning class and a noon class afterward, I come home and make for lunch The Most Delicious Sandwich. A thickly sliced heirloom tomato over fresh basil leaves and goat cheese on warm toast with salt and pepper. Truly awesome. When I cut up the ruffled tomato into slices, it looked like a voluptuous flower, petals extending from the center. Gorgeous, like eating a work of art. So simple, so delicious. Buoyed by my earlier success, I sit down to eat it, napkin in my lap, no distractions except the ramblings of my own mind. Which are distraction enough. By thinking alone, I can completely take myself away from what I'm eating—I get so involved in the thoughts that I don't even notice what I'm putting in my mouth. Incredible effort is required to keep my mind on what's in front of me.

I take a bite and my mind goes on a stroll...*Mmm, this tastes great. What an amazing sandwich. Look at it!* Fine, enjoying the scenery. At the next bite, I start to analyze why the sandwich is so good...*I can taste how fresh the tomato is, how the cheese is a little tangy, the basil subtle, and the toast at just the right temperature. Maybe I'll write this recipe up and send it to my friends. Isn't summer great? I love tomatoes. I should plant more tomatoes next year. But not in the same place, I should turn over the center bed and see how they do there. Lots of sun in that spot.* By then I've taken three more bites and haven't tasted any of them. Back to the sandwich. *Tastes yummy. I'm so happy to be eating this sandwich. It's nice to sit down and enjoy it.* By then I'm already thinking about what to say about the next bite.

Even with all my practice in yoga and meditation, reminding myself to come back to the breath, my focus zips away when food arrives. Eating needs to be like the breath: always bringing my awareness back to it, not just at the beginning and the end, but in the middle as well. May my attention rest on enjoying every bite as much as possible, honoring the food, my body, the process of eating, the sacredness of bringing a bit of the world inside myself to become part of me.

On Friday, arriving home from subbing my friend's afternoon class, I find myself standing in front of the kitchen cabinet where we keep the cereal and snacks, looking for just the right thing to eat. I've caught myself here a million times before, searching through the cabinet as if something will have magically appeared there since the last time I checked...a few minutes ago. As if some grocery fairy secretly stocked the cupboard while my back was turned. What am I looking for? Is the answer to the meaning of life back there?

Perhaps every time I go into the kitchen and look in the fridge or the freezer or open a cupboard, some unconscious part of myself fully expects that some wonderful foodstuff has inexplicably appeared, at last, by chance, on one of my shelves, with the words EAT ME emblazoned across it. Then I can take a tiny bite of it and be forever full.

Instead, gazing into the larder at the usual suspects—crackers, oat cereal, dried fruit—I am, as usual, disappointed.

I don't know what I'm looking for. A mystery food. Some kind of bun or roll with a generous filling of savory curried greens inside— something I can hold in my hand and enjoy any time, anywhere. Like a vegetarian pork bun, but less bready. The crust on the outside would be chewy, soft, slightly crunchy.

Every once in a while I get a major craving for my mystery food— even though I don't think I've ever had such a thing in my life. Maybe I'm craving spanakopita, one of those Mediterranean phyllo dough pies filled with savory-sour dill, greens, and cheese. But even that sounds not quite chewy enough. It's weird to crave something I've never eaten, that doesn't even exist!

It's almost compulsive. Okay, it's truly compulsive. Sitting around, minding my own business, all of a sudden I'll find myself in front of the kitchen cabinets, opening each one and peering inside, shutting it, and going on to the next. Some days I'll even get out the step stool and climb all the way to the top of the shelves to peer into the hidden corners. Maybe it's up there, just out of reach.

Sometimes something interesting shows up, a forgotten ziplock bag of roasted nuts, some tepid substitute promising only temporary fulfillment, if that. Sometimes I simply sigh, shut the door, and walk away. Occasionally something inspiring will catch my eye and I'll cook up a delicious meal—which still provides only temporary fulfillment, no matter how delicious. It's always a pale imitation of this infinitely satisfying food my mind has created. But I always go back to look. It's as if I remember some food from a more spiritual existence, some nectar of the gods that I long to taste once again. Maybe I'm searching for Persephone's pomegranate seeds, the ones that transform her life forever and leave her the wife of Hades himself. I keep searching for this magic snack, although some part of me knows it doesn't exist on this plane. Chocolate comes close, though.

My unconscious pursuit of the perfect food reminds me of "A Hunger Artist," a Kafka story I always found fascinating. The hunger artist travels from town to town, hangs out in a cage, and—wait for it—doesn't eat. People come from all over to watch him not eat. At the end of the story, someone finally asks the hunger artist why he fasts, and he says simply, "I never found a food I liked."

Fortunately, in a world full of Brussels sprouts braised with olive oil and sage, asparagus parmesan soufflé, and artisanal whole wheat bread full of dried cranberries and walnuts, I have found many foods I like. Indeed, that's never been a problem. But I haven't found the food I really long for.

What is this food in my head, anyway? Let's see…it's green and good for you and so delicious. It's prepared by angels with love. The minute you bite into it, it's savory, chewy, nourishing, and wholesome. You feel instantly revitalized. A small, tiny amount, just a few bites, rejuvenates every cell, deepens your breath, clears your mind, heals your wounds, and mends your heart. It's made from plants that voluntarily separate themselves from their stalks, laying themselves at the feet of the approaching gardener who gathers them. They eagerly offer their vital energies to nourish living spirits. The angels in their chef hats, singing mantras, cook it tenderly to retain all the benefits of the generous plants. It's barely sweet, barely salty, and contains all the freshness of spring herbs, summer fruit, spreading leaves, and burgeoning seeds. It comes premade in bags or boxes…

you just open it up, sit down, and enjoy. It's a full meal, enough maybe for a whole day, maybe for a week, maybe for your family, maybe for your friends and neighbors. It multiplies like loaves and fishes, in little biodegradable containers that vaporize instantly the moment you finish them, without any greenhouse emissions. Nothing to clean up!

The part about how this food doesn't actually exist? Apparently that is no joke. Unearthing this fantasy from my unconscious mind and exposing it to the light of day is an enormous relief. I never quite realized how fragile, how futile, how very spiritual in nature my longing for the perfect food is. Perhaps my search for that perfect food in my kitchen cupboards can at last come to an end. (I'm pretty sure it's not there…but maybe I should check just one more time?)

Maybe I can start to appreciate real food for what it is, rather than always wishing it were something else. The nature of nourishment in this world is transient, not lasting, not eternally fulfilling, and, to my great disappointment, not magically reproducing. Sigh. I suppose I must learn to accept this, too. If I want fulfillment, true fulfillment, I must experience it on a spiritual path, not at the dinner table. I won't find it in the fridge, the top shelf of the cabinets, or at the bottom of a bag of potato chips. Damn it.

Saturday morning brings my first full daylong meditation retreat with Jack Kornfield at Spirit Rock. Fall is so beautiful in the Marin hills; the valleys are all misty, and deer and wild turkeys tread softly through the redwoods. In my backpack, I've tucked a thermos full of kitchari to have something warm and nourishing at the lunch break.

After settling onto my meditation cushion and listening to Jack speak, I'm a little weirded out by how well he seems to read my mind. Before the lunch break, Jack has his helpers pass out raisins from tiny paper cups, asks us to take a couple, and leads us in a mindful eating exercise. *Has he been reading my journals? Is he, like, in my head?* As we all sit, raisins in hand, Jack has us look at the raisin and appreciate it (*Wow, this raisin is super-wrinkly, it has lots of divets, oh, look, you can tell where it broke off its stem, it was a grape once, on a vine in a field, cool*), its colors, shape, and size (*Huh, it's kind of translucent, a dark purply-brown, like a tiny stained-glass window*). He asks us to place it in our mouths and feel the sensations and texture of it (*feels soft, yet firm and bumpy*), and then finally to chew it and taste its flavors. "Notice where the mind goes," says Jack. "Is it already saying, 'I want another?'" A ripple of laughter echoes through the room. *How does he know?* "Taste the sweetness of it, let it fill your mouth. Be with its raisin-ness. Keep bringing the awareness back."

It's by far the sweetest raisin I've ever tasted. Did they do something to the raisins, inject them with sugar or something? *Or have I never paid such close attention to how a single raisin tastes?* I chew and concentrate, amazed by the amount of flavor and complexity in one tiny package. I'm surprised how, with his encouragement and the focus of everyone in the room on savoring a single raisin, my attention seems happy to remain with what's in my mouth instead of its usual meandering.

Jack suggests we eat our lunch with the same level of committed attentiveness.

"Once a day, one meal a day, sit down and eat mindfully." *He's totally on to me.* "We feed the body until it's full, but we also feed some other part of ourselves that eats anyway. Remember this: You are not the desires, but the space of awareness in which they arise."

In the dining hall, I sit down at one of the long tables, arrange a napkin over my lap and open the thermos. Pouring some of the kitchari into the lid of my thermos, I cup my hands over it, enjoying the steam and the scents of ginger, turmeric, and cumin. For a moment I imagine the broccoli growing out in the field, being picked by callused hands, and ending up here, in my soup. I send a blessing out to those hands. I take a tiny bite and close my eyes. *Mmm. So tasty.* I can taste all the flavors, including the ghee. Another bite. *Eyes closed, enjoy it.* And again. I pause. *This is going to take a while,* I realize.

By the tenth bite, I feel irritated. It's annoying to have to be so mindful while eating—it feels like such an effort. I can feel a lot of impatience coming up, like, *Why can't I just eat?* I don't want to pay attention, I want to be checked out, to be inattentive and avoid the present moment. Staying in the present moment means being with whatever comes up: sadness, uncertainty, tension, and yes, the occasional joy. The impulse to push it all away, to close it up in a little box, even knowing that the possibility of joy gets locked inside too, is almost too much to resist.

But I continue eating my soup with as much mindfulness as I can muster. Part of me still wants to fill myself up with big mindless spoonfuls, just like that girl I once was, eating green ice cream lying on the green carpet. But then I don't feel full, and full is the whole point. *It's okay,* I reassure myself. *Sometimes I can be mindful and sometimes I can "just eat." Take your time, Kimber. Be patient with yourself.*

I can aspire to more mindfulness. As much as I can stand.

On Sunday I break out the brand-new hula hoop that's been sitting wrapped up just the way the UPS guy left it at our house a few months ago. A special gift for my hips. Scissors in hand, I wrestle the bubble wrap and packing tape to the ground and then give it a turn around my waist. Hula hooping was easy when I was a kid. It'll be great.

I'm *terrible* at it. Standing in the backyard on our little patch of grass, my hips can barely keep the thing above the ground. It keeps falling at my feet, knocking into my ankles and shins. This hoop is defective. My gaze turns doubtfully to the forlorn pile of bubble wrap scraps now scattered by the breeze. It's going to be tough to send it back.

"Honey, will you try this?" I call Chris outside to help. "I think this hoop is broken."

Wearing her jeans and work boots, she swings it around her waist. It stays up effortlessly, as if some magnetic force were propelling it round and round.

"Nope, works just fine. It's easy."

Ugh. Damn naturally coordinated girlfriend.

"Give me that."

Slowly, the hoop stays up a little longer, bouncing off my hips a few extra swings before clattering around my feet. My heart's pumping like crazy. It's good exercise. As long as I stay in a beginner's mind, let myself make mistakes and not get frustrated with it, it might even be enjoyable. *Yoga was hard when you first tried it and you love it now. You can do this.*

By the end of the week, after three hula hooping sessions, I'm starting to get the hang of it. It actually stays on my waist and off the ground for a few minutes. With the CD player going, playing funk hits from the nineties, I could do this all day. Hula hooping meets my ideal criteria for exercise: fun and you don't have to get anywhere.

Over the last several weeks, the habit of daily sesame oil self-massage somehow fell out of my routine. I start it back up again, and my body feels so grateful. Friendliness toward my body comes more easily when I'm taking good care of it, touching it, soothing it, holding it—when I see it through my hands and eyes rather than amplified through the mirror's still-painful reflection. Not simply cleaning it and covering it up. Perhaps if I'd been doing self-massage from an early age, like brushing my teeth or washing my face, I wouldn't have ended up in such a life-or-death struggle with my body. My life has taken a big, deep, relaxing breath now that I've developed a friendlier relationship with my body, letting it support me, taking care of it, watching all the things it can do, enjoying it, and being patient with it. Teaching it to hula hoop again.

Lying on the grass and looking up into the fiery evening sky after a reasonably successful and exhausting hoop session, I close my eyes.

"Hey, body," I whisper. "Here's my commitment to you: to love you no matter what, no matter what shape or size you are, no matter what abilities you have, just because you're mine, because you're here."

My heart holds with love each student who comes to my class, no matter what they look like, what their ability. If I can hold that open, accepting space for others, why not hold it for myself?

For lunch on Monday I have a generous bowl of homemade vegetable noodle soup and some hot tea. Half an hour later, the same old feeling of being hungry sneaks up on me. Enough already! I'm not hungry. My body doesn't need more food.

This feeling, the hungry feeling that comes up right after eating, needs a new name. My stomach is full; the feeling of fullness, tightness in my lower belly is easy to feel. But I'm still getting a signal of rumbling, gnawing hunger. Where? In my esophagus? In my stomach? Feeling of hunger after eating, I hereby christen you..."Digestion." Sir Digestion, if you prefer. Yes, you will no longer fool me with your claims of "I'm dying, feed me more!" Instead of listening to your false claims, I will henceforward enjoy the sensation of fullness in my belly.

Now a little red light goes off in my head. The renaming process reminds me a little bit of the process I went through when I was anorexic, of telling myself that I wasn't hungry and denying that I felt hunger at all. What's different now? Can I set reasonable boundaries without locking myself in the old jailhouse again? The difference now is that I really have eaten, well and mindfully, a delicious meal of vegetables, noodles, broth, and tofu. My belly is truly full. No lying or repressing is going on here. In fact, I know for a fact that my body is working on digesting and integrating my tasty meal.

It makes sense. The feeling of digestion is so similar to the feeling when my stomach is empty that I can't distinguish between the two. Hunger comes up, I eat, my body digests, then the same (or similar) hungry sensation reasserts itself, so I eat again, and the same thing happens, over and over. This feeling is digestion: the full side of hunger, not the empty side. Now it's time to enjoy those rumbling post-meal sensations and take a few moments to savor being full.

chapter fourteen

Love My Body

Today in my Tuesday noon class, one of my regular yoga students, Trish, looks at me and asks if I've gotten slimmer.

Surprised, I say, "I don't know, I don't have a scale."

In front of everyone laying out their mats and getting ready for class to start, she says, "Can't you tell by how your clothes fit?"

Okay, now I feel totally stupid. *No, I haven't noticed, okay? Because all my pants are stretchy. Because during the infrequent moments when I look at my body in the mirror, I'm trying not to judge and criticize. Because I'm attempting something new—being kind to myself on the inside and not worrying so much about what I look like on the outside. Geez.*

The truth is I've been feeling kind of bloated lately. But I'm not about to say that in front of the whole class. What a great way to start out! Will my students wonder, *Hmm, if she's feeling bloated today, will class be easier or harder? Will she teach us "swollen boat pose"?*

Blushing, I self-consciously clear my throat and ask everyone to take their seats.

Too late, the correct response occurs to me. Next time I'll strike a pose, toss my hair, and say, "No darling, but I *feel* fabulous." Inner diva to the rescue.

Why, I wonder for probably the millionth time, do people think it's okay to comment on another person's weight? "Hey, Tina, seems like you've packed on a few pounds there. Better lay off the sweets, huh?" Or "Jimbo, looking good, what did you do with those ten pounds?" Why is weight a public issue?

Trish's comment lands like a smoldering cigarette on the dry brush of my self-image. My inner anorexic's voice pipes up, fanning the flames: *See, people are watching you, just like I've always said. They think you're fat and they're congratulating you for finally starting to lose those unsightly pounds. They agree with me: you should starve yourself again.*

My inner prisoner fires back, *Shut up, shut up, shut up! Let's eat some donuts, you'll feel better.* She grins and adds some crumpled paper to feed the tongues of smoke.

Love this body, my inner therapist chimes in, stepping in and pouring a big mug of tea over the growing flames. *Love it, just the way it is.* Sizzling, the steam drifts and disperses. I repeat her cooling words to myself, again and again.

The next morning while in the shower getting ready to go teach my Wednesday class in San Francisco, my mind assesses where I'm at in this journey to Fullness. We've hit rough spots and wild storms, the wind has died, we've gotten stuck in the whirlpool, lured by sirens, held captive by Calypso...no, no, this is not that book.

But like Odysseus's journey to Ithaca, some actual progress has been made:

1. I take more time while eating to appreciate my meal and really enjoy it.

2. I sit down more often while I eat and I'm not machine-eating or bingeing.

3. I'm not eating the moment my feet hit the welcome mat or right before bed at night.

4. My body and I are starting to trust and enjoy each other more; we're starting to become friends.

5. I listen more to my body's signals both in yoga practice and around eating.

6. My inner anorexic and Svetlana have piped down, while my inner diva and inner therapist speak up more.

7. Occasionally I am not hungry.

Over the weekend, Chris and I went to see a friend in her wonderful one-woman show about menopause. During one of her hilarious monologues about using food to cope with her mood swings (marshmallow fluff and Froot Loop sandwiches), relief swept over me to realize that I'm creating better habits around food and my body now (however painstaking it might be), because who wants to be stuck with their teenage body image and eating problems for the rest of their life? I now know that I don't want to be sixty years old and afraid to be alone with a bag of Cheetos, afraid I'll end up stalking and killing the cheesy squiggles, then futilely attempt to hide the evidence of orange crumbs and crushed plastic.

I am more than my fatal attraction to crunchy, salty snack foods. I want lifelong habits that feel fantastic. I want to be shiny at sixty, sunny at seventy, awesome at eighty, and naughty at ninety. I want my desires and my beliefs about myself and the world to be aligned whenever food passes through my lips.

Sitting down to eat a quick bite, I realize one thing that has improved a lot is breakfast. Cereal and bread used to be my morning staples—and hunger crept up long before noon. Nowadays, eggs and vegetables or plain yogurt, fruit, and walnuts serve as breakfast, which seems to have eliminated my hunger before lunch. Drinking my swamp drink or some carrot juice in the afternoon helps me get from lunch to dinner with less hunger, too. Under my awareness and attention, my hunger and I have developed a working relationship.

My whole self needs to work together, to not always have the inner anorexic, Svetlana, and the inner prison guard on one side of the rope, and the inner prisoner, inner therapist, and inner diva on the other, trying to tug one another across the muddy creek bed and into the shallow water. I have the urge to jump into the game and help the latter team, the good guys, the underdogs win. But can't they all sit down and have a civilized picnic on some grassy slope?

The inner anorexic can enjoy her single green apple, confidently serene that yes, indeed, she is eating less than anyone else. The prison guard can eat his fast food meal out of the bag. Svetlana eats something I've never seen before, a big cabbage roll that reminds her of her babka in Russia. My inner therapist has a veggie sandwich full of sprouts on whole wheat bread with sunflower seeds, and my inner prisoner, still in her long, drab hospital gown, carries a bakery box full of fantastically pink frosted cupcakes (she calls them "fairy cakes" in a faux British accent) that she shares around with every-one—except the anorexic, of course, who looks at her like she's bonkers.

My inner diva accepts a cupcake, lifts a fingerful of pink sugary fluffiness to her lips, and declares, "Divine, love! Come sit by me." She smoothes out a spot on the quilt next to her, where my inner prisoner happily plops down and curls up her knees. My inner diva has a bento box in her lap, a slender wooden box divided into compartments full of fragrant rice, steamed and pickled vegetables, sautéed fish, and roasted squash sprinkled with black sesame seeds. Her red chopsticks have delicately painted white cranes flying across their stems. That woman knows how to eat.

"Of course, dahling, enjoying a good meal is a delight. By the way, your soft hips are luscious. And have I mentioned lately? You're beautiful."

My inner anorexic finds eating inconvenient and annoying, and wonders why anyone bothers. But the part of me that is content with big soft hips seems to be winning. She's steady and determined. Sweet and confident. And outrageous. And just herself. She embodies the enjoyment of life I want to embrace more and more.

My wildly fabulous inner best friend, the diva, reminds me to love the body I'm in, shaped just so. "You wouldn't change the shape of your face or the color of your eyes, would you?" she asks. "Why pick on your hips?"

My job is simply to love these things as they are, without needing to alter them or be different. Isn't that what all of us have to do? Love ourselves and one another, just as we are? Whatever we're given— offer love in return.

The secret to fullness has been there all along, like when Dorothy discovered that she and her fancy red shoes had the power to return home the whole time. I've always had it within me. Finding fullness is embracing the journey, finding satisfaction in the process itself. The reward all along the way is self-discovery, stepping into a sense of living my life fully and authentically. To eat, exercise, play, make love, meditate, swim, and relax with the sense of taking care of myself. Fully infusing it with self-love—not concealing ever-deeper levels of self-hatred.

Stopping in the bathroom one last time, before heading out the door, I brush my teeth, watching the foamy smile in the mirror.

Everything about me, or any woman, is not reducible to outer beauty or, worse yet, the numbers on the scale. Life is not a beauty contest. As women grow older, when we give up on asking ourselves who's thinner or prettier, do we instead ask who looks younger? How can we become friends of the heart when we're competing with one another? What are we competing for? A lifetime supply of insecurity and dissatisfaction? No one wins the prettiest or the most beautiful forever. The "most" anything is only temporary. It's like waves competing to be the tallest in the ocean; for a second you pause at the top of the crest, and a moment later you're part of the vast watery depths again.

But beauty remains one of the easiest things to judge people by. We are very visual, first looking for gender, closely followed, or sometimes preceded, by race, and then attractiveness. Just looking at someone, you can't tell what they do or what they're thinking or whether, like you, they like to sing along with Ella Fitzgerald's Cole Porter album. But looking at someone's appearance, we sometimes try to guess whether they are lonely on Saturday nights or whether they had a date to their senior prom. Judging people by their appearance, their beauty, their age, or what clothes they're wearing is overrated. So is fighting my weight, my body, and the sands of time.

Finally, I'm out of the house and on BART headed into the city. The train's aboveground route runs past a homeless encampment visible between the MacArthur and 19th Street stations. From the center aisle, clutching the ceiling rail as fellow commuters sway around me, I notice that people are camping under the overpass, their life's belongings piled all around them. This morning as our train rumbles by, I look to see if anyone is there, and sure enough a tired-looking woman is sitting up in her sleeping bag, using a pink compact to apply mascara.

My eyes glimpse her for only a moment before we cruise underground. My thoughts spin. What would compel me to put on makeup when I didn't have a roof over my head? Is she making a valiant effort to hold on to her beauty despite her circumstances, to retain a sense of dignity? Or even in the midst of a struggle for food and shelter, perhaps she feels driven, compelled by the need to grasp at beauty, at youth. Does it relate to her survival, her ability to get her next meal? Or does it mean something else altogether? It's fascinating and disturbing at the same time. Before glimpsing her in front of her tiny mirror, I'd assumed that the ability/desire to wear makeup wasn't consistent with homelessness.

As we head underground, the train's exterior darkens and I catch a reflection of myself in the Plexiglas window. Just a few minutes ago my eyes were looking in the mirror, in my safe, warm house, not to apply mascara, but to at least make sure I was presentable to the world. Though separated by class and circumstances, she and I aren't so different.

In my late twenties, I embarked on frequent search-and-destroy missions against any and all gray hairs, but by my early thirties, surrender was the only option. I was seriously outnumbered. Why not embrace my crow's feet and gray hairs? Rather than lusting after expensive plastic surgery treatments, why not age gracefully, be willing to look my age, be unafraid to face the world with my wrinkles, moles, stretch marks, scars, whatever?

I'm entitled to love the world, to love myself as long as my body holds breath, and to love my body in the world. I want to honor the bodies of those around me, the stories they tell of laughter, work, days in the sun, turmoil, and joy. I know a number of older women my mother's age who won't put on a swimsuit, who won't enter the water, who won't be seen unless fully dressed, who will never again feel their body touched by sun, water, air, and sky. It's heartbreaking. Let me age gracefully, so I can inspire the women around me to sense their own inner worth, to embrace the sense that their bodies and hearts are entitled to the sublime pleasures life offers. For so long I thought I had to earn these pleasures by controlling my body. But we don't earn the right to enjoy our bodies, we are born to it. Let me love this body now and as long as it breathes.

Stepping through the sliding doors, off the train and into the stream of hunched commuters, my head feels a little taller, my heart a little more open, and my body more at ease. If I had an inner Mary Tyler Moore, she'd throw her hat in the air.

All the students in class today are women, of different shapes, sizes, colors, and ages. There's almost always a mix of genders in my class, but today all the guys stayed home. Marla is in her sixties, beautiful with gray hair and an aging body she both challenges and takes good care of. Suzanne is twenty-something, with light hair, thin and willowy. Kathleen could be anywhere between thirty and fifty, tightly curled dark hair, wide hips, a radiant smile and feisty attitude. Looking out at all their faces, concentrating, breathing, smiling or frowning, it's easy for me to see how beautiful each one of them is: each gorgeous and extraordinary and amazing in her own way, deeply complicated, intelligent, and capable. I know Michelle is writing a novel, and Stacy teaches kung fu at a dojo nearby and is going to China next week. Tamare loves music and loves my classes, seeking me out whenever she can find time to practice yoga. The few I don't know also have whole histories, rich stories, and a depth of character and people in their lives that even if we'd known each other for years I'd only tap the surface of.

Full

I don't care what my students look like, how much they weigh or how old they are or whether they wear makeup or shave or can do handstands in the middle of the room. Do they love their lives? Do they live connected to what is truly important to them? That's what matters.

It's growing easier to extend that same generous, expansive, non-judging approach to my own body and appearance. When the mirror goes close-up on my thighs or my butt, that old self-conscious, hyper-judgmental attitude starts to creep up on me. A deep breath holds it off for a moment. *Hello, Butt. How's it going? Busy day today?*

My butt and I are teammates, buddies, living in the same house, answering the door together. When the bell rings and we spy Miss Anorexic and Svetlana on the doorstep, we open the door and tell them, "Judgments are no longer welcome here. No solicitors, no critics, no deliveries today."

After class, since I'm already in the city, I join my mom on a shopping trip to some of the nearby boutique stores. Ensconced on a spacious couch, I scribble some thoughts into my journal until Mom calls me over to the dressing room where she's trying on clothes. I peek behind the burgundy tapestry curtains.

"See," she says, "this dress looks great in front. But look at these rolls of fat in back!" She points to how the light cotton gathers a bit around her skin in back.

"Mom," I sigh, "you're beautiful. Your back is beautiful."

She shrugs in disgust. She doesn't buy the dress.

Some good role models on how to love my body and age gracefully would be welcome around now. Just a few weeks ago, I attended an Ayurvedic workshop offered by an older Indian woman (she was probably my mother's age) wearing a beautiful seafoam-colored, midriff-baring sari with what I'm sure Mom would call "rolls of fat" hanging out. Watching as Dr. Prakriti talked about how Ayurveda recommended eating with the seasons, I was transfixed by how completely at ease she seemed, with her round belly, comfortable in her own skin, and able to enjoy her beauty at the front of a full room of people. She was stunning.

My mother looks in the mirror and sees only what she doesn't like. In this woman I love, there's an eerily familiar self-consciousness. An inner experience I will no longer perpetuate.

❄

At home that night before bed, I delve into my journal, to record a few thoughts for the day:

I am not my mom. (I know this, but a reminder is sometimes necessary.)

My relationship to food is no longer about weight or appearance.

It's about listening to my body's needs and observing its response to what I feed it. Watching how my body changes, and observing my reaction to those changes. Practicing being kind to myself no matter what. Even seeing my frustration in a kind, loving way. And knowing that my body is amazing and capable, and always has been. That's it: eating and body image are ways to know myself better.

The difference between feeling beautiful and feeling ugly is seeing myself with kind eyes, telling myself that I'm beautiful as I am, and giving myself permission to believe it. Beauty is in the eye of the beholder...I can hold the beauty within myself and live my life from that perspective, or I can hold a sense of ugliness and inadequacy and live from that place instead. No more comparing myself to others. May I see the beauty in others without denigrating my own.

This body needs me to say yes to it, just as it is right now. No more singing that same old jingle of body-shame and dieter's promised lands. I've sung it for too long, perhaps out of habit, or just not knowing what else to sing, like when my son makes up a bit of doggerel and repeats it endlessly.

In one of Jack Kornfield's books there's a story about a tribe in Africa in which every mother, before her baby is born, goes out under the trees around the village and listens. While the new life is growing inside her, she composes a song that she sings to her unborn child. Then she teaches it to the village, so that at the moment the baby is born, the whole village sings the child into the light. Throughout the child's life, whenever she needs to be reminded of who she is, who loves her, her place in the world, she sings the song, or a loved one sings it to her, bringing her back to herself with each note. And eventually, on her deathbed, her song is sung to her as she breathes her last breath, each member of her tribe entrusting her to the spirits with her song in their hearts.

I need a song to bring myself back: the song that reminds me that I am beautiful and loved and whole. That I have a place here. That I belong in this life. I forgot my song for too long. I forgot who I was.

Maybe my song will go something like: Choose this life. Choose this body. Say yes to all of it. Say yes to the beauty and the good and the ugly and the difficult. Choose what you have, what you are. Choose this moment. Choose to love and remember. You are full. You are alive.

I choose this body just as it is. Choose it, own it, claim it as my own, as what I want, as what I've chosen. I take full responsibility for it. Throw away excuses like, "I have no willpower when it comes to chocolate," and instead say, "I choose this chocolate, I choose to eat it, I choose to have a body that eats and likes chocolate and looks like it eats chocolate!"

Every time something goes in my mouth, a choice is made. I choose this body that enjoys bread and ice cream and olive oil and butter, and lots of fresh organic fruits and vegetables, and coffee and Superfood, and fruit crisp, and herbal tea and milk. Every day, I could decide not to eat those things, and instead, every day, I choose to have a body which is a no-deprivation zone. Funny, in reality I made that choice a long time ago, when I first stopped being anorexic, but it's taken me this long to decide to own that choice, instead of holding on to the idea that someday I'll be thin again.

WHY I CHOOSE THIS BODY

- It's tall.

- It tans easily.

- It's strong and flexible.

- It's rounded and soft some places, firm in others…it has variety.

- It has a big steady seat to sit on.

- It enjoys good, fresh food.

- It enjoys sunlight.

- It enjoys exercise.

- It's pretty and fun.

- It gets me where I want to go, with grace and style.

- It enjoys being surrounded by water.

- It all works together well.

- It has a good mix of symmetry and asymmetry, which keeps things interesting.

- Sometimes it's silly and goofy.

- Sometimes it surprises me with what it can do.

- Within it, I can feel my own aliveness.

Looking at this list, would I ever trade this body in for someone else's? No way. Whether my body meets some outer standard of beauty is beside the point. It carries and plays with my son. It lets me make love to my sweet partner.

Living in this beautiful body is my choice. I choose this joy, the joy of embracing my embodiment, without qualification. I choose this perfection, the fullness of my own experience, the fullness of my own freedom to say yes to what is right in front of me, to say yes to this body, to this moment, to the choice to love myself just as I am, no longer holding back for some better time, some more ideal state.

The heaviness in my eyes tells me sleep is coming fast. Chris fell asleep ages ago. Closing my journal with the pen still inside, I slide it next to the alarm clock, shut off the light, snuggle into the warmth of her back, and let my thoughts dissolve into dreams.

Something totally mind-blowing has happened. I still can't believe it. Not long ago I received a sweet, nonchalant e-mail from a new student who works for a yoga clothing company I'd never heard of. She wanted to get together for lunch and tell me a little about the company and a "special relationship" they offer yoga instructors. I usually try to meet up with students when they ask, mostly because as a yoga student I always enjoyed meeting casually with the teachers whose classes I loved.

One overcast Thursday after my noon class, I meet Amber at a casual French café within walking distance of the yoga studio, located in a yuppie-industrial section of town. We order at the counter and settle into wicker chairs to talk about yoga and her new job garnering interest for a yoga clothing company. She hints around that her company invites fitness instructors to be "ambassadors" in the communities where they open stores. The instructors teach free classes at the store for the public and employees, and in return the company gives them free clothes and uses them in a photo shoot to advertise the new store. If I'm interested, I could be the first ambassador for the store they expect to open in Berkeley later this spring.

Excuse me? I'm trying to be cool about it, but I can't believe my ears. Yes, teaching classes, no problem; free clothes, I can accept that, I'm sure. Photo shoot? I can't have heard right. Do they really want to put my picture out there in the world, my body, my face? Isn't that something teenagers and skinny models do?

I'm sure she said photo shoot. Of me. In their clothes. All my body image insecurities go zinging off: *I'll have to go on a diet...I'll have to exercise more...I'll have to lose some weight.*

I look at the woman across from me in amazement. What she's telling me is that she thinks I would be great in a photo shoot for her company's clothing. Me, right now, just as I am, eating goat cheese salad and toasted bread, not me starving myself for a week or wracked with insecurity about how I look. Me just like this. Not some idealized me, not me after four weeks of dieting boot camp. This me, sitting here in front of her. Can't she see my giant hips?

Yes, Kimber, apparently she knows about your hips. Apparently she doesn't care. Does not care. Can you let that sink in to your brain awhile? No matter how big you happen to think your hips are, she thinks they'd be great in a photo shoot.

As we're leaving, Amber gives me a quick hug and tells me to think about her offer. Minutes pass before my brain can make sense of what just happened. Walking to the car, I can hear my inner anorexic and Svetlana plotting to slim me down for the spotlight—but they no longer run the show. My inner therapist leans back on her couch and smiles knowingly, while my inner diva looks like she's just eaten the canary. "That's right, darling. They see your hips and love them. You look fabulous just the way you are. About time the world took notice!"

The photo shoot takes place a few weeks later on a cold, rainy February afternoon. Our little band—Marty, the cameraman, Geri, a consultant from the San Francisco store, Amber, and I—stand on a hidden overlook at the top of Dwight Avenue in Berkeley. The University of California campus and, much to my amusement, the law school where my favorite class was "Poetry for the People," are below. Dressed in sleeveless, form-fitting, spanking new yoga clothes appropriate for a warm and vigorous workout, I freeze my ass off.

Amber stands nearby, just out of sight of the camera lens, holding my heavy winter coat and stepping forward to bundle me in it whenever the sun closes behind another cloud, or the rain sprinkles us. At the edge of the road, just above a plum tree in its full blossoming petticoats, I move from pose to pose—reverse warrior, bound side angle, tree pose, half moon pose—smiling into the wind and hoping the goose bumps on my arms don't show up in the final shots.

"Can you try not to smile so much?" the photographer calls to me at one point. "We don't need so much teeth."

My mouth can't help it. The whole thing is hilarious, ridiculous, like some dream come true, gone fantastically wrong. Me and my big thighs are doing yoga poses, half-dressed, in forty-degree rain, and letting someone take pictures of it! And I'm delighted by the whole thing. Ha!

Later that week Amber e-mails me a bunch of the best pictures from the shoot. She writes: "Here are the amazing photos of you. You should be proud of yourself. I am. As we are all too judgmental of ourselves, keep in mind we will choose only the best, and the ones you feel comfortable with."

My finger double-clicks the folder. Will I hate them? Will I pull my hair out and beg her not to let any of them see the light of day? Will I cry and wail and...*Just remember to breathe, Kimber. And be kind, look at these like a friend.* I scroll through the thumbnails on my computer screen. There I am, black pants, pink shirt, no goose bumps to be seen. Big smile, long hair streaming back. They're... fine. Lovely. Some of them are even beautiful. I ask Amber to discard one of them because the pose looks uncomfortable (ouch, was I doing that?), and another because a strategically placed tree in the background is rising up rather pornographically between my legs. But the rest of them, I tell her, are great.

Wow, my mind believes the photos turned out well. Is this me? Has my inner diva finally taken control? For the first time I liked a group of photos of myself. Photos that are going to be used in an ad campaign. Whoa.

In May, when the store in Berkeley opens, they hang a giant poster of me from the photo shoot over the bra shelf, me leaning back over my front leg in a wide stance, arms clasped behind. Two years later, they take it down and give it to me. I look at it sometimes. Is that really me? Is that the same me I look at in the mirror? Can I look at myself and see the same beauty in the mirror that I see in the poster? Part of me says, *Yep, that's me.* And part says, *That was just a moment in time. Let it go. Get back to the work of loving yourself now.*

Over the weekend we head up to Yosemite for my birthday. We bring up bags full of all kinds of yummy food to cook in the cabin. We fuel ourselves to hike up to see the big trees one day and hang out by the river the next. Along the rocky banks of the Merced on Sunday afternoon, we lay out big beach towels and enjoy our picnic of vegetarian BLTs (they're better than they sound). As I put the containers away in the backpack and Cooper plays in his swim trunks a few yards away near the edge of the water, I watch a big black mosquito alight on his cheek.

"Cooper! Come here, quick!"

Hearing the urgency in my voice he turns around and takes a few hurried steps toward me. Without thinking, I smack him across the cheek where the mosquito is sucking on his face. The look on his face when his eyes meet mine is utter betrayal.

Holy shit. My child thinks I just slapped him for no reason. I've never laid a hand on him for *any* reason. He thinks…

"Oh crap, honey, I'm so sorry…"

I reach for him, shaking my hand, showing him the smear of insect and blood across my palm. I'm horrified. *What did I just do?* I can't breathe.

"Oh my God I'm so sorry are you okay I didn't mean it! Mosquito, see?"

His eyes widen. His expression shifts from hurt to incredulity to the faintest smile. And suddenly we're laughing. Out of relief or absurdity, who knows? Every time we look at each other, and the bloody, smushed bug on my hand, we burst out in more breathless laughter.

Chris, worried by the commotion, strides over, concerned.

"What's going on?"

But I can't talk clearly enough to get the story out straight. Holding my belly with one hand, I shake the red splotch on the other in her face, as if that will explain everything.

"Slap…Bug…Cooper…"

She can't help but laugh with us now that Cooper and I have tears running down our cheeks. We lie back on the rocks and release our breath into the sky.

Later back at the cabin, Cooper and Chris go outside to see if the tiny creek might harbor some critters, and I pick up one of the magazines that previous visitors have left there. This one has a picture of Julia Roberts in a green dress. I look at it more closely and notice how skinny she seems. *Thank God I don't have to be that skinny for my work.*

That's the first time I've had a spontaneous reaction to a model that wasn't based on envy or defensiveness ("Man, I wish I looked like that," or "She's probably just airbrushed to look like that"). Instead, just the simple recognition of how much work it must take to look like that all the time (with or without airbrushing), and relief that it's not my fate. I get to enjoy eating well, whatever my body wants.

Physical appearance is not the most important thing about me or anyone else. What matters is the heart and the spirit. The body is important and its pleasures are wonderful and sweet, but they are not all there is. My life is about deepening my spirit, opening my heart, and helping others do the same. My body needs me to recognize its outer form, to tend it, take care of it, honor it, and also recognize that it is impermanent, not my whole self. As the sacred vehicle I live in, it allows me to explore and interact and be present in the world. It allows me to discover beauty in myself and everywhere. And have wild, joyous belly laughs.

chapter fifteen

Share the Love

"Do you think of your body as your best friend?" I ask my friend Marjorie one afternoon as we drive down I-5 to Los Angeles for a three-day advanced yoga workshop with John Friend.

She grows thoughtful. I told her about little Emily's "body equals best friend" moment and how I was working on cultivating that kind of friendship with my body. Marjorie and I have been friends for years and I've learned much from her no-nonsense wisdom and honesty. She'll know whether the body-as-best-friend metaphor will resonate with other women too.

"I used to think of my body as my best friend." Marjorie looks out the window at the startlingly green hills, a gift from winter rains on this normally sun-parched stretch of highway. "When I played water polo in college, I loved how readily my body responded to the constant training. I felt strong and connected. Invincible."

She grows quiet, her eyes searching the grassy landscape.

"It's changed tremendously over the years. With all my various injuries and now aging, that connection was severed." She turns her palms up on her lap and gazes into them. "I hate to say it, but right now I mostly feel a sense of frustration with my body's limitations."

I chew my lower lip as my eyes follow the dotted white line of the highway.

"Well, what if your body really were your best friend? Do you give up on your friends when they get injured or disabled?" My hands resting lightly on the steering wheel, I wonder out loud, "Do we ditch our friends when they start to show gray hairs? Do we say, 'You suck, you can't do a cartwheel. How dare you feel pain or get wrinkles?' If our friendships grow deeper over time and through difficulties, why shouldn't our relationship with our bodies work the same way? What if you could cultivate an unconditional friendship with your body that endured through all your body's changes, gaining weight, losing weight, having a baby, breastfeeding, getting older, menopause, illness, disability, everything? That instead of feeling alienated from your body, these changes brought you closer to your body?"

Marjorie laughs. "Yeah, right."

"When a friend gets sick, we bring them soup and books and help them heal in every way we know how. When a friend gains weight, we reassure her that she's always beautiful to us, and tell her no, you look great just the way you are. When a friend complains about aging, we tell her, honestly, that we don't know what wrinkles she's talking about, that she looks lovely, that age is just a number. We can start by just treating our bodies like the sweet, lifelong friends that they are, let them know we value their companionship, and focus on what they can do, not on what they can't."

"Or what they aren't," Marjorie says. "You wouldn't compare your best friend to some airbrushed photo in a magazine. Or to some skinnier, younger friend."

"And you'd never insult your best friend to her face. If someone insulted her, telling her she's fat and ugly, you'd go on endlessly about what a total asshole they were, how they probably had serious mental problems, and that if she believed it for a moment, she is as insane as they are. You'd take her out dancing and shake your booties together until she remembered how beautiful she is."

"In fact," Marjorie adds, "if you really loved your best friend, you probably wouldn't even think bad things about her. You'd see nothing but how amazing she is."

I nod. "So, why do we go around acting like it's okay to insult ourselves in the mirror? What would you say to your best friend if she was having a bad hair day, or if she told you she looked terrible? If you were a good friend—and not the kind who says, 'Yeah, babe, you look like crap'—you'd say, 'Oh, hon, you're just a little tired. Get some good sleep tonight and you'll feel better.' Or, 'You look great, I love your hair, you're a goddess no matter what.'"

Marjorie and I crack up thinking of what we could say to ourselves in the mirror instead of our usual litany of complaints and criticisms.

1. Hey, beautiful. (A classic, this is one my next-door neighbor always greets me with when I'm not with Chris.)

2. You sexy thing. (Wink, wink.)

3. What a fine-looking woman! (Satisfying self-assessment.)

4. You look fabulous, darling. (Vintage Billy Crystal.)

5. Now that's what this mirror was made to see! (Not a total fabrication.)

6. You gorgeous goddess. (Divine.)

7. Looking good. (Appreciative and affirming.)

8. You're the first, you're the last, my everything... (Cue Barry White music.)

Many of these, we decide, require a hair toss, a look over the shoulder, and a sultry glance into the mirror.

"What if the lighting is bad?" Marjorie considers. "Bad lighting makes me look like the Crypt Keeper."

"Mmm. Yeah, we need a rule about that. Bad mirrors suck. If you don't like the reflection you see, it's not your fault. Horror-show lighting happens…you don't have to take it personally."

"Don't believe a bad mirror," Marjorie smiles. "That's what your best friend would say."

We lean back into the headrests, laughing.

"The thing about a best friend," says Marjorie, taking a deep breath, "is that she knows your stories. She knows when you're being too hard on yourself and when you're not trying hard enough. She's not afraid to say so either, but lovingly." Her hand traces the warm edge of the dashboard. "That's it—she loves you through thick and thin, forgives your flaws and mistakes, and she reminds you when you forget who you really are. We can do that for ourselves. And each other."

We lapse into silence for a few minutes as the petals from the nearby almond orchards swirl across the road, collecting in drifts along the shoulders.

I speak. "You know, if we relate to our *own* bodies with more love, we make it more likely that Emily will be able to grow up and always feel like her body is her best friend."

"I like that." Marjorie tilts her head. "She inspires us to love our bodies now; we inspire her to keep loving her body later. What's the opposite of a vicious circle? A tender square? A compassionate triangle? How about a loving polygon?" She laughs, looking over her glasses at me. "A *virtuous* circle, that's it. Sounds so pure. Whatever, it works for me."

After our first yoga session the next day, Marjorie and I meet for sushi with our friend Denise and a new friend Eva. Sitting down at the polished table, I tell them about the yoga workshop I want to put together to help women deal with body image in a friendlier and more loving way.

"What do you think it is about yoga that helps us be nicer to ourselves?" I ask, pulling my chopsticks from their paper holder and balancing them lightly in my hand. "Yoga's made a huge difference in my ability to listen to my body and become more in tune with my inner and outer well-being. What else?"

Marjorie unfolds her napkin into her lap and scoots her chair forward.

"For me it taps into a deep animal pleasure, a basic sensory experience of being in my body. It reminds me that being in the body is what life is all about."

Nodding, Denise says, "It's like being a kid again, in your body, feeling the pleasure and the possibility. Going upside-down, twisting, balancing, it alters your perspective on what's real and what matters."

Eva leans her forearms against the table. "The power in yoga is that it doesn't matter if you want to change or think you don't need to…"

"…or deserve to…" Marjorie adds.

"…it changes you." Eva tells us that when she first started yoga she found herself constantly repeating the words "I can't do that" in every pose, even if she was actually doing the pose. She started to realize how often she repeated that phrase throughout her life.

"It's the shift from the head to the heart," Marjorie observes. "Instead of getting caught up in the self-talk that's running the show, we begin to see that all the mental patterns are optional."

"That's right," Eva continues. "Once I'd noticed my 'I can't' mind, I could stop listening to it and stop believing it. I almost never say 'I can't' anymore. And I can do more than I ever guessed." She taps the end of her chopsticks lightly against the edge of the table. "There's something about the practice of yoga you fall in love with. It's hard to explain what touches you so deeply about it."

I share how when I first started taking lots of yoga classes, I would sneak off to a class and make up stories about where I'd been. "I was just grocery shopping, honey, see, here's the milk!" It felt like I was having an affair, or becoming a junkie. "I need a yoga fix, now. Please—just ninety minutes."

Steaming bowls of fragrant rice and vegetables arrive, and we pass them around the table. As we settle down to eating, Marjorie tells us about seeing a picture of herself that had been taken years ago during a beach yoga retreat, doing an arm balance in the sand.

"It was horrible." She grimaces. "I looked awful in my bikini, and the pose was all wrong. I hated that picture. But my teacher insisted that it was lovely. 'See the effort, the concentration, the beauty in your expression?' She said, 'Marjorie, you're a teacher, too. If you can't see the beauty in your own face and feel comfortable with a picture taken of yourself, then who can?' It was such a good reminder for me."

"I hate seeing photos of myself," Eva agrees. "They can send me spiraling out for a week."

"Years ago, I had a Twister party at my house…" I say as I warm my hands around the mug of green tea. Everyone at the table bursts out laughing.

"No one should be allowed to hold a camera during Twister," says Denise.

"Exactly. A friend later gave me a stack of pictures, and of course one was of my butt, taken from behind. It was huge! Like a still shot from *The Butt That Ate Manhattan*. I was horrified. I immediately started planning a stringent diet, figuring out how I could starve myself again. But first I would burn that pair of pants in a ritual bonfire, during which I would sell my soul to the devil in exchange for making me wickedly skinny again.

"After my initial freak-out, I got to thinking about it. I realized that the Twister party had happened months ago. I had been totally fine in the meantime, not obsessed with my body, not feeling bad about my body at all. And then this one picture comes along and BLAM. I gave up my well-being and all my acceptance and love for my body to this one picture. I gave all my power away to an inanimate object and let it determine how I should feel about myself. I realized how crazy it was to surrender all my power to one photo."

"Those shifts add up," nods Eva. "You get one insight and you add another, and another onto that. But it's not all one breakthrough and everything changes. One insight is just the beginning."

"You have to use your insights to create a new pattern, a new habit. One you actually want," I add.

"The way water creates a canyon," Marjorie murmurs, gazing at the pot of lucky bamboo in the center of the table. "You have lots of little awakenings that pull the dust away from the rocks, and you make room for more insight to flow through. Until you have a whole river."

We finish our meal and sit back in our chairs. Full.

"Join me for a special Love Your Body Workshop next month," I announce in my classes the following week. At the end of many Buddhist practices, there is a moment when you bring your hands together in front of your heart and ask, "May this practice benefit all beings." The time has come to share my journey with other women, to see if we can inspire and support one another in cultivating friendly and loving relationships toward our bodies.

The afternoon of the workshop arrives, and I prepare my friend Bonnie's backyard studio, sweeping the bamboo floor with an industrial-size dust mop, and murmuring prayers about clearing away obstacles to awareness. Inside the studio, tucked away in the folds of a grass-lined neighborhood, surrounded by lumbering pines and fig trees, you feel a sense of placelessness; you could be anywhere, prepared to meet yourself at last in the lap of the world, in the palm of this moment.

Ten women of all shapes, sizes, and ages arrive, and we settle into a circle under the skylights with our name tags, blankets, and yoga mats scattered across the floor. We listen as each woman recounts the journey that brings her here: for one, a health crisis, another aging, another, like me, a recovering anorexic, and another recovering from an abusive childhood. For some, a positive relationship with their body feels like a fairytale dream; for others, a positive relationship feels possible, real, and growing with each day. I tell them my history of disordered eating, and share how affected I was that day at Cooper's preschool, hearing Emily's dad recount her assertion that her body was her best friend, and by the woman at the college gym, whose hands worshipped her own body.

"We forget sometimes," I say as I let my hands settle onto my thighs, "that what you say about your body and how you treat your body affects the people around you. If you hate your body and treat your body poorly, people sense it. Sometimes they even imitate it, the way children unconsciously mirror their parents. If you love your body, and if you show up and step into the world embodying a spirit of love toward your body, others sense that love and learn to imitate it instead."

Looking out at their beautiful faces, I share that I had realized that loving my body wasn't just about me. I have a responsibility, not just to myself and my own body, but to other women, and to Emily. That responsibility extends to my mother, and my sister, and all my students, and to anyone I interact with: May everyone in my life see me embrace my body and my whole self with love. If I don't do that, I'm not just letting myself down, I'm letting everyone else down, too. It might feel like a daunting task, to think of it that way, but it inspires me to remember that loving my body is important work, not selfish or self-obsessed.

I shift my legs underneath me and lean into the circle.

"By supporting one another and in our hearts doing the inner work of learning to love ourselves, we make it easier for Emily to grow up and always feel that her body is her best friend. Perhaps she, and girls like her, won't have to go through the same struggles that so many of us have been through. Through our efforts, we make it more likely that she will have more inner and outer support in her life, that all around her she'll see women who love themselves, and that she'll see a woman who loves herself every time she looks in the mirror."

I laugh conspiratorially. "I have this fantasy that we'll start happy naked women flash mobs, all different kinds of women, showing up in gyms with oil and lotion, sitting in front of mirrors and lovingly touching their bodies. Showing other women it can be done. It's loving-your-body performance art!"

The room sparks with shrieks of delight...but do I also detect some horror?

"Don't worry," I reassure them, "that's not the next part of the workshop. You may never feel comfortable doing that, and that's fine. But can you do everything but that? Can you love yourself completely in the privacy of your own space? Can you let your love for yourself be an example to everyone around you?"

The room grows still, contemplating the possibilities.

One student, Patricia, who had lived in Japan for two years, tells us the story of her first experience at a Japanese public bathhouse.

"I was completely embarrassed to be naked in front of a group of women, including my female friends, and all the other bathers, strangers I'd never seen before in my life. My Japanese friends were totally at ease, having grown up visiting the baths. I went in, pink and blushing from head to toe, and saw five or six women on low stools in front of faucets and basins, in their sixties, seventies, and eighties, all sitting together, totally naked, chatting and scrubbing one another's backs. It was no big deal. I was blown away. It was incredible to see how deeply comfortable they were with their own bodies and with one another. Without saying anything, they gave me permission to feel at ease in my body, too."

"Accepting and being comfortable with your body is a huge intermediate step for many of us," I echo. "One that usually has to come long before you can consider the possibility of loving your body. The first step is letting go of criticism and judgment toward the body. No more name-calling or comparisons. That alone would be a huge accomplishment for many of us.

"The second step is acceptance, a sense of the body as normal and fine, and a willingness to engage in a neutral way with your body. Being comfortable and unashamed naked or in a swimsuit in a public space is a good testing ground. Then we can move to a more loving space, one of kindness and enjoyment within our bodies. But we have to give ourselves the time and the space to find our way, and hold within our hearts a vision of what's possible."

I lay a wide piece of butcher paper on the floor and draw a big circle in the middle of it. Inside the circle I write "New Rules About Bodies and Body Image."

"We internalize lots of rules about what our bodies are supposed to look like and how we're supposed to feel about our bodies.

Unhappy, stupid, unrealistic rules, like, you're not supposed to have flab, you're not supposed to have cellulite, you're not worth loving if you're not two sizes smaller than you are now. We impose many of these rules on ourselves and one another, even as we're desperately trying to unlearn them.

"Imagine if we could start over and make entirely new rules for ourselves around bodies and body image, what new rule would you invent?"

I invite everyone to grab a colored marker and write their new rule into a bubble off the main one. As everyone adds their ideas, the page transforms into a wild flower, with crazy petals spraying from the center. Here are our rules:

1. Self-care, self-love is not self-indulgent: You don't need an excuse to look after yourself.

2. Eat lunch. Don't skip lunch.

3. Feel. Feel good in your body. Don't judge feelings.

4. Celebrate all bodies.

5. Nourish yourself. Health is sexy.

6. Learn and practice massage on friends and family.

7. Inner beauty is more valuable than outer beauty.

8. Curvy or flat, flabby or toned, all bodies are fine.

9. Hair anywhere, everywhere, is okay.

10. Whether or not you love your body does not have to have anything to do with how it looks. Love your body no matter what.

That last rule, that's mine. Ditching conditions is the key to loving our bodies no matter how much weight we gain or lose, whether we can do handstands or need to spend hours or days in bed nursing our wounds and illnesses. We don't have to wait until we feel better to be our body's best friend. Even today, when I've eaten too much ice cream, when I've noticed another crease under my eye and its neighbor, a newly arrived pimple. Loving my body because it's my body, because I'm worth loving.

"You might think, what's the point of making up these rules, they don't change anything." I circle the tip of my finger across the poster, encompassing our efforts. "You can change the rules of your own life. Change how you treat your own body. Live by your own rules."

The sun streaks brightly through the skylights, revealing tiny dust motes floating through our circle. We breathe together for a moment, and I ask everyone to get into a comfortable seated position.

"Close your eyes, and ask yourself the question: Right now, how do I feel about my body, does it feel like it's my best friend? How do I want to feel toward my body?

"Imagine that you are able to cultivate a deep sense of love and friendship toward your body. Imagine that you're able to feel toward your body the way you want, to create a relationship with the body that embraces all the changes it goes through. What would that look and feel like? What do you need to shift in your mind and heart to make this change possible?"

I ask them to contemplate these questions for a moment, and when they're ready, to write down their thoughts and even share their insights with the group.

After a few minutes, Talya, a tall and willowy newspaper editor, lays her journal down beside her.

"My body and I are like acquaintances or distant cousins: people who see each other every day from a distance, who know each other's name, and who like each other, but don't know much about whether the other one likes music or art, hiking, or playing on the beach. It's weird, I don't know my body very well, it feels like a stranger to me. There's potential there for some kind of friendship, but we have to get to know each other first. Bodywork, yoga, going on long walks with my dog, even just checking in with how my body feels during the day will help me bridge that gap. Maybe I should send my body text messages to check up on how it's doing: *Hey body, how RU?* For many years now, I've been healing my mind, and I hadn't realized how badly I needed to take care of my body and learn its language. I was mean to my body, ignoring it, and now I'm trying to be more loving. Every day if I can."

It's Tina's turn to speak. With two recently adopted kids at home and not enough time for herself, I know Tina is struggling. She looks at me with tears in her eyes.

"I don't know how to be a friend to my body. I always felt like my body wasn't curvy enough. And then later I developed chronic fatigue, and my frustration with my body reached a peak when I found out I couldn't have a child. All my life I told myself, I'm a woman, I'm going to have a baby and my breasts are finally going to be big and round and beautiful, and I'm going to breastfeed. All of that was denied me, and it's still so painful. I adore my kids, and I wouldn't change anything about them, but I still feel this deep level of anger toward my body."

Infertility is something I know very little about. Cooper was conceived after just three months of attempts. But I do know what it's like to feel betrayed and disappointed by your body.

I begin cautiously, laying my hand reassuringly on Tina's knee.

"The feeling of betrayal when we're injured or when our body isn't performing for us in the way that we had expected and hoped is something we all experience at various times. I don't know that particular experience. But you are not alone. Several years ago I broke my foot, and I remember feeling so frustrated and angry at my body, like, 'How can you do this to me?'

"If we're working with the premise that my body is my best friend, then what do we do when our best friend has let us down? We have to talk about it: 'You're my best friend, and I feel betrayed.'"

I turn to the group.

"We have to speak and listen. 'This is what I expected of you, this is what you did, and this is what happened.' We take responsibility for our mind's expectations and openly listen to our body's reasons for not meeting them. We have to accept what's happened and be willing to move forward. In a close friendship, discussing a rift often results in both friends knowing each other better, and the relationship grows stronger as a result of the difficulty, rather than weaker. The relationship heals in the broken places. And then we forgive. Remember to give yourself credit. You've come a long way already in your body. You're in this together."

My knees and hips tell me that we've been sitting for a long time and it's time to do some yoga practice. I lead them through a gentle sequence while sharing what worked to shift my relationship with my body to one of greater friendship and affection.

"The most important way in which I cultivate my friendship with my body is yoga practice. In fact, treating my body to yoga is the main way I take care of my mind as well. Basically, I do yoga instead of taking Prozac. I've never taken antidepressants, but I definitely notice that if I skip my yoga practice several days in a row, not only does my body start to whine and complain, but my mind revs up the old Critic-o-matic: 'You don't brush your teeth hard enough, you should spend more time flossing, why don't you know when to keep your mouth shut, I told you not to put those red socks in with the white towels, you nitwit!' The inside of my head is a much nicer place to live when I do yoga every day.

"My brain needs it, my cells need it, my muscles and bones need it. If I miss a practice occasionally, once a week or so, it's not a big deal. My yoga practice gives me a deep awareness of my body's needs and a profound respect for what it's able to do.

"The Buddhist practice of loving-kindness, *maitri* or *metta*, has also helped tremendously. Pema Chödrön calls *maitri* the cultivation of 'unconditional friendship with yourself,' the simple practice of relating to your mind with a basic attitude of friendliness. I've been applying it to my body: I try to notice my habits around my body, what I say about it and to it, holding whatever I notice very gently, with friendliness, love, and nonjudgment. In *Eat, Pray, Love*, Elizabeth Gilbert describes a moment when she accidentally sees a reflection of herself in the mirror of a hotel lobby, and moves toward the familiar face, thinking that she's about to encounter and embrace a friend of hers she hasn't seen in a while. She's startled and pleased to suddenly realize it's her own face. Can you see your best friend in the mirror? Or even just someone you'd like to get to know better, and treat well?

"The third practice that's changed how I relate to my body is self-massage with natural oils. I first learned about it from my philosophy teacher, Carlos Pomeda, who's an older Spanish scholar. I remember him saying, 'I do self-massage every day.' I tried to wrap my mind around that. I realized if Carlos can do this, surely I can, too.

"Then when I did my first Ayurvedic cleanse with Mark Altar, he asked us to do self-massage every day with warmed, raw, organic sesame oil. I loved it. Every morning, sometimes before I shower, sometimes after, I massage my entire body with natural oils. It's also very powerful to repeat a blessing or mantra while you do it. I use *Om Namah Shivaya*—'I honor the divine within myself.' Some folks prefer almond oil, and if you ask an Ayurvedic consultant, you can get a recommendation about what oil would be good for your body type. In fact, you probably have olive oil at home, you could do this today.

"The fourth practice that has helped me be a better friend to myself has been mirror practice: looking in the mirror and thinking of five good things I can say to my reflection. John Gottman, a marriage specialist, says that for every one negative interaction in a relationship, we need five positive ones in order to balance it out. So for every one negative thought you have toward yourself…you get the idea. If you're like me, you're going to be busy reminding yourself of your five positive things often.

"See the beautiful in yourself. I've even started to invite in a practice of seeing the goddess in myself. My friend Marjorie, who's helped me think through a lot of these ideas, told me the other day that she was at work and had to run off to meet a date. She went into the bathroom at her work, which has terrible, uber-stylish lighting, and all she could see were huge bags under her eyes and straggly hair. She turned away from the mirror, bent forward and ran her hands through her hair upside-down, gently pinched her cheeks, and took a deep breath. She turned back to look in the mirror, posed with her arm behind her head, and said, 'Hey, goddess.' And she saw it. The goddess looking back at her. She felt fantastic and her date went beautifully. That's a really different way to relate to the mirror than we usually do. Can we start to take even the tiniest little steps in that direction, to try it out, try it on?

"The last thing is: Let go of relationships and situations that don't support your growing friendliness toward your body. Avoid friends who like to criticize and obsess about weight and appearance, their own or anyone else's. Tell family members that you'd be happy to talk to them about anything else. If someone insists on talking about it, tell them about your new resolve to become better friends with your body. Spend time with friends who reflect back to you your own beauty and worthiness. Gather to yourself what serves you and let go of what doesn't serve you.

"Chris, my dear partner, looked over the materials for today and said, 'You didn't include how important it is to have a partner who loves your body.' I said, 'Yes, that's true, but you can't just go out and buy one at the drugstore.' Having an adoring partner is a very helpful thing and if you can arrange that in your life, I recommend it. Don't put up with dissatisfaction with your body from partners. Find someone who loves you whatever shape or size or weight you are."

The sun has shifted, casting broad shadows across our bodies. I ask everyone to lie on their backs, knees bent.

"Place your hand at the center of your chest, and feel your heart beating, the softness of your skin. Offer your body a sense of reassurance, in words or through a feeling. Tell your body, I love you, I want to love you, I want to get to know you better, I want us to celebrate and enjoy life together, I want to feel whole. Tell your body whatever it needs to hear, tell yourself whatever words are most reassuring. Let each breath be a gift to yourself."

I hear their breath soften and lengthen.

"May love pour into your body like rain on a parched landscape, softening you down to the roots and making space for you to grow from the inside out."

chapter sixteen

The Goddess Within

I am not hungry today. This journey began out of curiosity, wondering why my hunger was so persistent. And slowly along the way, my hunger ebbed. It hasn't vacated the premises entirely, but I know when to expect it and why: usually right around my period, in the morning before breakfast, or after a long stretch of teaching. It comes and goes, like hot and cold, and I've learned to be okay with that. The truth is my need for nourishment is only partially met by the colorful mounds of food on my plate, no matter how delicious. *How* I feed myself is at least as important as *what*. And how I treat myself and value this body and vast life I share with so many other amazing beings…that's where the big, hand-drawn X marks the spot labeled "Fullness."

By examining my hunger, talking about it, letting it guide me, I've learned more than I thought possible about myself. I've found that body image and hunger are largely internal, passive experiences. "I'm hungry" happens inside the black box of my head, and leaves me feeling that there's nothing to be done about it but eat a big meal.

Unless we're visibly starving, no one sees another's hunger, just like no one sees the magazine images that we carry around in our heads and compare ourselves to. Weirdly, those magazine images feel passive, too, as if I had rented an apartment plastered in old Cindy Crawford and Farrah Fawcett posters, now barely visible under images of Lady Gaga dressed as an aristocratic alien and Rihanna wrapped in thick black duct tape. Some part of me felt I wasn't entitled to strip the walls bare and hang something different.

Today I mentally pull those endless layers of dusty posters off the walls, fill in the cracks, smooth on a coat of fresh paint, and hang new pictures of myself enjoying life. Pictures of me practicing yoga, hula hooping, meditating, playing ball with Cooper in the yard, with Chris's arms around me in an embrace.

The invisible has become visible, bringing into the light my discomfort with hunger and with my body image, and as I suspected, they are completely intertwined, like a trellis interwoven with jasmine. My dislike of my body left me feeling dissatisfied with myself and my life, mired in a profound sense of unworthiness that left me hungry for more. Having made peace with my body, ending the comparisons, holding myself with love, my hunger has subsided and a sense of well-being has filled its place.

There's a part of me that knows to enjoy this time now. I'm feeling good, enjoying my body. The neighbor who calls me "Beautiful" said today, "Looking great as usual!" and I responded, "Thank you," finding a special sweetness there.

Last night while getting ready for bed, I noticed a new wrinkle that's forming by my lip, on the left upper side, and I can see that it's one of many getting ready to move into the neighborhood. Even so, I'm reveling in a feeling of renewed youth, enjoying whatever bit of beauty is present at this moment, no longer paralyzed with the self-consciousness and self-hatred that inhabited me for so many years. I was obsessed with being perfect and beautiful, like a porcelain doll, forgetting that the purpose of life is to live fully, not to die perfect.

❄

It's time for the ultimate test of my new body image. The mirror test. I've known all along I would circle back to this place, but my mind wasn't ready yet. Can I, looking into a full-length mirror, lovingly apply oil to my whole body, including my butt, hips, and thighs? I've had several years of regular practice—massaging oil onto my body daily, repeating mantras of seeing my own divine nature. But always in the shower, or with my back turned to the mirror over the sink. A trembling nervousness arises, like I'm about to perform a solo on stage. Has anything changed, or will my hands become cold, clammy, and paralyzed as they approach East Thigh and West Thigh? Can I love the woman I see in the mirror?

My plan of action: rather than sitting naked in the sterile atmosphere of the bathroom or the disheveled mess of the closet—the only two places big mirrors hang in our house—"the stage" will be in the yoga room, in front of a free-standing mirror. My little yoga studio, the sparsely furnished spare bedroom in our house, is a powerful place for me; it was there, during my yoga practice, that my body began to feel like home.

First I cover the windows with blankets—I like the neighbors, but not that much—turn on the heater, and lay a large beach towel on the floor, a stool in the center of it, and another colorful beach towel on top. Then I light a candle, fire up a stick of my favorite sandalwood incense, and rearrange my altar, with its stones and statues, a drawing of a dragonfly from a student, a picture of Pema to the left, a photo of me doing dancer's pose in front of an uprooted giant sequoia to the right, and off to the side, my handmade hunger goddess, holding her precious trinkets. A fingertip pulled along the surface tells me the free-standing mirror is dirty. I briefly consider ignoring the dust, but realize I want the mirror to be clean and radiant, to truly reflect whatever beauty I might be capable of seeing.

I make myself a cup of tea, get my pajamas ready to step into afterwards, and warm the bottle of sesame oil in a bowl of hot water. And now, music. It takes me no time to choose one of my favorite CDs, by a kirtan band that performs a version of *Om Namo Bhagavate Vasudevaya* that I adore. In it, the female vocalist sings a poetic translation of a line from the Persian poet Hafez: "Because the beloved one lives inside of you, I gather you close against my heart." Singing this chant opens my heart to Chris and Cooper and every-one I love, and fills me with the longing to open toward myself.

Turning up the volume, I stand back, and gaze at my clothed self in the mirror. Ready? *Ready.* Slowly I remove my necklace, earrings, bracelet, rings, and set them carefully on the desk. I undress in the mirror as if for a lover, first my top, then my pants, and then my undergarments. Sitting on the stool, shy at first, swaying to the music, I pour a handful of warm oil into my palms and smooth it along my arms. They feel strong and supple. I drizzle oil down my chest and belly and across my thighs, and soak in the feeling of warmth on my skin, the feeling of taking care of myself this way. I catch a glimpse of my hips and thighs and I feel a shudder of aware-ness, a bubbling up of my inner critical voices, the old habit of com-paring this body to something outside myself. Rubbing oil on my knees, I sense a choice: I can follow those voices down their old path or settle into this new one: me, the mirror, the music, the desire to see beauty in myself. I take in a deep breath. It's not a hard choice. Not anymore.

Smiling into the mirror, I see my expression: bedazzled, amused, delighted. My smile widens and I laugh. I beam back at my reflection and can't help laughing again; my smile is now stuck on bright.

Rubbing oil onto my hips and my thighs, I remember why I love them. They're curvy and strong, they're soft and nice to look at. My hands move to my butt, and as I see them moving across my skin, it feels, miraculously, like just another part of this beautiful, whole body that is mine. *I love you*, I whisper to my body. *Thank you... Thank you.*

Singing along with the mantras, *Sri Ma* (meaning Dearest Divine Mother, among other things), and that old favorite, *Om Namah Shivaya*, I drench my hands in oil and soak my elbows, ankles, and feet, those parched places, in the warm ointment. I lift up one leg and then the other to get better access to my butt, and continue laying on the oil in circles and strokes, using my elbows against the sides and tops of my thighs, and when my favorite song starts, I push the stool out of the way and dance.

"Because the one I love lives inside of you, I lean as close to you as I can." I brush my fingers through my hair and point to myself in the mirror. Dark, wavy hair, big smile, long arms, breasts like small handfuls, succulent belly. My hips spiral, my thighs turn, my butt jumps. I laugh and sing and sway. I can see her right there. The goddess is here.

The glow of my body dims somewhat overnight, but I look fondly into the mirror of the yoga room the next morning as I sweep the floor, chasing the dust bunnies out of the corners, preparing for my practice. An old longing arises to write about this journey that my hands have taken, finally offering love to the unloved parts of me inside and out. I want to tell the story of how I met my hunger and let it teach me how to feel full. I light the candle on the altar and lay out my mat, sighing to myself: *I don't have time to write a book about anorexia, or yoga, or applied spirituality. Or rather, I do have time, but I*

can't make myself do it. The truth is, I have the time, and I can make myself write, but—I'm afraid to cultivate the self-discipline and control required to write an entire book.

When I think about committing myself to writing every day, my imagination pulls the inner anorexic and Svetlana up from the back of my mind, where they stand close together, whispering and plotting their long-awaited coup. Not so intimidated by them, and not willing to put up with their antics, I ask what they're up to. "We," they look at each other and nod, "know all about self-discipline." Their eyes drop to their feet, clasping their hands behind their backs.

"Yeah, that's true," I concede, "but I don't trust you enough to let you steer the boat. You'll hold me captive, make a massive U-turn, and head us back to that desert island where I was starving to death."

"Give us another chance. Look, you don't want to starve yourself anymore. We get that. Let us help you. Self-discipline is what we're good at. You can't do this without us."

I take a deep breath and, placing my feet at the top of my mat, begin my warm-up sequence of sun salutations.

They're right. I've spent years writing down little spurts of ideas here and there, tons of journal entries and musings. If the book is going to happen, I have to buckle down and get serious about the process of writing. But I'm afraid to cultivate any kind of intense self-discipline that might involve restriction or deprivation again, afraid that it will open up the Pandora's box of my anorexic mindset, and I'll catapult myself into that painful, hungry world again, the one I've worked so hard to escape.

My inner therapist emerges from the shadows and reaches for the anorexic's hand. "It's okay," she says. "We can work together on this. You've come so far. You have a fundamental sense of friendliness and worthiness now that you didn't have before. You treat your body with kindness and concern, and see the beauty in it. You can tap into your inner strength. You know how to keep from turning it on yourself."

The diva appears, in a fabulous, high-collared coat, and puts her arm through Svetlana's. "I'll keep an eye on them, too, darling. We're all in this together." She reaches up and kisses Svetlana on the cheek. "If you don't play nice, no more tea parties for you." Svetlana looks worried for a moment, and then smiles awkwardly, like she's recently become accustomed to gentle teasing.

I know how to write a book: how to be focused and determined, self-directed and highly motivated. That's exactly what I did while starving myself, constantly pushing myself, "encouraging" myself, nurturing along the dream of thinness, using every ounce of spare energy for its success. And I've spent all these years being afraid to use that motivating energy, because of how terrifyingly powerful that energy is. After all, I used it to try to kill myself.

But moving through my standing poses, warrior two, side angle, triangle, half moon, following my breath, I realize that my vital power isn't inherently bad or negative at all—it's my ability to turn my dreams into reality. Like the energy of my body, it's just energy; the question is how I use it. *Choose a better dream*, my heart whispers.

A sob catches in my throat, and I lower myself gently to the floor. I squandered this energy, abused it by focusing it against myself and against life, rather than in support of my imagination and joy. When I decided to control my body using the weapon of self-hatred that society placed in my hands, I put the full force of my own power into its arc. I spent years using my tremendous human will for evil, not for good. Like a disgraced comic book superhero, I've been afraid to access this power ever since, terrified it might unleash the same mayhem on my body as before.

I have to differentiate between the power itself and the end to which I use it. For the first time in memory, there's a wellspring of trust and love within me. And a deep knowing. This power to make my dreams real in the world and do everything possible to achieve my longing is not something to suppress, but something to harness, enjoy, and appreciate.

In my hungry fifteen-year-old body, each morning found me thinking about my weight and how to avoid eating that day. Instead, why not wake up in the morning with gratitude for being alive, for having such a wonderful life and great family, and think about what I'm going to write today?

As an anorexic, every little thing around me was a reminder of my campaign against my body: mirrors reminded me of the fat that stubbornly clung to my body, food reminded me to look away, the numbers lined up on the clock whispered *be thin or die.* Instead, everything can remind me to write, post-its on my computer, in my bag, everywhere I might see them. *Love your body. Write from love. Share your stories. The only thing holding me back is myself. I am and have everything I need.*

My anorexic self was superdisciplined: exercising even when I was sick or tired. Nothing distracted me from my goal. Now I can be devotedly disciplined. Time to write will come first (after family, of course). Appointments, phone calls, surfing the Internet, answering e-mails—everything else has to wait. Rewards can be hula hooping breaks or naps outside in the sun.

When I'm best friends with my body, anything is possible. I can exercise or lie around all day, or go on a long hike, or hang out by the pool in the sun, or lounge in the sand at the beach, or eat, or not eat, in a totally different way than I ever have before. Out of love, not fear or shame or self-hatred.

You and me, body, we're in this together.

This morning, while I'm heating water for tea, a dream reemerges from the night before, featuring my chorus line of inner characters, onstage, in Vegas showgirl costumes, embracing one another at the waist, doing high kicks to the best of their ability. They were all there—in high feathers and stunning sequins, my inner anorexic clasping my prison escapee, who in turn supported her old nemesis, the prison guard, his arm crossed behind my inner therapist's back, and her arm around Svetlana, swinging her hips enthusiastically alongside my inner diva. Their heights and sizes vary widely, giving the show a comical tinge, but I could tell they'd practiced their high kicks for many hours and appeared to have wholeheartedly enjoyed rehearsing this number together.

At the final crescendo, they bowed and flourished in the spotlight, brandishing extravagant headpieces and exhilarated grins. From my seat in the audience, I leapt to my feet and applauded vigorously, tears in my eyes, delighted to see them all dancing as one and obviously having a marvelous time. I'm surprised I didn't wake myself up laughing and clapping.

Pouring my tea, I walk out the back door and down the steps into the garden. Morning is garden time, when the sun illuminates the dew clinging to every branch and leaf. I settle into an aging wooden deck chair and blow steam off the edge of my cup. The robinia tree above me unfurled its leaves weeks ago, into the cool March breeze. Soon, fragrant pink flowers will billow from it, but there's no sign of them yet. They're hiding, in the tree's DNA, in tiny cells and membranes, waiting to emerge fully.

Sitting back, my gaze fills with the sky, the garden's translucent coral lilies, and my cat's attempt to trap a tiny spider in the spiky grass. I hope Cooper's friend Emily will be able to grow up with a sense of trust and love toward her body, stronger with each passing year. In my life, those tender qualities toward myself have been hard won, and I wish her an easier journey than mine. I want Emily to grow up in a society where she is encouraged and supported in her love and connection to her body. Where puberty is a magical time of transformation and self-discovery, a deepening of her connection to herself. Where her friendship with her body grows strong like the roots of our robinia tree, pushing into the earth, extending with freedom and delight into every leaf and branch. Where her journey as a young woman is eased and comforted by her love for her body, and she enjoys her body inside and out as she moves through all the stages of her life.

This is the vision I want to help make possible, and I know what to do: be my body's best friend. Like that wonderful quote from Gandhi: Be the change you wish to see in the world. By embodying love for my body, I shift the world. By teaching other women to do the same, together we tilt the whole world in the direction of love.

Epilogue

One sunny August Monday, Mom arrives at the airport on one of her semiregular visits. I swing by in the car to pick her up and catch her up on Cooper's acrobatics classes and tennis lessons.

Mom mentions that her cat and dog still disagree about who gets to sleep on the bed. "And we're getting that crack fixed in the living room wall. By the way, do you notice anything different?"

I glance over at her from the driver's seat. Her hand rests lightly on the skin around her throat, thumb on one side of her jaw, index finger on the other.

"They got rid of all this. And tightened things up here. It turned out great. I've got pictures, you'll see what a good job they did."

Glaring at the road in front of me, I will tears not to come.

I can hear her digging through her fringed leather bag.

"They're in here somewhere, I'll show you when we get to the house."

"Mom…" I manage to choke out.

"Hmm?"

"I can't look at your pictures."

"Of course not right now. Later, when you're not driving."

"No. Never. I can't ever look at your pictures."

The cumulative frustration of all the years of hiding anything painful from my mom breaches the lump in my throat. The tears pour out. Driving while crying, is that illegal? I take a deep breath.

"Mom, you know how you hate it when I talk about being anorexic? Well, I can't stand to hear about your plastic surgery. I can't stand to hear about how you want to change your body, how you don't like the way you look, how much you're fighting growing older. I want a good role model for growing older, for aging gracefully, not..."

"Well, both your grandmothers aged gracefully..." She sighs. "I don't know why I'm the way I am, why I want my body to look different."

"I don't begrudge you your happiness about your surgery, Mom. But I can't listen to it. I've spent half my life trying to learn how to love my body the way it is and hearing you criticize your body, which is likely to be my body in the future, is more than I can handle. When you criticize yourself, I start criticizing my own body. I've worked hard to stop thinking like an anorexic, and I can't even talk to you about it because it upsets you so much."

"I didn't know that you were anorexic. What do you want me to say? Did you tell your father? What did he say?"

"He said he didn't know at the time and that he was sorry I went through it. Could you at least say that?"

She clears her throat. We both stare through the windshield at the white lines on the road.

"I didn't know at the time. I'm sorry you went through that. I really didn't know."

She turns away to look out the window and I reach across the seat for her hand.

"I know, Mom. Thank you."

We drive on and I fish a tissue out from the box under the seat. Relief and disbelief wash over my body. If only we could talk this honestly more often.

As we approach the interstate on-ramp, Mom brightens.

"Hey look, there's a sign for the zoo! We should take Cooper there."

I inwardly roll my eyes. Classic Mom: divert-and-distract-from-topic-when-things-get-too-real. But she's made a step forward today: no denials. And an inkling of self-awareness. We can work with that.

"Sure, Mom. Maybe tomorrow afternoon. Want to get some lunch?"

Kimber Simpkins is a writer and yoga teacher transplanted from the Midwest to Northern California. Her successful shift from hating her body to loving it surprised no one more than herself, and it continues to inspire her students and readers everywhere. When not on her yoga mat or thinking up ways to treat her body as a friend, Kimber may be found playing, meditating, or hula-hooping in her backyard garden. You can find out more about Kimber, including her Love Your Body workshops, at http://www.kimberyoga. com.

Start a conversation—*What does it mean to be truly* full?

Take your reading experience to the next level and start a group discussion with the *Full* Reading Group Guide, **available for free download at https://www.newharbinger.com/fullguide**.

Perfect for book clubs, sharing with friends, or simply to enhance your own reading enjoyment, the *Full* Reading Group Guide will inspire you to feed your soul.

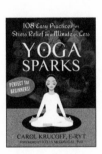
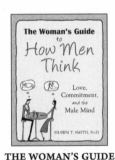